UNIVERSITY CASEBOOK SERIES®

2014 STATUTORY APPENDIX AND CASE SUPPLEMENT

LABOR LAW

CASES AND MATERIALS

FIFTEENTH EDITION

by

COX, BOK, GORMAN, AND FINKIN

SUPPLEMENT

by

ROBERT A. GORMAN
Kenneth W. Gemmill Professor of Law Emeritus
University of Pennsylvania

MATTHEW W. FINKIN
Albert J. Harno and Edward W. Cleary Chair in Law
University of Illinois

TIMOTHY P. GLYNN
Miriam T. Rooney Professor of Law and
Director of US Healthcare Compliance Certification Program
Seton Hall

D1318368

© 2001, 2004 FOUNDATION PRESS
© 2005, 2006, 2008, 2009, 2011, 2012 THOMSON REUTERS/FOUNDATION PRESS
© 2013 LEG, Inc. d/b/a West Academic Publishing
© 2014 LEG, Inc. d/b/a West Academic
  444 Cedar Street, Suite 700
  St. Paul, MN 55101
  1-877-888-1330

Printed in the United States of America

ISBN: 978-1-62810-078-5

Mat #41645123

TABLE OF CONTENTS

PART ONE. THE EVOLUTION OF LABOR RELATIONS LAWS

PART TWO. THE ESTABLISHMENT OF THE COLLECTIVE BARGAINING RELATIONSHIP

PART TEN. RECONSIDERING THE LABOR ACT IN THE CONTEMPORARY CONTEXT

TABLE OF CASES

The principal cases are in bold type.

UNIVERSITY CASEBOOK SERIES®

2014 STATUTORY APPENDIX AND CASE SUPPLEMENT

LABOR LAW

CASES AND MATERIALS

FIFTEENTH EDITION

by

COX, BOK, GORMAN, AND FINKIN

SHERMAN ACT

26 Stat. 209 (1890), as amended, 15 U.S.C. §§ 1 et seq. (1988).

Sec. 1. Every contract, combination in the form of a trust or otherwise, or conspiracy, in restraint of trade or commerce among the several States, or with foreign nations, is hereby declared to be illegal. Every person who shall make any such contract or engage in any such combination or conspiracy, shall be deemed guilty of a misdemeanor, and, on conviction thereof, shall be punished by fine not exceeding five thousand dollars, or by imprisonment not exceeding one year, or by both said punishments, in the discretion of the court.

Sec. 2. Every person who shall monopolize, or attempt to monopolize, or combine or conspire with any other person or persons, to monopolize any part of the trade or commerce among the several States, or with foreign nations, shall be deemed guilty of a misdemeanor, and, on conviction thereof, shall be punished by fine not exceeding five thousand dollars, or by imprisonment not exceeding one year, or by both said punishments, in the discretion of the court.

Sec. 3. Every contract, combination in form of trust or otherwise, or conspiracy, in restraint of trade or commerce in any territory of the United States or of the District of Columbia, or in restraint of trade or commerce between any such territory and another, or between any such territory or territories and any State or States or the District of Columbia, or with foreign nations, or between the District of Columbia and any State or States or foreign nations, is hereby declared illegal. Every person who shall make any such contract or engage in any such combination or conspiracy, shall be deemed guilty of a misdemeanor, and, on conviction thereof, shall be punished by fine not exceeding five thousand dollars, or by imprisonment not exceeding one year, or by both said punishments, in the discretion of the court.

Sec. 4. The several circuit courts of the United States are hereby invested with jurisdiction to prevent and restrain violations of this act; and it shall be the duty of the several district attorneys of the United States, in their respective districts, under the direction of the Attorney General, to institute proceedings in equity to prevent and restrain such violations. Such proceedings may be by way of petition setting forth the case and praying that such violation shall be enjoined or otherwise prohibited. When the parties complained of shall have been duly notified of such petition the court shall proceed, as soon as may be, to the hearing and determination of the case; and pending such petition and before final decree, the court may at any time make such temporary restraining order or prohibition as shall be deemed just in the premises.

Sec. 5. Whenever it shall appear to the court before which any proceeding under section 4 of this act may be pending, that the ends of justice require that other parties should be brought before the court, the court may cause them to be summoned, whether they reside in the district in which the court is held or not; and subpoenas to that end may be served in any district by the marshal thereof.

Sec. 6. Any property owned under any contract or by any combination, or pursuant to any conspiracy (and being the subject thereof) mentioned in section 1 of this act, and being in the course of transportation from one State to another, or to a foreign country, shall be forfeited to the United States, and may be seized and condemned by like proceedings as those provided by law for the forfeiture, seizure, and condemnation of property imported into the United States contrary to law.

Sec. 7. Any person who shall be injured in his business or property by any other person or corporation by reason of anything forbidden or declared to be unlawful by this act, may sue therefor in any Circuit Court of the United States in the district in which the defendant resides or is found, without respect to the amount in controversy, and shall recover three-fold the damages sustained, and the costs of suit, including a reasonable attorney's fee.

Sec. 8. That the word "person," or "persons" wherever used in this act shall be deemed to include corporations and associations existing under or authorized by the laws of either the United States, the laws of any State or the laws of any foreign country.

Clayton Act

38 Stat. 730 (1914), as amended, 15 U.S.C. §§ 12 et seq. (1988).

Be it enacted by the Senate and House of Representatives of the United States of America in Congress assembled, That "anti-trust laws," as used herein, includes the Act entitled "An Act to protect trade and commerce against unlawful restraints and monopolies", approved July second, eighteen hundred and ninety [Sherman Act, supra.] * * *

* * *

Sec. 6. That the labor of a human being is not a commodity or article of commerce. Nothing contained in the anti-trust laws shall be construed to forbid the existence and operation of labor, agricultural, or horticultural organizations, instituted for the purposes of mutual help, and not having capital stock or conducted for profit, or to forbid or restrain individual members of such organizations from lawfully carrying out the legitimate objects thereof; nor shall such organizations, or the members thereof, be held or construed to be illegal combinations or conspiracies in restraint of trade, under the anti-trust laws.

* * *

Sec. 16. That any person, firm, corporation, or association shall be entitled to sue for and have injunctive relief, in any court of the United States having jurisdiction over the parties, against threatened loss or damage by a violation of the anti-trust laws, including sections two, three, seven and eight of this Act, when and under the same conditions and principles as injunctive relief against threatened conduct that will cause loss or damage is granted by courts of equity, under the rules governing such proceedings, and upon the execution of proper bond against damages for an injunction improvidently granted and a showing that the danger of irreparable loss or damage is immediate, a preliminary injunction may issue: *Provided*, That nothing herein contained shall be construed to entitle any person, firm, corporation, or association, except the United States, to bring suit in equity for injunctive relief against any common carrier subject to the provisions of the Act to regulate commerce, approved February fourth, eighteen hundred and eighty-seven, in respect of any matter subject to the regulation, supervision, or other jurisdiction of the Interstate Commerce Commission.

* * *

Sec. 20. That no restraining order or injunction shall be granted by any court of the United States, or a judge or the judges thereof, in any case between an employer and employees, or between employers and employees, or between employees, or between persons employed and persons seeking employment, involving, or growing out of, a dispute concerning terms or conditions of employment, unless necessary to prevent irreparable injury to property, or to a property right, of the party making the application, for which injury there is no adequate remedy at law, and such property or property right must be described with particularity in the application, which must be in writing and sworn to by the applicant or by his agent or attorney.

And no such restraining order or injunction shall prohibit any person or persons, whether singly or in concert, from terminating any relation of employment, or from ceasing to perform any work or labor, or from recommending, advising, or persuading others by peaceful means so to do; or from attending at any place where any such person or persons may lawfully be, for the purpose of peacefully obtaining or communicating information, or from peacefully persuading any person to work or to abstain from working; or from ceasing to patronize or to employ any party to such dispute, or from recommending, advising, or persuading others by peaceful and lawful means so to do; or from paying or giving to, or withholding from, any person engaged in such dispute, any strike benefits or other moneys or things of value; or from peaceably assembling in a lawful manner, and for lawful purposes; or from doing any act or thing which might lawfully be done in the absence of such dispute by any party thereto; nor shall any of the acts specified in this paragraph be considered or held to be violations of any law of the United States.

* * *

NORRIS-LAGUARDIA ACT

47 Stat. 70 (1932), 29 U.S.C. §§ 101–15 (1988).

Sec. 1. No court of the United States, as herein defined, shall have jurisdiction to issue any restraining order or temporary or permanent injunction in a case involving or growing out of a labor dispute, except in a strict conformity with the provisions of this Act; nor shall any such restraining order or temporary or permanent injunction be issued contrary to the public policy declared in this Act.

Sec. 2. In the interpretation of this Act and in determining the jurisdiction and authority of the courts of the United States, as such jurisdiction and authority are herein defined and limited, the public policy of the United States is hereby declared as follows:

Whereas under prevailing economic conditions, developed with the aid of governmental authority for owners of property to organize in the corporate and other forms of ownership association, the individual unorganized worker is commonly helpless to exercise actual liberty of contract and to protect his freedom of labor, and thereby to obtain acceptable terms and conditions of employment, wherefore, though he should be free to decline to associate with his fellows, it is necessary that he have full freedom of association, self-organization, and designation of representatives of his own choosing, to negotiate the terms and conditions of his employment, and that he shall be free from the interference, restraint, or coercion of employers of labor, or their agents, in the designation of such representatives or in self-organization or in other concerted activities for the purpose of collective bargaining or other mutual aid or protection; therefore, the following definitions of, and limitations upon, the jurisdiction and authority of the courts of the United States are hereby enacted.

Sec. 3. Any undertaking or promise, such as is described in this section, or any other undertaking or promise in conflict with the public policy declared in section 2 of this Act, is hereby declared to be contrary to the public policy of the United States, shall not be enforceable in any court of the United States and shall not afford any basis for the granting of legal or equitable relief by any such court, including specifically the following:

Every undertaking or promise hereafter made, whether written or oral, express or implied, constituting or contained in any contract or agreement of hiring or employment between any individual, firm, company, association, or corporation, and any employee or prospective employee of the same whereby

(a) Either party to such contract or agreement undertakes or promises not to join, become, or remain a member of any labor organization or of any employer organization; or

(b) Either party to such contract or agreement undertakes or promises that he will withdraw from an employment relation in the event that he joins, becomes, or remains a member of any labor organization or of any employer organization.

Sec. 4. No court of the United States shall have jurisdiction to issue any restraining order or temporary or permanent injunction in any case involving or growing out of any labor dispute to prohibit any person or persons participating or interested in such dispute (as these terms are herein defined) from doing, whether singly or in concert, any of the following acts:

(a) Ceasing or refusing to perform any work or to remain in any relation of employment;

(b) Becoming or remaining a member of any labor organization or of any employer organization, regardless of any such undertaking or promise as is described in section 3 of this Act;

(c) Paying or giving to, or withholding from, any person participating or interested in such labor dispute, any strike or unemployment benefits or insurance, or other moneys or things of value;

(d) By all lawful means aiding any person participating or interested in any labor dispute who is being proceeded against in, or is prosecuting, any action or suit in any court of the United States or of any State;

(e) Giving publicity to the existence of, or the facts involved in, any labor dispute, whether by advertising, speaking, patrolling, or by any other method not involving fraud or violence;

(f) Assembling peaceably to act or to organize to act in promotion of their interests in a labor dispute;

(g) Advising or notifying any person of an intention to do any of the Acts heretofore specified;

(h) Agreeing with other persons to do or not to do any of the acts heretofore specified; and

(i) Advising, urging, or otherwise causing or inducing without fraud or violence the acts heretofore specified, regardless of any such undertaking or promise as is described in section 3 of this Act.

Sec. 5. No court of the United States shall have jurisdiction to issue a restraining order or temporary or permanent injunction upon the ground that any of the persons participating or interested in a labor dispute constitute or are engaged in an unlawful combination or conspiracy because of the doing in concert of the acts enumerated in section 4 of this Act.

Sec. 6. No officer or member of any association or organization, and no association or organization participating or interested in a labor dispute, shall be held responsible or liable in any court of the United States for the unlawful acts of individual officers, members, or agents, except upon clear proof of actual participation in, or actual authorization of, such acts, or of ratification of such acts after actual knowledge thereof.

Sec. 7. No court of the United States shall have jurisdiction to issue a temporary or permanent injunction in any case involving or growing out of a labor dispute, as herein defined, except after hearing the testimony of witnesses in open court (with opportunity for cross-examination) in support of the allegations of a complaint made under oath, and testimony in opposition thereto, if offered, and except after findings of fact by the court, to the effect—

(a) That unlawful acts have been threatened and will be committed unless restrained or have been committed and will be continued unless restrained, but no injunction or temporary restraining order shall be issued on account of any threat or unlawful act excepting against the person or persons, association, or organization making the threat or committing the unlawful act or actually authorizing or ratifying the same after actual knowledge thereof;

(b) That substantial and irreparable injury to complainant's property will follow:

(c) That as to each item of relief granted greater injury will be inflicted upon complainant by the denial of relief than will be inflicted upon defendants by the granting of relief;

(d) That complainant has no adequate remedy at law; and

(e) That the public officers charged with the duty to protect complainant's property are unable or unwilling to furnish adequate protection.

Such hearing shall be held after due and personal notice thereof has been given, in such manner as the court shall direct, to all known persons against whom relief is sought, and also to the chief of those public officials of the county and city within which the unlawful acts have been threatened or committed charged with the duty to protect complainant's property: *Provided, however*, That if a complainant shall also allege that, unless a temporary restraining order shall be issued without notice, a substantial and irreparable injury to complainant's property will be unavoidable, such a temporary restraining order may be issued upon testimony under oath, sufficient, if sustained, to justify the court in issuing a temporary injunction upon a hearing after notice. Such a temporary restraining order shall be effective for no longer than five days and shall become void at the expiration of said five days. No temporary restraining order or temporary injunction shall be issued except on condition that complainant shall first file an undertaking with adequate security in an amount to be fixed by the court sufficient to recompense those enjoined for any loss, expense, or damage caused by the improvident or erroneous issuance of such order or injunction, including all reasonable costs (together with a reasonable attorney's fee) and expense of defense against the order or against the granting of any injunctive relief sought in the same proceeding and subsequently denied by the court.

The undertaking herein mentioned shall be understood to signify an agreement entered into by the complainant and the surety upon which a decree may be rendered in the same suit or proceeding against said complainant and surety, upon a hearing to assess damages of which hearing complainant and surety shall have reasonable notice, the said complainant and surety submitting themselves to the jurisdiction of the court for that purpose. But nothing herein contained shall deprive any party having a claim or cause of action under or upon such undertaking from electing to pursue his ordinary remedy by suit at law or in equity.

Sec. 8. No restraining order or injunctive relief shall be granted to any complainant who has failed to comply with any obligation imposed by law which is involved in the labor dispute in question, or who has failed to make every reasonable effort to settle such dispute either by negotiation or with the aid of any available governmental machinery of mediation or voluntary arbitration.

Sec. 9. No restraining order or temporary or permanent injunction shall be granted in a case involving or growing out of a labor dispute, except on the basis of findings of fact made and filed by the court in the record of the case prior to the issuance of such restraining order or injunction; and every restraining order or injunction granted in a case involving or growing out of a labor dispute shall include only a prohibition of such specific act or acts as may be expressly complained of in the bill of complaint or petition filed in such case and as shall be expressly included in said findings of fact made and filed by the court as provided herein.

Sec. 10. Whenever any court of the United States shall issue or deny any temporary injunction in a case involving or growing out of a labor dispute, the court shall, upon the request of any party to the proceedings and on his filing the usual bond for costs, forthwith certify as in ordinary cases the record of the case to the circuit court of appeals for its review. Upon the filing of such record in the circuit court of appeals, the appeal shall be heard and the temporary injunctive order affirmed, modified, or set aside with the greatest possible expedition, giving the proceedings precedence over all other matters except older matters of the same character.

Sec. 11.*   In all cases arising under this Act in which a person shall be charged with contempt in a court of the United States (as herein defined), the accused shall enjoy the right to a speedy and public trial by an impartial jury of the State and district wherein the contempt shall have been committed: *Provided*, That this right shall not apply to contempts committed in the presence of the court or so near thereto as to interfere directly with the administration of justice or to apply to the misbehavior, misconduct, or disobedience of any officer of the court in respect to the writs, orders, or process of the court.

Sec. 12.*   The defendant in any proceeding for contempt of court may file with the court a demand for the retirement of the judge sitting in the proceeding, if the contempt arises from an attack upon the character or conduct of such judge and if the attack occurred elsewhere than in the presence of the court or so near thereto as to interfere directly with the administration of justice. Upon the filing of any such demand the judge shall thereupon proceed no further, but another judge shall be designated in the same manner as is provided by law. The demand shall be filed prior to the hearing in the contempt proceeding.

Sec. 13. When used in this Act, and for the purposes of this Act—

(a) A case shall be held to involve or to grow out of a labor dispute when the case involves persons who are engaged in the same industry, trade, craft, or occupation; or have direct or indirect interests therein; or who are employees of the same employer; or who are members of the same or an affiliated organization of employers or employees; whether

---

*   Sections 11 and 12 were repealed in 1948, 62 Stat. 862. The text of Section 11 is now in 18 U.S.C. § 3692 (1982); Rule 42 of the Federal Rules of Criminal Procedure now governs the matters formerly treated in Section 12.

such dispute is (1) between one or more employers or associations of employers and one or more employees or associations of employees; (2) between one or more employers or associations of employers and one or more employers or associations of employers; or (3) between one or more employees or associations of employees and one or more employees or associations of employees; or when the case involves any conflicting or competing interests in a "labor dispute" (as hereinafter defined) of "persons participating or interested" therein (as hereinafter defined).

(b) A person or association shall be held to be a person participating or interested in a labor dispute if relief is sought against him or it, and if he or it is engaged in the same industry, trade, craft, or occupation in which such dispute occurs, or has a direct or indirect interest therein, or is a member, officer, or agent of any association composed in whole or in part of employers or employees engaged in such industry, trade, craft, or occupation.

(c) The term "labor dispute" includes any controversy concerning terms or conditions of employment, or concerning the association or representation of persons in negotiating, fixing, maintaining, changing, or seeking to arrange terms or conditions of employment, regardless of whether or not the disputants stand in the proximate relation of employer and employee.

(d) The term "court of the United States" means any court of the United States whose jurisdiction has been or may be conferred or defined or limited by Act of Congress, including the courts of the District of Columbia.

Sec. 14. If any provision of this Act or the application thereof to any person or circumstance is held unconstitutional or otherwise invalid, the remaining provisions of the Act and the application of such provisions to other persons or circumstances shall not be affected thereby.

Sec. 15. All Acts and parts of Acts in conflict with the provisions of this Act are hereby repealed.

RAILWAY LABOR ACT

44 Stat., Part II, 577 (1926), as amended;
45 U.S.C. §§ 151–88 (1988).

TITLE I

Sec.1. When used in this Act and for the purposes of this Act—

First. The term "carrier" includes any express company, sleeping-car company, carrier by railroad, subject to the Interstate Commerce Act, and any company which is directly or indirectly owned or controlled by or under common control with any carrier by railroad and which operates any equipment or facilities or performs any service (other than trucking service) in connection with the transportation, receipt, delivery, elevation, transfer in transit, refrigeration or icing, storage, and handling of property transported by railroad, and any receiver, trustee, or other individual or body, judicial or otherwise, when in the possession of the business of any such "carrier": *Provided, however,* That the term "carrier" shall not include any street, interurban, or suburban electric railway, unless such railway is operating as a part of a general steam-railroad system of transportation, but shall not exclude any part of the general steam-railroad system of transportation now or hereafter operated by any other motive power. The Interstate Commerce Commission is authorized and directed upon request of the Mediation Board or upon complaint of any party interested to determine after hearing whether any line operated by electric power falls within the terms of this proviso. The term "carrier" shall not include any company by reason of its being engaged in the mining of coal, the supplying of coal to a carrier where delivery is not beyond the mine tipple, and the operation of equipment or facilities therefor, or in any of such activities.

Second. The term "Adjustment Board" means the National Railroad Adjustment Board created by this Act.

Third. The term "Mediation Board" means the National Mediation Board created by this Act.

Fourth. The term "commerce" means commerce among the several States or between any State, Territory, or the District of Columbia and any foreign nation, or between any Territory or the District of Columbia and any State, or between any Territory and any other Territory, or between any Territory and the District of Columbia, or within any Territory or the District of Columbia, or between points in the same State but through any other State or any Territory or the District of Columbia or any foreign nation.

Fifth. The term "employee" as used herein includes every person in the service of a carrier (subject to its continuing authority to supervise and direct the manner of rendition of his service) who performs any work defined as that of an employee or subordinate official in the orders of the Interstate Commerce Commission now in effect, and as the same may be amended or interpreted by orders hereafter entered by the Commission pursuant to the authority which is conferred upon it to enter orders amending or interpreting such existing orders: *Provided, however,* That no occupational classification made by order of the

Interstate Commerce Commission shall be construed to define the crafts according to which railway employees may be organized by their voluntary action, nor shall the jurisdiction or powers of such employee organizations be regarded as in any way limited or defined by the provisions of this Act or by the orders of the Commission. The term "employee" shall not include any individual while such individual is engaged in the physical operations consisting of the mining of coal, the preparation of coal, the handling (other than movement by rail with standard railroad locomotives) of coal not beyond the mine tipple, or the loading of coal at the tipple.

Sixth. The term "representative" means any person or persons, labor union, organization, or corporation designated either by a carrier or group of carriers or by its or their employees, to act for it or them.

Seventh. The term "district court" includes the United States District Court for the District of Columbia; and the term "circuit court of appeals" includes the United States Court of Appeals for the District of Columbia.

This Act may be cited as the "Railway Labor Act."

Sec. 2. The purposes of the Act are:

(1) To avoid any interruption to commerce or to the operation of any carrier engaged therein; (2) to forbid any limitation upon freedom of association among employees or any denial, as a condition of employment or otherwise, of the right of employees to join a labor organization; (3) to provide for the complete independence of carriers and of employees in the matter of self-organization; (4) to provide for the prompt and orderly settlement of all disputes concerning rates of pay, rules, or working conditions; (5) to provide for the prompt and orderly settlement of all disputes growing out of grievances or out of the interpretation or application of agreements covering rates of pay, rules, or working conditions.

First. It shall be the duty of all carriers, their officers, agents, and employees to exert every reasonable effort to make and maintain agreements concerning rates of pay, rules, and working conditions, and to settle all disputes, whether arising out of the application of such agreements or otherwise, in order to avoid any interruption to commerce or to the operation of any carrier growing out of any dispute between the carrier and the employees thereof.

Second. All disputes between a carrier or carriers and its or their employees shall be considered, and, if possible, decided, with all expedition, in conference between representatives designated and authorized so to confer, respectively, by the carrier or carriers and by the employees thereof interested in the dispute.

Third. Representatives, for the purposes of this Act, shall be designated by the respective parties without interference, influence, or coercion by either party over the designation of representatives by the other; and neither party shall in any way interfere with, influence, or coerce the other in its choice of representatives. Representatives of employees for the purposes of this Act need not be persons in the employ of the carrier, and no carrier shall, by interference, influence, or coercion seek in any manner to prevent the designation by its employees as their representatives of those who or which are not employees of the carrier.

Fourth. Employees shall have the right to organize and bargain collectively through representatives of their own choosing. The majority of any craft or class of employees shall have the right to determine who shall be the representative of the craft or class for the purposes of this Act. No carrier, its officers or agents, shall deny or in any way question the right of its employees to join, organize, or assist in organizing the labor organization of their choice, and it shall be unlawful for any carrier to interfere in any way with the organization of its employees, or to use the funds of the carrier in maintaining or assisting or contributing to any labor organization, labor representative, or other agency of collective bargaining, or in performing any work therefor, or to influence or coerce employees in an effort to induce them to join or remain or not to join or remain members of any labor organization or to deduct from the wages of employees any dues, fees, assessments, or other contributions payable to labor organizations, or to collect or to assist in the collection of any such dues, fees, assessments, or other contributions: *Provided,* That nothing in this Act shall be construed to prohibit a carrier from permitting an employee, individually, or local representatives of employees from conferring with management during working hours without loss of time, or to prohibit a carrier from furnishing free transportation to its employees while engaged in the business of a labor organization.

Fifth. No carrier, its officers, or agents shall require any person seeking employment to sign any contract or agreement promising to join or not to join a labor organization; and if any such contract has been enforced prior to the effective date of this Act, then such carrier shall notify the employees by an appropriate order that such contract has been discarded and is no longer binding on them in any way.

Sixth. In case of a dispute between a carrier or carriers and its or their employees, arising out of grievances or out of the interpretation or application of agreements concerning rates of pay, rules, or working conditions, it shall be the duty of the designated representative or representatives of such carrier or carriers and of such employees, within ten days after the receipt of notice of a desire on the part of either party to confer in respect to such dispute, to specify a time and place at which such conference shall be held: *Provided,* (1) That the place so specified shall be situated upon the line of the carrier involved or as otherwise mutually agreed upon; and (2) that the time so specified shall allow the designated conferees reasonable opportunity to reach such place of conference, but shall not exceed twenty days from the receipt of such notice: *And provided further,* That nothing in this Act shall be construed to supersede the provisions of any agreement (as to conferences) then in effect between the parties.

Seventh. No carrier, its officers, or agents shall change the rates of pay, rules, or working conditions of its employees, as a class as embodied in agreements except in the manner prescribed in such agreements or in section 6 of this Act.

Eighth. Every carrier shall notify its employees by printed notices in such form and posted at such times and places as shall be specified by the Mediation Board that all disputes between the carrier and its employees will be handled in accordance with the requirements of this Act, and in such notices there shall be printed verbatim, in large type, the third, fourth, and fifth paragraphs of this section. The provisions of said paragraphs are hereby made a part of the contract of employment between the carrier and each employee, and shall be held binding upon the parties, regardless of any other express or implied agreements between them.

Ninth. If any dispute shall arise among a carrier's employees as to who are the representatives of such employees designated and authorized in accordance with the requirements of this Act, it shall be the duty of the Mediation Board, upon request of either party to the dispute, to investigate such dispute and to certify to both parties, in writing, within thirty days after the receipt of the invocation of its services, the name or names of the individuals or organizations that have been designated and authorized to represent the employees involved in the dispute, and certify the same to the carrier. Upon receipt of such certification the carrier shall treat with the representative so certified as the representative of the craft or class for the purposes of this Act. In such an investigation, the Mediation Board shall be authorized to take a secret ballot of the employees involved, or to utilize any other appropriate method of ascertaining the names of their duly designated and authorized representatives in such manner as shall insure the choice of representatives by the employees without interference, influence, or coercion exercised by the carrier. In the conduct of any election for the purposes herein indicated the Board shall designate who may participate in the election and establish the rules to govern the election, or may appoint a committee of three neutral persons who after hearing shall within ten days designate the employees who may participate in the election. The Board shall have access to and have power to make copies of the books and records of the carriers to obtain and utilize such information as may be deemed necessary by it to carry out the purposes and provisions of this paragraph.

Tenth. The willful failure or refusal of any carrier, its officers, or agents to comply with the terms of the third, fourth, fifth, seventh, or eighth paragraph of this section shall be a misdemeanor, and upon conviction thereof the carrier, officer, or agent offending shall be subject to a fine of not less than $1,000 nor more than $20,000 or imprisonment for not more than six months, or both fine and imprisonment, for each offense, and each day during which such carrier, officer, or agent shall willfully fail or refuse to comply with the terms of the said paragraphs of this section shall constitute a separate offense. It shall be the duty of any United States attorney to whom any duly designated representative of a carrier's employees may apply to institute in the proper court and to prosecute under the direction of the Attorney General of the United States, all necessary proceedings for the enforcement of the provisions of this section, and for the punishment of all violations thereof and the costs and expenses of such prosecution shall be paid out of the appropriation for the expenses of the courts of the United States: *Provided*, That nothing in this Act shall be construed to require an individual employee to render labor or service without his consent, nor shall anything in this Act be construed to make the quitting of his labor by an individual employee an illegal act; nor shall any court issue any process to compel the performance by an individual employee of such labor or service, without his consent.

Eleventh. Notwithstanding any other provisions of this chapter, or of any other statute or law of the United States, or Territory thereof, or of any State, any carrier or carriers as defined in this chapter and a labor organization or labor organizations duly designated and authorized to represent employees in accordance with the requirements of this chapter shall be permitted—

(a) to make agreements, requiring, as a condition of continued employment, that within sixty days following the beginning of such employment, or the effective date of such agreements, whichever is the later, all employees shall become members of the labor organization representing their craft or class: *Provided*, That no such agreement shall require such condition of employment with respect to employees to whom membership is not available upon the same terms and conditions as are generally applicable to any other member or with respect to employees to whom membership was denied or terminated for any reason other than the failure of the employee to tender the periodic dues, initiation fees, and assessments (not including fines and penalties) uniformly required as a condition of acquiring or retaining membership.

(b) to make agreements providing for the deduction by such carrier or carriers from the wages of its or their employees in a craft or class and payment to the labor organization representing the craft or class of such employees, of any periodic dues, initiation fees, and assessments (not including fines and penalties) uniformly required as a condition of acquiring or retaining membership: *Provided*, That no such agreement shall be effective with respect to any individual employee until he shall have furnished the employer with a written assignment to the labor organization of such membership dues, initiation fees, and assessments, which shall be revocable in writing after the expiration of one year or upon the termination date of the applicable collective agreement, whichever occurs sooner.

* * *

Sec. 3. First. There is hereby established a Board, to be known as the "National Railroad Adjustment Board", the members of which shall be selected within thirty days after June 21, 1934, and it is hereby provided—

(a) That the said Adjustment Board shall consist of thirty-four members, seventeen of whom shall be selected by the carriers and seventeen by such labor organizations of the employees, national in scope, as have been or may be organized in accordance with the provisions of section 2 of this Act.

(b) The carriers, acting each through its board of directors or its receiver or receivers, trustee or trustees, or through an officer or officers designated for that purpose by such board, trustee or trustees, or receiver or receivers, shall prescribe the rules under which its representatives shall be selected and shall select the representatives of the carriers on the Adjustment Board and designate the division on which each such representative shall serve, but no carrier or system of carriers shall have more than one voting representative on any division of the Board.

(c) Except as provided in the second paragraph of subsection (h) of this section, the national labor organizations as defined in paragraph (a) of this section, acting each through the chief executive or other medium designated by the organization or association thereof, shall prescribe the rules under which the labor members of the Adjustment Board shall be selected and shall select such members and designate the division on which each member shall serve; but no labor organization shall have more than one voting representative on any division of the Board.

* * *

(h) The said Adjustment Board shall be composed of four divisions, whose proceedings shall be independent of one another, and the said divisions as well as the number of their members shall be as follows:

First division: To have jurisdiction over disputes involving train- and yard-service employees of carriers; that is, engineers, firemen, hostlers, and outside hostler helpers, conductors, trainmen, and yard-service employees. This division shall consist of eight members, four of whom shall be selected and designated by the carriers and four of whom shall be selected and designated by the labor organizations * * *.

Second division: To have jurisdiction over disputes involving machinists, boilermakers, blacksmiths, sheet-metal workers, electrical workers, car men, the helpers and apprentices of all the foregoing, coach cleaners, power-house employees, and railroad-shop laborers. This division shall consist of ten members, five of whom shall be selected by the carriers and five by the national labor organizations of the employees.

Third division: To have jurisdiction over disputes involving station, tower, and telegraph employees, train dispatchers, maintenance-of-way men, clerical employees, freight handlers, express, station, and store employees, signal men, sleeping-car conductors, sleeping-car porters, and maids and dining-car employees. This division shall consist of ten members, five of whom shall be selected by the carriers and five by the national labor organizations of employees.

Fourth division: To have jurisdiction over disputes involving employees of carriers directly or indirectly engaged in transportation of passengers or property by water, and all other employees of carriers over which jurisdiction is not given to the first, second, and third divisions. This division shall consist of six members, three of whom shall be selected by the carriers and three by the national labor organizations of the employees.

(i) The disputes between an employee or group of employees and a carrier or carriers growing out of grievances or out of the interpretation or application of agreements concerning rates of pay, rules, or working conditions, including cases pending and unadjusted on the date of approval of this Act, shall be handled in the usual manner up to and including the chief operating officer of the carrier designated to handle such disputes; but, failing to reach an adjustment in this manner, the disputes may be referred by petition of the parties or by either party to the appropriate division of the Adjustment Board with a full statement of the facts and all supporting data bearing upon the disputes.

(j) Parties may be heard either in person, by counsel, or by other representatives, as they may respectively elect, and the several divisions of the Adjustment Board shall give due notice of all hearings to the employee or employees and the carrier or carriers involved in any disputes submitted to them.

(k) Any division of the Adjustment Board shall have authority to empower two or more of its members to conduct hearings and make findings upon disputes, when properly submitted, at any place designated by the division: *Provided, however*, That except as provided in paragraph (h) of this section, final awards as to any such dispute must be made by the entire division as hereinafter provided.

* * *

(m) The awards of the several divisions of the Adjustment Board shall be stated in writing. A copy of the awards shall be furnished to the respective parties to the controversy, and the awards shall be final and binding upon both parties to the dispute. In case a dispute arises involving an interpretation of the award the division of the Board upon request of either party shall interpret the award in the light of the dispute.

(n) A majority vote of all members of the division of the Adjustment Board eligible to vote shall be competent to make an award with respect to any dispute submitted to it.

(o) In case of an award by any division of the Adjustment Board in favor of petitioner, the division of the Board shall make an order, directed to the carrier, to make the award effective and, if the award includes a requirement for the payment of money, to pay the employee the sum to which he is entitled under the award on or before a day named. In the event any division determines that an award favorable to the petitioner should not be made in any dispute referred to it, the division shall make an order to the petitioner stating such determination.

(p) If a carrier does not comply with an order of a division of the Adjustment Board within the time limit in such order, the petitioner, or any person for whose benefit such order was made, may file in the District Court of the United States for the district in which he resides or in which is located the principal operating office of the carrier, or through which the carrier operates, a petition setting forth briefly the causes for which he claims relief, and the order of the division of the Adjustment Board in the premises. Such suit in the District Court of the United States shall proceed in all respects as other civil suits, except that on the trial of such suit the findings and order of the division of the Adjustment Board shall be conclusive on the parties, and except that the petitioner shall not be liable for costs in the district court nor for costs at any subsequent stage of the proceedings, unless they accrue upon his appeal, and such costs shall be paid out of the appropriation for the expenses of the courts of the United States. If the petitioner shall finally prevail he shall be allowed a reasonable attorney's fee, to be taxed and collected as a part of the costs of the suit.

The district courts are empowered, under the rules of the court governing actions at law, to make such order and enter such judgment, by writ of mandamus or otherwise, as may be appropriate to enforce or set aside the order of the division of the Adjustment Board: *Provided, however*, That such order may not be set aside except for failure of the division to comply with the requirements of this chapter, for failure of the order to conform, or confine itself, to matters within the scope of the division's jurisdiction, or for fraud or corruption by a member of the division making the order.

(q) If any employee or group of employees, or any carrier, is aggrieved by the failure of any division of the Adjustment Board to make an award in a dispute referred to it, or is aggrieved by any of the terms of an award or by the failure of the division to include certain terms in such award, then such employee or group of employees or carrier may file in any United States district court in which a petition under paragraph (p) could be filed, a petition for review of the division's order. A copy of the petition shall be forthwith transmitted by the clerk of the court to the Adjustment Board. The Adjustment Board shall file in the court the record of the proceedings on which it based its action. The court shall have jurisdiction to affirm the order of the division, or to set it aside, in whole or in part, or it may remand the proceeding to the division for such further action as it may direct. On such review, the findings and order of the division shall be conclusive on the parties, except that the order of the division may be set aside, in whole or in part, or remanded to the division, for failure of the division to comply with the requirements of this chapter, for failure of the order to conform, or confine itself, to matters within the scope of the division's jurisdiction, or for fraud or corruption by a member of the division making the order. The judgment of the court shall be subject to review as provided in sections 1291 and 1254 of title 28, United States Code.

(r) All actions at law based upon the provisions of this section shall be begun within two years from the time the cause of action accrues under the award of the division of the Adjustment Board, and not after.

* * *

Second. Nothing in this section shall be construed to prevent any individual carrier, system, or group of carriers and any class or classes of its or their employees, all acting through their representatives, selected in accordance with the provisions of this Act, from mutually agreeing to the establishment of system, group, or regional boards of adjustment for the purpose of adjusting and deciding disputes of the character specified in this section. In the event that either party to such a system, group, or regional board of adjustment is dissatisfied with such arrangement, it may upon ninety days' notice to the other party elect to come under the jurisdiction of the Adjustment Board.

* * *

Sec. 4.   First. * * * There is hereby established, as an independent agency in the executive branch of the Government, a board to be known as the "National Mediation Board," to be composed of three members appointed by the President, by and with the advice and consent of the Senate, not more than two of whom shall be of the same political party.

Each member of the Mediation Board in office on January 1, 1965, shall be deemed to have been appointed for a term of office which shall expire on July 1 of the year his term would have otherwise expired. The terms of office of all successors shall expire three years after the expiration of the terms for which their predecessors were appointed; but any member appointed to fill a vacancy occurring prior to the expiration of the term of which his predecessor was appointed shall be appointed only for the unexpired term of his predecessor. * * *

A member of the Board may be removed by the President for inefficiency, neglect of duty, malfeasance in office, or ineligibility, but for no other cause.

* * *

Sec. 5. **First.** The parties, or either party, to a dispute between an employee or group of employees and a carrier may invoke the services of the Mediation Board in any of the following cases:

(a) A dispute concerning changes in rates of pay, rules, or working conditions not adjusted by the parties in conference.

(b) Any other dispute not referable to the National Railroad Adjustment Board and not adjusted in conference between the parties or where conferences are refused.

The Mediation Board may proffer its services in case any labor emergency is found by it to exist at any time.

In either event the said Board shall promptly put itself in communication with the parties to such controversy, and shall use its best efforts, by mediation, to bring them to agreement. If such efforts to bring about an amicable settlement through mediation shall be unsuccessful, the said Board shall at once endeavor as its final required action (except as provided in paragraph third of this section and in section 10 of this Act) to induce the parties to submit their controversy to arbitration, in accordance with the provisions of this Act.

If arbitration at the request of the Board shall be refused by one or both parties, the Board shall at once notify both parties in writing that its mediatory efforts have failed and for thirty days thereafter, unless in the intervening period the parties agree to arbitration, or an emergency board shall be created under section 10 of this Act, no change shall be made in the rates of pay, rules, or working conditions or establish practices in effect prior to the time the dispute arose.

* * *

Sec. 6. Carriers and representatives of the employees shall give at least thirty days' written notice of an intended change in agreements affecting rates of pay, rules, or working conditions, and the time and place for the beginning of conference between the representatives of the parties interested in such intended changes shall be agreed upon within ten days after the receipt of said notice, and said time shall be within the thirty days provided in the notice. In every case where such notice of intended change has been given, or conferences are being held with reference thereto, or the services of the Mediation Board have been requested by either party, or said Board has proffered its services, rates of pay, rules, or working conditions shall not be altered by the carrier until the controversy has been finally acted upon as required by section 5 of this Act, by the Mediation Board, unless a period of ten days has elapsed after termination of conferences without request for or proffer of the services of the Mediation Board.

Sec. 7. First. Whenever a controversy shall arise between a carrier or carriers and its or their employees which is not settled either in conference between representatives of the parties or by the appropriate adjustment board or through mediation, in the manner provided in the preceding sections, such controversy may, by agreement of the parties to such controversy, be submitted to the arbitration of a board of three (or, if the parties to the controversy so stipulate, of six) persons: *Provided, however*, That the failure or refusal of either party to submit a controversy to arbitration shall not be construed as a violation of any legal obligation imposed upon such party by the terms of this Act or otherwise.

Second. Such board of arbitration shall be chosen in the following manner:

(a) In the case of a board of three, the carrier or carriers and the representatives of the employees, parties respectively to the agreement to arbitrate, shall each name one arbitrator; the two arbitrators thus chosen shall select a third arbitrator. If the arbitrators chosen by the parties shall fail to name the third arbitrator within five days after their first meeting, such third arbitrator shall be named by the Mediation Board.

(b) In the case of a board of six, the carrier or carriers and the representatives of the employees, parties respectively to the agreement to arbitrate, shall each name two arbitrators; the four arbitrators thus chosen shall, by a majority vote, select the remaining two arbitrators. If the arbitrators chosen by the parties shall fail to name the two arbitrators within fifteen days after their first meeting, the said two arbitrators, or as many of them as have not been named, shall be named by the Mediation Board.

Third. (a) When the arbitrators selected by the respective parties have agreed upon the remaining arbitrator or arbitrators, they shall notify the Mediation Board, and, in the event of their failure to agree upon any or upon all of the necessary arbitrators within the period fixed by this Act, they shall, at the expiration of such period, notify the Mediation Board of the arbitrators selected, if any, or of their failure to make or complete such selection.

(b) The board of arbitration shall organize and select its own chairman and make all necessary rules for conducting its hearings: *Provided, however*, That the board of arbitration shall be bound to give the parties to the controversy a full and fair hearing, which shall include an opportunity to present evidence in support of their claims, and an opportunity to present their case in person, by counsel, or by other representative as they may respectively elect.

* * *

Sec. 9. First. The award of a board of arbitration, having been acknowledged as herein provided, shall be filed in the clerk's office of the district court designated in the agreement to arbitrate.

Second. An award acknowledged and filed as herein provided shall be conclusive on the parties as to the merits and facts of the controversy submitted to arbitration, and unless, within ten days after the filing of the award, a petition to impeach the award, on the grounds hereinafter set forth, shall be filed in the clerk's office of the court in which the award has been filed, the court shall enter judgment on the award, which judgment shall be final and conclusive on the parties.

Third. Such petition for the impeachment or contesting of any award so filed shall be entertained by the court only on one or more of the following grounds:

(a) That the award plainly does not conform to the substantive requirements laid down by this Act for such awards, or that the proceedings were not substantially in conformity with this Act;

(b) That the award does not conform, nor confine itself, to the stipulations of the agreement to arbitrate; or

(c) That a member of the board of arbitration rendering the award was guilty of fraud or corruption; or that a party to the arbitration practiced fraud or corruption which fraud or corruption affected the result of the arbitration. *Provided, however,* That no court shall entertain any such petition on the ground that an award is invalid for uncertainty; in such case the proper remedy shall be a submission of such award to a reconvened board, or subcommittee thereof, for interpretation, as provided by this Act: *Provided further,* That an award contested as herein provided shall be construed liberally by the court, with a view to favoring its validity, and that no award shall be set aside for trivial irregularity or clerical error, going only to form and not to substance.

* * *

Sec. 10. If a dispute between a carrier and its employees be not adjusted under the foregoing provisions of this Act and should, in the judgment of the Mediation Board, threaten substantially to interrupt interstate commerce to a degree such as to deprive any section of the country of essential transportation service, the Mediation Board shall notify the President, who may thereupon, in his discretion, create a board to investigate and report respecting such dispute. Such board shall be composed of such number of persons as to the President may seem desirable: *Provided, however,* That no member appointed shall be pecuniarily or otherwise interested in any organization of employees or any carrier. The compensation of the members of any such board shall be fixed by the President. Such board shall be created separately in each instance and it shall investigate promptly the facts as to the dispute and make a report thereon to the President within thirty days from the date of its creation.

* * *

After the creation of such board, and for thirty days after such board has made its report to the President, no change, except by agreement, shall be made by the parties to the controversy in the conditions out of which the dispute arose.

* * *

TITLE II

Sec. 201.   All of the provisions of title I of this Act, except the provisions of section 3 thereof, are extended to and shall cover every common carrier by air engaged in interstate or foreign commerce, and every carrier by air transporting mail for or under contract with the United States Government, and every air pilot or other person who performs any work as an employee or subordinate official of such carrier or carriers, subject to its or their continuing authority to supervise and direct the manner of rendition of his service.

Sec. 202.   The duties, requirements, penalties, benefits, and privileges prescribed and established by the provisions of title I of this Act, except section 3 thereof, shall apply to said carriers by air and their employees in the same manner and to the same extent as though such carriers and their employees were specifically included within the definition of "carrier" and "employee", respectively, in section 1 thereof.

Sec. 203.   The parties or either party to a dispute between an employee or a group of employees and a carrier or carriers by air may invoke the services of the National Mediation Board and the jurisdiction of said Mediation Board is extended to any of the following cases:

(a) A dispute concerning changes in rates of pay, rules, or working conditions not adjusted by the parties in conference.

(b) Any other dispute not referable to an adjustment board, as hereinafter provided, and not adjusted in conference between the parties, or where conferences are refused.

The National Mediation Board may proffer its services in case any labor emergency is found by it to exist at any time.

The services of the Mediation Board may be invoked in a case under this title in the same manner and to the same extent as are the disputes covered by section 5 of title I of this Act.

Sec. 204.   The disputes between an employee or group of employees and a carrier or carriers by air growing out of grievances, or out of interpretation or application of agreements concerning rates of pay, rules, or working conditions, including cases pending and unadjusted on the date of approval of this Act before the National Labor Relations Board, shall be handled in the usual manner up to and including the chief operating officer of the carrier designated to handle such disputes; but, failing to reach an adjustment in this manner, the disputes may be referred by petition of the parties or by either party to an appropriate adjustment board, as hereinafter provided, with a full statement of the facts and supporting data bearing upon the disputes.

It shall be the duty of every carrier and of its employees, acting through their representatives, selected in accordance with the provisions of this title, to establish a board of adjustment of jurisdiction not exceeding the jurisdiction which may be lawfully exercised by system, group, or regional boards of adjustment, under the authority of section 3, Title I, of this Act.

Such boards of adjustment may be established by agreement between employees and carriers either on any individual carrier, or system, or group of carriers by air and any class or classes of its or their employees; or pending the establishment of a permanent National Board of Adjustment as hereinafter provided. Nothing in this Act shall prevent said carriers by air, or any class or classes of their employees, both acting through their representatives selected in accordance with provisions of this title, from mutually agreeing to the establishment of a National Board of Adjustment of temporary duration and of similarly limited jurisdiction.

* * *

NATIONAL LABOR RELATIONS ACT*

49 Stat. 449 (1935), as amended; 29 U.S.C. §§ 151–69 (1988).

FINDINGS AND POLICIES

Sec. 1. The denial by **some** employers of the right of employees to organize and the refusal by **some** employers to accept the procedure of collective bargaining lead to strikes and other forms of industrial strife or unrest, which have the intent or the necessary effect of burdening or obstructing commerce by (a) impairing the efficiency, safety, or operation of the instrumentalities of commerce; (b) occurring in the current of commerce; (c) materially affecting, restraining, or controlling the flow of raw materials or manufactured or processed goods from or into the channels of commerce, or the prices of such materials or goods in commerce; or (d) causing diminution of employment and wages in such volume as substantially to impair or disrupt the market for goods flowing from or into the channels of commerce.

The inequality of bargaining power between employees who do not possess full freedom of association or actual liberty of contract, and employers who are organized in the corporate or other forms of ownership association substantially burdens and affects the flow of commerce, and tends to aggravate recurrent business depressions, by depressing wage rates and the purchasing power of wage earners in industry and by preventing the stabilization of competitive wage rates and working conditions within and between industries.

Experience has proved that protection by law of the right of employees to organize and bargain collectively safeguards commerce from injury, impairment, or interruption, and promotes the flow of commerce by removing certain recognized sources of industrial strife and unrest, by encouraging practices fundamental to the friendly adjustment of industrial disputes arising out of differences as to wages, hours, or other working conditions, and by restoring equality of bargaining power between employers and employees.

Experience has further demonstrated that certain practices by some labor organizations, their officers, and members have the intent or the necessary effect of burdening or obstructing commerce by preventing the free flow of goods in such commerce through strikes and other forms of industrial unrest or through concerted activities which impair the interest of the public in the free flow of such commerce. The elimination of such practices is a necessary condition to the assurance of the rights herein guaranteed.

It is hereby declared to be the policy of the United States to eliminate the causes of certain substantial obstructions to the free flow of commerce and to mitigate and eliminate these obstructions when

---

* The text of the original Wagner Act of 1935 is printed in roman type; the Taft–Hartley amendments of 1947 are in boldface type; the Landrum–Griffin amendments of 1959 are in italics; the 1974 amendments are underscored. Deleted matter is in brackets; bracketed matter in regular roman type was deleted in 1947, and bracketed matter in boldface type was deleted in 1959. Other amendments and deletions are specifically noted.

they have occurred by encouraging the practice and procedure of collective bargaining and by protecting the exercise by workers of full freedom of association, self-organization, and designation of representatives of their own choosing, for the purpose of negotiating the terms and conditions of their employment or other mutual aid or protection.

DEFINITIONS

Sec. 2. When used in this Act—

(1) The term "person" includes one or more individuals, labor organizations, partnerships, associations, corporations, legal representatives, trustees, trustees in bankruptcy, or receivers.

(2) The term "employer" includes any person acting [in the interest of] **as an agent** of an employer, directly or indirectly, but shall not include the United States **or any wholly owned Government corporation, or any Federal Reserve Bank,** or any State or political subdivision thereof, [**or any corporation or association operating a hospital, if no part of the net earnings inures to the benefit of any private shareholder or individual,**]* or any person subject to the Railway Labor Act, as amended from time to time, or any labor organization (other than when acting as an employer), or anyone acting in the capacity of officer or agent of such labor organization.

(3) The term "employee" shall include any employee, and shall not be limited to the employees of a particular employer, unless the Act explicitly states otherwise, and shall include any individual whose work has ceased as a consequence of, or in connection with, any current labor dispute or because of any unfair labor practice, and who has not obtained any other regular and substantially equivalent employment, but shall not include any individual employed as an agricultural laborer, or in the domestic service of any family or person at his home, or any individual employed by his parent or spouse, **or any individual having the status of an independent contractor, or any individual employed as a supervisor, or any individual employed by an employer subject to the Railway Labor Act, as amended from time to time, or by any other person who is not an employer as herein defined.**

(4) The term "representatives" includes any individual or labor organization.

(5) The term "labor organization" means any organization of any kind, or any agency or employee representation committee or plan, in which employees participate and which exists for the purpose, in whole or in part, of dealing with employers concerning grievances, labor disputes, wages, rates of pay, hours of employment, or conditions of work.

(6) The term "commerce" means trade, traffic, commerce, transportation, or communication among the several States, or between the District of Columbia or any Territory of the United States and any State or other Territory, or between any foreign country and any State, Territory, or the District of Columbia, or within the District of Columbia or any Territory, or between points in the same State but

---

* The bracketed matter was deleted in 1974, by 88 Stat. 395 (1974).

through any other State or any Territory or the District of Columbia or any foreign country.

(7) The term "affecting commerce" means in commerce, or burdening or obstructing commerce or the free flow of commerce, or having led or tending to lead to a labor dispute burdening or obstructing commerce or the free flow of commerce.

(8) The term "unfair labor practice" means any unfair labor practice listed in section 8.

(9) The term "labor dispute" includes any controversy concerning terms, tenure or conditions of employment, or concerning the association or representation of persons in negotiating, fixing, maintaining, changing, or seeking to arrange terms or conditions of employment, regardless of whether the disputants stand in the proximate relation of employer and employee.

(10) The term "National Labor Relations Board" means the National Labor Relations Board provided for in section 3 of this Act.

(11) The term "supervisor" means any individual having authority, in the interest of the employer, to hire, transfer, suspend, lay off, recall, promote, discharge, assign, reward, or discipline other employees, or responsibly to direct them, or to adjust their grievances, or effectively to recommend such action, if in connection with the foregoing the exercise of such authority is not of a merely routine or clerical nature, but requires the use of independent judgment.

(12) The term "professional employee" means—

(a) any employee engaged in work (i) predominantly intellectual and varied in character as opposed to routine mental, manual, mechanical, or physical work; (ii) involving the consistent exercise of discretion and judgment in its performance; (iii) of such a character that the output produced or the result accomplished cannot be standardized in relation to a given period of time; (iv) requiring knowledge of an advanced type in a field of science or learning customarily acquired by a prolonged course of specialized intellectual instruction and study in an institution of higher learning or a hospital, as distinguished from a general academic education or from an apprenticeship or from training in the performance of routine mental, manual, or physical processes; or

(b) any employee, who (i) has completed the courses of specialized intellectual instruction and study described in clause (iv) of paragraph (a), and (ii) is performing related work under the supervision of a professional person to qualify himself to become a professional employee as defined in paragraph (a).

(13) In determining whether any person is acting as an "agent" of another person so as to make such other person responsible for his acts, the question of whether the specific

acts performed were actually authorized or subsequently ratified shall not be controlling.

(14) The term "health care institution" shall include any hospital, convalescent hospital, health maintenance organization, health clinic, nursing home, extended care facility, or other institution devoted to the care of sick, infirm, or aged person.

NATIONAL LABOR RELATIONS BOARD

Sec. 3.* (a) The National Labor Relations Board (hereinafter called the "Board") created by this Act prior to its amendment by the Labor Management Relations Act, 1947, is continued as an agency of the United States, except that the Board shall consist of five instead of three members, appointed by the President by and with the advice and consent of the Senate. Of the two additional members so provided for, one shall be appointed for a term of five years and the other for a term of two years. Their successors, and the successors of the other members, shall be appointed for terms of five years each, excepting that any individual chosen to fill a vacancy shall be appointed only for the unexpired term of the member whom he shall succeed. The President shall designate one member to serve as Chairman of the Board. Any member of the Board may be removed by the President, upon notice and hearing, for neglect of duty or malfeasance in office, but for no other cause.

(b) **The Board is authorized to delegate to any group of three or more members any or all of the powers which it may itself exercise.** *The Board is also authorized to delegate to its regional directors its powers under section 9 to determine the unit appropriate for the purpose of collective bargaining, to investigate and provide for hearings, and determine whether a question of representation exists, and to direct an election or take a secret ballot under subsection (c) or (e) of section 9 and certify the results thereof, except that upon the filing of a request therefor with the Board by any interested person, the Board may review any action of a regional director delegated to him under this paragraph, but such a review shall not, unless specifically ordered by the Board, operate as a stay of any action taken by the regional director.* **A vacancy in the Board shall not impair the right of the remaining members to exercise all of the powers of the Board, and three members of the Board shall, at all times, constitute a quorum of the Board, except that two members shall constitute a quorum of any group designated pursuant to the first sentence hereof. The Board shall have an official seal which shall be judicially noticed.**

(c) The Board shall at the close of each fiscal year make a report in writing to Congress and to the President [stating in detail the cases it has heard, the decisions it has rendered, the names, salaries, and duties of all employees and officers in the employ or under the supervision of

---

* The changes made in Sections 3 and 4 by the Taft–Hartley amendments were so extensive, that the typeface designations for these two sections show only the 1947 and 1959 amendments.

the Board, and an account of all moneys it has disbursed.]* summarizing significant case activities and operations for that fiscal year.

(d) **There shall be a General Counsel of the Board who shall be appointed by the President, by and with the advice and consent of the Senate, for a term of four years. The General Counsel of the Board shall exercise general supervision over all attorneys employed by the Board (other than administrative law judges ** and legal assistants to Board members) and over the officers and employees in the regional offices. He shall have final authority, on behalf of the Board, in respect of the investigation of charges and issuance of complaints under section 10, and in respect of the prosecution of such complaints before the Board, and shall have such other duties as the Board may prescribe or as may be provided by law.** *In case of a vacancy in the office of the General Counsel the President is authorized to designate the officer or employee who shall act as General Counsel during such vacancy, but no person or persons so designated shall so act (1) for more than forty days when the Congress is in session unless a nomination to fill such vacancy shall have been submitted to the Senate, or (2) after the adjournment sine die of the session of the Senate in which such nomination was submitted.*

Sec. 4. **(a) Each member of the Board and the General Counsel of the Board [shall receive a salary of $12,000 per annum,] shall be eligible for reappointment, and shall not engage in any other business, vocation, or employment. The Board shall appoint an executive secretary, and such attorneys, examiners, and regional directors, and such other employees as it may from time to time find necessary for the proper performance of its duties. The Board may not employ any attorneys for the purpose of reviewing transcripts of hearings or preparing drafts of opinions except that any attorney employed for assignment as a legal assistant to any Board member may for such Board member review such transcripts and prepare such drafts. No administrative law judge's report shall be reviewed, either before or after its publication, by any person other than a member of the Board or his legal assistant, and no administrative law judge shall advise or consult with the Board with respect to exceptions taken to his findings, rulings, or recommendations. The Board may establish or utilize such regional, local, or other agencies, and utilize such voluntary and uncompensated services, as may from time to time be needed. Attorneys appointed under this section may, at the direction of the Board, appear for and represent the Board in any case in court. Nothing in this Act shall be construed to authorize the Board to appoint individuals for the purpose of conciliation or mediation, or for economic analysis.**

(b) All of the expenses of the Board, including all necessary traveling and subsistence expenses outside the District of

---

*   The bracketed matter was deleted in part in 1975 and in part in 1982, and the matter following was added in 1982.

**   The title "administrative law judge" was adopted in 5 U.S.C. § 3105, in 1972.

Columbia incurred by the members or employees of the Board under its orders, shall be allowed and paid on the presentation of itemized vouchers therefor approved by the Board or by any individual it designates for that purpose.

Sec. 5.   The principal office of the Board shall be in the District of Columbia, but it may meet and exercise any or all of its powers at any other place. The Board may, by one or more of its members or by such agents or agencies as it may designate, prosecute any inquiry necessary to its functions in any part of the United States. A member who participates in such an inquiry shall not be disqualified from subsequently participating in a decision of the Board in the same case.

Sec. 6.   The Board shall have authority from time to time to make, amend, and rescind, **in the manner prescribed by the Administrative Procedure Act,** such rules and regulations as may be necessary to carry out the provisions of this Act. [Such rules and regulations shall be effective upon publication in the manner which the Board shall prescribe.]

RIGHTS OF EMPLOYEES

Sec. 7.   Employees shall have the right to self-organization, to form, join, or assist labor organizations, to bargain collectively through representatives of their own choosing, and to engage in other concerted activities for the purpose of collective bargaining or other mutual aid or protection, **and shall also have the right to refrain from any or all of such activities except to the extent that such right may be affected by an agreement requiring membership in a labor organization as a condition of employment as authorized in section 8(a)(3).**

UNFAIR LABOR PRACTICES

Sec. 8.   (a) It shall be an unfair labor practice for an employer—

(1) to interfere with, restrain, or coerce employees in the exercise of the rights guaranteed in section 7;

(2) to dominate or interfere with the formation or administration of any labor organization or contribute financial or other support to it: *Provided*, That subject to rules and regulations made and published by the Board pursuant to section 6, an employer shall not be prohibited from permitting employees to confer with him during working hours without loss of time or pay;

(3) by discrimination in regard to hire or tenure of employment or any term or condition of employment to encourage or discourage membership in any labor organization: *Provided*, That nothing in this Act, or in any other statute of the United States, shall preclude an employer from making an agreement with a labor organization (not established, maintained, or assisted by any action defined in **section 8(a) of** this Act as an unfair labor practice) to require as a condition of employment membership therein **on or after the thirtieth day following the beginning of such employment or the effective date of such agreement, whichever is the later, (i)** if such labor organization is the

representative of the employees as provided in section 9(a), in the appropriate collective-bargaining unit covered by such agreement when made, **[and has at the time the agreement was made or within the preceding twelve months received from the Board a notice of compliance with Section 9(f), (g), (h)], and (ii) unless following an election held as provided in section 9(e) within one year preceding the effective date of such agreement, the Board shall have certified that at least a majority of the employees eligible to vote in such election have voted to rescind the authority of such labor organization to make such an agreement:** *Provided further*, **That no employer shall justify any discrimination against an employee for nonmembership in a labor organization (A) if he has reasonable grounds for believing that such membership was not available to the employee on the same terms and conditions generally applicable to other members, or (B) if he has reasonable grounds for believing that membership was denied or terminated for reasons other than the failure of the employee to tender the periodic dues and the initiation fees uniformly required as a condition of acquiring or retaining membership;**

(4) to discharge or otherwise discriminate against an employee because he has filed charges or given testimony under this Act;

(5) to refuse to bargain collectively with the representatives of his employees, subject to the provisions of section 9(a).

(b) **It shall be an unfair labor practice for a labor organization or its agents—**

(1) to restrain or coerce (A) employees in the exercise of the rights guaranteed in section 7: *Provided,* **That this paragraph shall not impair the right of a labor organization to prescribe its own rules with respect to the acquisition or retention of membership therein; or (B) an employer in the selection of his representatives for the purposes of collective bargaining or the adjustment of grievances;**

(2) to cause or attempt to cause an employer to discriminate against an employee in violation of subsection (a)(3) or to discriminate against an employee with respect to whom membership in such organization has been denied or terminated on some ground other than his failure to tender the periodic dues and the initiation fees uniformly required as a condition of acquiring or retaining membership;

---

* The (ii) provision was added in 1951 by 65 Stat. 601.

(3) to refuse to bargain collectively with an employer, provided it is the representative of his employees subject to the provisions of section 9(a);

(4) *(i)*to engage in, or to induce or encourage [the employees of any employer] *any individual employed by any person engaged in commerce or in an industry affecting commerce* to engage in, a strike or a [concerted] refusal in the course of [their] *his* employment to use, manufacture, process, transport, or otherwise handle or work on any goods, articles, materials, or commodities or to perform any services[,]; *or (ii) to threaten, coerce, or restrain any person engaged in commerce or in an industry affecting commerce,* where *in either case* an object thereof is—

(A) forcing or requiring any employer or self-employed person to join any labor or employer organization [or any employer or other person to cease using, selling, handling, transporting, or otherwise dealing in the products of any other producer, processor, or manufacturer, or to cease doing business with any other person;] *or to enter into any agreement which is prohibited by section 8(e);*

(B) forcing or requiring any [any employer or other] *person to cease using, selling, handling, transporting, or otherwise dealing in the products of any other producer, processor, or manufacturer, or to cease doing business with any other person, or* forcing or requiring any other employer to recognize or bargain with a labor organization as the representative of his employees unless such labor organization has been certified as the representative of such employees under the provisions of section 9[;]; *Provided, That nothing contained in this clause (B) shall be construed to make unlawful, where not otherwise unlawful, any primary strike or primary picketing;*

(C) forcing or requiring any employer to recognize or bargain with a particular labor organization as the representative of his employees if another labor organization has been certified as the representative of such employees under the provisions of section 9;

(D) forcing or requiring any employer to assign particular work to employees in a particular labor organization or in a particular trade, craft, or class rather than to employees in another labor organization or in another trade, craft, or class, unless such employer is failing to conform to an order or certification of the Board determining the bargaining representative for employees performing such work:

Provided, **That nothing contained in this subsection (b) shall be construed to make unlawful a refusal by any person to enter upon the premises of any employer (other than his own employer), if the employees of such employer are engaged in a strike ratified or approved by a representative of such employees whom such employer is required to recognize under this Act:** *Provided further, That for the purposes of this paragraph (4) only, nothing contained in such paragraph shall be construed to prohibit publicity, other than picketing, for the purpose of truthfully advising the public, including consumers and members of a labor organization, that a product or products are produced by an employer with whom the labor organization has a primary dispute and are distributed by another employer, as long as such publicity does not have an effect of inducing any individual employed by any person other than the primary employer in the course of his employment to refuse to pick up, deliver, or transport any goods, or not to perform any services, at the establishment of the employer engaged in such distribution:*

(5) to require of employees covered by an agreement authorized under subsection (a)(3) the payment, as a condition precedent to becoming a member of such organization, of a fee in an amount which the Board finds excessive or discriminatory under all the circumstances. In making such a finding, the Board shall consider, among other relevant factors, the practices and customs of labor organizations in the particular industry, and the wages currently paid to the employees affected; [and]

(6) to cause or attempt to cause an employer to pay or deliver or agree to pay or deliver any money or other thing of value, in the nature of an exaction, for services which are not performed or not to be performed[.]; *and*

(7) to picket or cause to be picketed, or threaten to picket or cause to be picketed, any employer where an object thereof is forcing or requiring an employer to recognize or bargain with a labor organization as the representatives of his employees, or forcing or requiring the employees of an employer to accept or select such labor organization as their collective bargaining representative, unless such labor organization is currently certified as the representative of such employees:

(A) where the employer has lawfully recognized in accordance with this Act any other labor organization and a question concerning representation may not appropriately be raised under section 9(c) of this Act.

(B) where within the preceding twelve months a valid election under section 9(c) of this Act has been conducted, or

(C) where such picketing has been conducted without a petition under section 9(c) being filed within a reasonable period of time not to exceed thirty days from the commencement of such picketing: Provided, That when such a petition has been filed the Board shall forthwith,

without regard to the provisions of section 9(c)(1) or the absence of a showing of a substantial interest on the part of the labor organization, direct an election in such unit as the Board finds to be appropriate and shall certify the results thereof: Provided further, That nothing in this subparagraph (C) shall be construed to prohibit any picketing or other publicity for the purpose of truthfully advising the public (including consumers) that an employer does not employ members of, or have a contract with, a labor organization, unless an effect of such picketing is to induce any individual employed by any other person in the course of his employment, not to pick up, deliver or transport any goods or not to perform any services.

Nothing in this paragraph (7) shall be construed to permit any act which would otherwise be an unfair labor practice under this section 8(b).

(c) The expressing of any views, argument, or opinion, or the dissemination thereof, whether in written, printed, graphic, or visual form, shall not constitute or be evidence of an unfair labor practice under any of the provisions of this Act, if such expression contains no threat of reprisal or force or promise of benefit.

(d) For the purposes of this section, to bargain collectively is the performance of the mutual obligation of the employer and the representative of the employees to meet at reasonable times and confer in good faith with respect to wages, hours, and other terms and conditions of employment, or the negotiation of an agreement, or any question arising thereunder, and the execution of a written contract incorporating any agreement reached if requested by either party, but such obligation does not compel either party to agree to a proposal or require the making of a concession: *Provided*, That where there is in effect a collective-bargaining contract covering employees in an industry affecting commerce, the duty to bargain collectively shall also mean that no party to such contract shall terminate or modify such contract, unless the party desiring such termination or modification—

(1) serves a written notice upon the other party to the contract of the proposed termination or modification sixty days prior to the expiration date thereof, or in the event such contract contains no expiration date, sixty days prior to the time it is proposed to make such termination or modification;

(2) offers to meet and confer with the other party for the purpose of negotiating a new contract or a contract containing the proposed modifications;

(3) notifies the Federal Mediation and Conciliation Service within thirty days after such notice of the existence of a dispute, and simultaneously therewith notifies any State or Territorial agency established to

mediate and conciliate disputes within the State or Territory where the dispute occurred, provided no agreement has been reached by that time; and

(4) continues in full force and effect, without resorting to strike or lock-out, all the terms and conditions of the existing contract for a period of sixty days after such notice is given or until the expiration date of such contract, whichever occurs later:

The duties imposed upon employers, employees, and labor organizations by paragraphs (2), (3), and (4) shall become inapplicable upon an intervening certification of the Board, under which the labor organization or individual, which is a party to the contract, has been superseded as or ceased to be the representative of the employees subject to the provisions of section 9(a), and the duties so imposed shall not be construed as requiring either party to discuss or agree to any modification of the terms and conditions contained in a contract for a fixed period, if such modification is to become effective before such terms and conditions can be reopened under the provisions of the contract. Any employee who engages in a strike within [the sixty-day] any notice period specified in this subsection, or who engages in any strike within the appropriate period specified in subsection (g) of this section, shall lose his status as an employee of the employer engaged in the particular labor dispute, for the purposes of sections 8, 9, and 10 of this Act, but such loss of status for such employee shall terminate if and when he is reemployed by such employer. Whenever the collective bargaining involves employees of a health care institution, the provisions of this section 8(d) shall be modified as follows:

(A) The notice of section 8(d)(1) shall be ninety days; the notice of section 8(d)(3) shall be sixty days; and the contract period of section 8(d)(4) shall be ninety days.

(B) Where the bargaining is for an initial agreement following certification or recognition, at least thirty days' notice of the existence of a dispute shall be given by the labor organization to the agencies set forth in section 8(d)(3).

(C) After notice is given to the Federal Mediation and Conciliation Service under either clause (A) or (B) of this sentence, the Service shall promptly communicate with the parties and use its best efforts, by mediation and conciliation, to bring them to agreement. The parties shall participate fully and promptly in such meetings as may be undertaken by the Service for the purpose of aiding in a settlement of the dispute.

(e) It shall be an unfair labor practice for any labor organization and any employer to enter into any contract or agreement, express or implied, whereby such employer ceases or refrains or agrees to cease or refrain from handling, using, selling, transporting or otherwise dealing in any of the products of any other employer, or to cease doing business with any other person, and any contract or agreement entered into heretofore or hereafter containing such an agreement shall be to such extent unenforcible and void: Provided, That nothing in this subsection

(e) shall apply to an agreement between a labor organization and an employer in the construction industry relating to the contracting or subcontracting of work to be done at the site of the construction, alteration, painting, or repair of a building, structure, or other work: Provided further, That for the purposes of this subsection (e) and section 8(b)(4)(B) the terms "any employer", "any person engaged in commerce or an industry affecting commerce", and "any person" when used in relation to the terms "any other producer, processor, or manufacturer", "any other employer", or "any other person" shall not include persons in the relation of a jobber, manufacturer, contractor, or subcontractor working on the goods or premises of the jobber or manufacturer or performing parts of an integrated process of production in the apparel and clothing industry: Provided further, That nothing in this Act shall prohibit the enforcement of any agreement which is within the foregoing exception.

(f)* It shall not be an unfair labor practice under subsections (a) and (b) of this section for an employer engaged primarily in the building and construction industry to make an agreement covering employees engaged (or who, upon their employment, will be engaged) in the building and construction industry with a labor organization of which building and construction employees are members (not established, maintained, or assisted by any action defined in section 8(a) of this Act as an unfair labor practice) because (1) the majority status of such labor organization has not been established under the provisions of section 9 of this Act prior to the making of such agreement, or (2) such agreement requires as a condition of employment, membership in such labor organization after the seventh day following the beginning of such employment or the effective date of the agreement, whichever is later, or (3) such agreement requires the employer to notify such labor organization of opportunities for employment with such employer, or gives such labor organization an opportunity to refer qualified applicants for such employment, or (4) such agreement specifies minimum training or experience qualifications for employment or provides for priority in opportunities for employment based upon length of service with such employer, in the industry or in the particular geographical area: Provided, That nothing in this subsection shall set aside the final proviso to section 8(a)(3) of this Act: Provided further, That any agreement which would be invalid, but for clause (1) of this subsection, shall not be a bar to a petition filed pursuant to section 9(c) or 9(e).

(g) A labor organization before engaging in any strike, picketing, or other concerted refusal to work at any health care institution shall, not less than ten days prior to such action, notify the institution in writing and the Federal Mediation and Conciliation Service of that intention, except that in the case of bargaining for an initial agreement following certification or recognition the notice required by this subsection shall not be given until the expiration of the period specified in clause (B) of the last sentence of section 8(d) of this Act. The notice shall state the

---

*   Sec. 8(f) was inserted in the Act by subsec. (a) of Sec. 705 of Public Law 86–257. Sec. 705(b) provides:

Nothing contained in the amendment made by subsection (a) shall be construed as authorizing the execution or application of agreements requiring membership in a labor organization as a condition of employment in any State or Territory in which such execution or application is prohibited by State or Territorial law.

date and time that such action will commence. The notice, once given, may be extended by the written agreement of both parties.

REPRESENTATIVES AND ELECTIONS

Sec. 9. (a) Representatives designated or selected for the purposes of collective bargaining by the majority of the employees in a unit appropriate for such purposes, shall be the exclusive representatives of all the employees in such unit for the purposes of collective bargaining in respect to rates of pay, wages, hours of employment, or other conditions of employment: *Provided,* That any individual employee or a group of employees shall have the right at any time to present grievances to their employer **and to have such grievances adjusted, without the intervention of the bargaining representative, as long as the adjustment is not inconsistent with the terms of a collective-bargaining contract or agreement then in effect:** *Provided further,* **That the bargaining representative has been given opportunity to be present at such adjustment.**

(b) The Board shall decide in each case whether, in order to assure to employees the fullest freedom in exercising the rights guaranteed by this Act, the unit appropriate for the purposes of collective bargaining shall be the employer unit, craft unit, plant unit, or subdivision thereof: *Provided,* **That the Board shall not (1) decide that any unit is appropriate for such purposes if such unit includes both professional employees and employees who are not professional employees unless a majority of such professional employees vote for inclusion in such unit; or (2) decide that any craft unit is inappropriate for such purposes on the ground that a different unit has been established by a prior Board determination, unless a majority of the employees in the proposed craft unit vote against separate representation or (3) decide that any unit is appropriate for such purposes if it includes, together with other employees, any individual employed as a guard to enforce against employees and other persons rules to protect property of the employer or to protect the safety of persons on the employer's premises; but no labor organization shall be certified as the representative of employees in a bargaining unit of guards if such organization admits to membership, or is affiliated directly or indirectly with an organization which admits to membership, employees other than guards.**

[(c) Whenever a question affecting commerce arises concerning the representation of employees, the Board may investigate such controversy and certify to the parties, in writing, the name or names of the representatives that have been designated or selected. In any such investigation, the Board shall provide for an appropriate hearing upon due notice, either in conjunction with a proceeding under section 10 or otherwise, and may take a secret ballot of employees, or utilize any other suitable method to ascertain such representatives.]

(c)(1) Whenever a petition shall have been filed, in accordance with such regulations as may be prescribed by the Board—

(A) by an employee or group of employees or any individual or labor organization acting in their behalf alleging that a substantial number of employees (i) wish to be represented for collective bargaining and that their employer declines to recognize their representative as the representative defined in section 9(a), or (ii) assert that the individual or labor organization, which has been certified or is being currently recognized by their employer as the bargaining representative, is no longer a representative as defined in section 9(a); or

(B) by an employer, alleging that one or more individuals or labor organizations have presented to him a claim to be recognized as the representative defined in section 9(a);

the Board shall investigate such petition and if it has reasonable cause to believe that a question of representation affecting commerce exists shall provide for an appropriate hearing upon due notice. Such hearing may be conducted by an officer or employee of the regional office, who shall not make any recommendations with respect thereto. If the Board finds upon the record of such hearing that such a question of representation exists, it shall direct an election by secret ballot and shall certify the results thereof.

(2) In determining whether or not a question of representation affecting commerce exists, the same regulations and rules of decision shall apply irrespective of the identity of the persons filing the petition or the kind of relief sought and in no case shall the Board deny a labor organization a place on the ballot by reason of an order with respect to such labor organization or its predecessor not issued in conformity with section 10(c).

(3) No election shall be directed in any bargaining unit or any subdivision within which, in the preceding twelve-month period, a valid election shall have been held. Employees [on strike] *engaged in an economic strike* who are not entitled to reinstatement shall [not] be eligible to vote *under such regulations as the Board shall find are consistent with the purposes and provisions of this Act in any election conducted within twelve months after the commencement of the strike.* In any election where none of the choices on the ballot receives a majority, a run-off shall be conducted, the ballot providing for a selection between the two choices receiving the largest and second largest number of valid votes cast in the election.

(4) Nothing in this section shall be construed to prohibit the waiving of hearings by stipulation for the purpose of a consent election in conformity with regulations and rules of decision of the Board.

(5) In determining whether a unit is appropriate for the purposes specified in subsection (b) the extent to which the employees have organized shall not be controlling.

(d) Whenever an order of the Board made pursuant to section 10(c) is based in whole or in part upon facts certified following an investigation pursuant to subsection (c) of this section and there is a petition for the enforcement or review of such order, such certification and the record of such investigation shall be included in the transcript of the entire record required to be filed under section 10(e) or 10(f), and thereupon the decree of the court enforcing, modifying, or setting aside in whole or in part the order of the Board shall be made and entered upon the pleadings, testimony, and proceedings set forth in such transcript.

(e)*(1) Upon the filing with the Board, by 30 per centum or more of the employees in a bargaining unit covered by an agreement between their employer and a labor organization made pursuant to section 8(a)(3), of a petition alleging they desire that such authority be rescinded, the Board shall take a secret ballot of the employees in such unit, and shall certify the results thereof to such labor organization and to the employer.

(2) No election shall be conducted pursuant to this subsection in any bargaining unit or any subdivision within which, in the preceding twelve-month period, a valid election shall have been held.

[Subsections (f), (g) and (h) were deleted by the Labor–Management Reporting and Disclosure Act.]

PREVENTION OF UNFAIR LABOR PRACTICES

Sec. 10. (a) The Board is empowered, as hereinafter provided, to prevent any person from engaging in any unfair labor practice (listed in section 8) affecting commerce. This power shall not be affected by any other means of adjustment or prevention that has been or may be established by agreement, law, or otherwise: *Provided,* **That the Board is empowered by agreement with any agency of any State or Territory to cede to such agency jurisdiction over any cases in any industry (other than mining, manufacturing, communications, and transportation except where predominantly local in character) even though such cases may involve labor disputes affecting commerce, unless the provision of the State of Territorial statute applicable to the determination of such cases by such agency is inconsistent with the corresponding provision of this Act or has received a construction inconsistent therewith.**

(b) Whenever it is charged that any person has engaged in or is engaging in any such unfair labor practice, the Board, or any agent or agency designated by the Board for such purposes, shall have power to issue and cause to be served upon such person a complaint stating the charges in that respect, and containing a notice of hearing before the Board or a member thereof, or before a designated agent or agency, at a place therein fixed, not less than five days after the serving of said

---

* As enacted in 1947, Section 9(e) had three subsections. In 1951, the first subsection was deleted and the two remaining subsections were renumbered (1) and (2). 65 Stat. 601. The deleted subsection required, as a condition to the inclusion of a union-shop provision in a collective agreement, that a majority of employees authorize such inclusion in a Board-conducted election.

complaint: *Provided*, **That no complaint shall issue based upon any unfair labor practice occurring more than six months prior to the filing of the charge with the Board and the service of a copy thereof upon the person against whom such charge is made, unless the person aggrieved thereby was prevented from filing such charge by reason of service in the armed forces, in which event the six-month period shall be computed from the day of his discharge.** Any such complaint may be amended by the member, agent, or agency conducting the hearing or the Board in its discretion at any time prior to the issuance of an order based thereon. The person so complained of shall have the right to file an answer to the original or amended complaint and to appear in person or otherwise and give testimony at the place and time fixed in the complaint. In the discretion of the member, agent, or agency conducting the hearing or the Board, any other person may be allowed to intervene in the said proceeding and to present testimony. [In any such proceeding the rules of evidence prevailing in courts of law or equity shall not be controlling.] **Any such proceeding shall, so far as practicable, be conducted in accordance with the rules of evidence applicable in the district courts of the United States under the rules of civil procedure for the district courts of the United States, adopted by the Supreme Court of the United States pursuant to section 2072 of Title 28.**

(c) The testimony taken by such member, agent, or agency or the Board shall be reduced to writing and filed with the Board. Thereafter, in its discretion, the Board upon notice may take further testimony or hear argument. If upon [all] **the preponderance of** the testimony taken the Board shall be of the opinion that any person named in the complaint has engaged in or is engaging in any such unfair labor practice, then the Board shall state its findings of fact and shall issue and cause to be served on such person an order requiring such person to cease and desist from such unfair labor practice, and to take such affirmative action including reinstatement of employees with or without back pay, as will effectuate the policies of this Act: *Provided*, **That where an order directs reinstatement of an employee, back pay may be required of the employer or labor organization, as the case may be, responsible for the discrimination suffered by him:** *And provided further*, **That in determining whether a complaint shall issue alleging a violation of section 8(a)(1) or section 8(a)(2), and in deciding such cases, the same regulations and rules of decision shall apply irrespective of whether or not the labor organization affected is affiliated with a labor organization national or international in scope.** Such order may further require such person to make reports from time to time showing the extent to which it has complied with the order. If upon [all] **the preponderance of** the testimony taken the Board shall not be of the opinion that the person named in the complaint has engaged in or is engaging in any such unfair labor practice, then the Board shall state its findings of fact and shall issue an order dismissing the said complaint. **No order of the Board shall require the reinstatement of any individual as an employee who has been suspended or discharged, or the payment to him of any back pay, if such individual was suspended or discharged for cause. In case the** evidence is presented before a member of the Board, or before an administrative law judge or judges* thereof, such member, or such judge or judges, as the case may be, shall issue and cause to be served on the parties to the proceeding a proposed report, together with a recommended order, which shall be filed with the Board, and if no exceptions are filed within twenty days after service thereof upon such parties, or within such further period as the Board may authorize, such recommended order shall become the order of the Board and become effective as therein prescribed.

(d) Until [**a transcript of**] the record in a case shall have been filed in a court, as hereinafter provided, the Board may at any time, upon reasonable notice and in such manner as it shall deem proper, modify or set aside, in whole or in part, any finding or order made or issued by it.

(e) The Board shall have power to petition any [United States] court of appeals of the United States [(including the United States court of appeals for the District of Columbia)] or if all the courts of appeals to which application may be made are in vacation, any [United States] district court *of the United States*, within any circuit or district, respectively, wherein the unfair labor practice in question occurred or wherein such person resides or transacts business, for the enforcement of such order and for appropriate temporary relief or restraining order, and shall [certify and] file in the court [a transcript of] the [entire] record in the proceedings, [including the pleadings and testimony upon which such order was entered and the findings and order of the Board.] *as printed in section 2112 of Title 28.* Upon [such filing] *the filing of such petition*, the court shall cause notice thereof to be served upon such person, and thereupon shall have jurisdiction of the proceeding and of the question determined therein, and shall have power to grant such temporary relief or restraining order as it deems just and proper, and to make and enter [upon the pleadings, testimony, and proceedings set forth in such transcript] a decree enforcing, modifying, and enforcing as so modified, or setting aside in whole or in part the order of the Board. No objection that has not been urged before the Board, its member, agent, or agency, shall be considered by the court, unless the failure or neglect to urge such objection shall be excused because of extraordinary circumstances. The findings of the Board with respect to questions of fact if supported by **substantial** evidence **on the record considered as a whole** shall be conclusive. If either party shall apply to the court for leave to adduce additional evidence and shall show to the satisfaction of the court that such additional evidence is material and that there were reasonable grounds for the failure to adduce such evidence in the hearing before the Board, its member, agent, or agency, the court may order such additional evidence to be taken before the Board, its member, agent, or agency, and to be made a part of [the transcript] *record.* The Board may modify its findings as to the facts, or make new findings, by reason of additional evidence so taken and filed, and it shall file such modified or new findings, which findings with respect to questions of fact if supported by **substantial** evidence **on the record considered as a whole** shall be conclusive, and shall file its

---

* The title "administrative law judge" was adopted in 5 U.S.C. § 3105, in 1972.

recommendations, if any, for the modification or setting aside of its original order. *Upon the filing of the record with it* the jurisdiction of the court shall be exclusive and its judgment and decree shall be final, except that the same shall be subject to review by the appropriate circuit court of appeals if application was made to the district court as hereinabove provided, and by the Supreme Court of the United States upon writ of certiorari or certification as provided in section 1254 of Title 28.

(f) Any person aggrieved by a final order of the Board granting or denying in whole or in part the relief sought may obtain a review of such order in any United States court of appeals in the circuit wherein the unfair labor practice in question was alleged to have been engaged in or wherein such person resides or transacts business, or in the United States Court of Appeals for the District of Columbia, by filing in such court a written petition praying that the order of the Board be modified or set aside. A copy of such petition shall be forthwith [served upon the Board] *transmitted by the clerk of the court to the Board* and thereupon the aggrieved party shall file in the court [a transcript of] the [entire] record in the proceeding, certified by the Board, [including the pleading and testimony upon which the order complained of was entered, and the findings and order of the Board.] *as provided in section 2112 of Title 28.* Upon [such filing,] *the filing of such petition*, the court shall proceed in the same manner as in the case of an application by the Board under subsection (e) *of this section*, and shall have the same exclusive jurisdiction to grant to the Board such temporary relief or restraining order as it deems just and proper, and in like manner to make and enter a decree enforcing, modifying, and enforcing as so modified, or setting aside in whole or in part the order of the Board; the findings of the Board with respect to questions of fact if supported by **substantial** evidence **on the record considered as a whole** shall in like manner be conclusive.

(g) The commencement of proceedings under subsection (e) or (f) of this section shall not, unless specifically ordered by the court, operate as a stay of the Board's order.

(h) When granting appropriate temporary relief or a restraining order, or making and entering a decree enforcing, modifying, and enforcing as so modified, or setting aside in whole or in part an order of the Board, as provided in this section, the jurisdiction of courts sitting in equity shall not be limited by sections 101 to 115 of title 29, United States Code.*

(i) [Repealed.]

(j) The Board shall have power, upon issuance of a complaint as provided in subsection (b) charging that any person has engaged in or is engaging in an unfair labor practice, to petition any United States district court within any district wherein the unfair labor practice in question is alleged to have occurred or wherein such person resides or transacts business, for appropriate temporary relief or restraining order. Upon the filing of any such petition the court shall cause notice thereof to be served upon such person, and thereupon shall

---

*   The Norris–LaGuardia Act of 1932.

have jurisdiction to grant to the Board such temporary relief or restraining order as it deems just and proper.

(k) Whenever it is charged that any person has engaged in an unfair labor practice within the meaning of paragraph (4)(D) of section 8(b), the Board is empowered and directed to hear and determine the dispute out of which such unfair labor practice shall have arisen, unless, within ten days after notice that such charge has been filed, the parties to such dispute submit to the Board satisfactory evidence that they have adjusted, or agreed upon methods for the voluntary adjustment of, the dispute. Upon compliance by the parties to the dispute with the decision of the Board or upon such voluntary adjustment of the dispute, such charge shall be dismissed.

(*l*) Whenever it is charged that any person has engaged in an unfair labor practice within the meaning of paragraph (4)(A), (B), or (C) of section 8(b), *or section 8(e) or section 8(b)(7)* the preliminary investigation of such charge shall be made forthwith and given priority over all other cases except cases of like character in the office where it is filed or to which it is referred. If, after such investigation, the officer or regional attorney to whom the matter may be referred has reasonable cause to believe such charge is true and that a complaint should issue, he shall, on behalf of the Board, petition any United States district court within any district where the unfair labor practice in question has occurred, is alleged to have occurred, or wherein such person resides or transacts business, for appropriate injunctive relief pending the final adjudication of the Board with respect to such matter. Upon the filing of any such petition the district court shall have jurisdiction to grant such injunctive relief or temporary restraining order as it deems just and proper, notwithstanding any other provision of law: *Provided further*, That no temporary restraining order shall be issued without notice unless a petition alleges that substantial and irreparable injury to the charging party will be unavoidable and such temporary restraining order shall be effective for no longer than five days and will become void at the expiration of such period[.]: *Provided further, That such officer or regional attorney shall not apply for any restraining order under section 8(b)(7) if a charge against the employer under section 8(a)(2) has been filed and after the preliminary investigation, he has reasonable cause to believe that such charge is true and that a complaint should issue.* Upon filing of any such petition the courts shall cause notice thereof to be served upon any person involved in the charge and such person, including the charging party, shall be given an opportunity to appear by counsel and present any relevant testimony: *Provided further*, That for the purposes of this subsection district courts shall be deemed to have jurisdiction of a labor organization (1) in the district in which such organization maintains its principal office, or (2) in any district in which its duly authorized officers or agents are engaged in promoting or protecting the interests of employee members. The service of legal process upon such officer or agent shall constitute service upon the labor organization and make such organization a party to the suit. In situations where such relief is appropriate the procedure specified herein shall apply to charges with respect to sections 8(b)(4)(D).

(m) Whenever it is charged that any person has engaged in an unfair labor practice within the meaning of subsection (a)(3) or (b)(2) of section 8, such charge shall be given priority over all other cases except cases of like character in the office where it is filed or to which it is referred and cases given priority under subsection (l) of this section.

INVESTIGATORY POWERS

Sec. 11. For the purpose of all hearings and investigations, which, in the opinion of the Board, are necessary and proper for the exercise of the powers vested in it by section 9 and section 10—

(1) The Board, or its duly authorized agents or agencies, shall at all reasonable times have access to, for the purpose of examination, and the right to copy any evidence of any person being investigated or proceeded against that relates to any matter under investigation or in question. The Board, or any member thereof, shall upon application of any party to such proceedings, forthwith issue to such party subpoenas requiring the attendance and testimony of witnesses or the production of any evidence in such proceeding or investigation requested in such application. **Within five days after the service of a subpena on any person requiring the production of any evidence in his possession or under his control, such person may petition the Board to revoke, and the Board shall revoke, such subpena if in its opinion the evidence whose production is required does not relate to any matter under investigation, or any matter in question in such proceedings, or if in its opinion such subpena does not describe with sufficient particularity the evidence whose production is required.** Any member of the Board, or any agent or agency designated by the Board for such purposes, may administer oaths and affirmations, examine witnesses, and receive evidence. Such attendance of witnesses and the production of such evidence may be required from any place in the United States or any Territory or possession thereof, at any designated place of hearing.

(2) In case of contumacy or refusal to obey a subpena issued to any person, any district court of the United States or the United States courts of any Territory or possession, or the District Court of the United States for the District of Columbia, within the jurisdiction of which the inquiry is carried on or within the jurisdiction of which said person guilty of contumacy or refusal to obey is found or resides or transacts business, upon application by the Board shall have jurisdiction to issue to such person an order requiring such person to appear before the Board, its member, agent, or agency, there to produce evidence if so ordered, or there to give testimony touching the matter under investigation or in question; and any failure to obey such order of the court may be punished by said court as a contempt thereof.

[(3) No person shall be excused from attending and testifying or from producing books, records, correspondence, documents, or other evidence in obedience to the subpena of the Board, on the ground that the testimony or evidence required of him may tend to incriminate him or subject him to a penalty or forfeiture; but no individual shall be prosecuted or subjected to any penalty or forfeiture for or on account of any transaction, matter, or thing concerning which he is compelled, after having claimed his privilege against self-incrimination, to testify or produce evidence, except that such individual so testifying shall not be exempt from prosecution and punishment for perjury committed in so testifying.]*

(4) Complaints, orders, and other process and papers of the Board, its member, agent, or agency, may be served either personally or by registered mail or by telegraph or by leaving a copy thereof at the principal office or place of business of the person required to be served. The verified return by the individual so serving the same setting forth the manner of such service shall be proof of the same, and the return post office receipt or telegraph receipt therefor when registered and mailed or telegraphed as aforesaid shall be proof of service of the same. Witnesses summoned before the Board, its member, agent, or agency, shall be paid the same fees and mileage that are paid witnesses in the courts of the United States, and witnesses whose depositions are taken and the persons taking the same shall severally be entitled to the same fees as are paid for like services in the courts of the United States.

(5) All process of any court to which application may be made under this Act may be served in the judicial district wherein the defendant or other person required to be served resides or may be found.

(6) The several departments and agencies of the Government, when directed by the President, shall furnish the Board, upon its request, all records, papers, and information in their possession relating to any matter before the Board.

Sec. 12. Any person who shall willfully resist, prevent, impede, or interfere with any member of the Board or any of its agents or agencies in the performance of duties pursuant to this Act shall be punished by a fine of not more than $5,000 or by imprisonment for not more than one year, or both.

LIMITATIONS

Sec. 13. Nothing in this Act, **except as specifically provided for herein,** shall be construed so as either to interfere with or impede or diminish in any way the right to strike, **or to affect the limitations or qualifications on that right.**

Sec. 14. (a) Nothing herein shall prohibit any individual employed as a supervisor from becoming or remaining a member of a labor organization, but no employer subject to this Act shall be compelled to deem individuals defined herein as supervisors as employees for the purpose of any law, either national or local, relating to collective bargaining.

(b) Nothing in this Act shall be construed as authorizing the execution or application of agreements requiring membership in a labor organization as a condition of employment in any State or Territory in which such execution or application is prohibited by State or Territorial law.

---

* Section 11(3) was repealed in 1970, by 84 Stat. 930. Similar immunity provisions were substituted; see 18 U.S.C. §§ 6001, 6002, 6004 (1970).

(c)(1) The Board, in its discretion, may, by rule of decision or by published rules adopted pursuant to the Administrative Procedure Act, decline to assert jurisdiction over any labor dispute involving any class or category of employers, where, in the opinion of the Board, the effect of such labor dispute on commerce is not sufficiently substantial to warrant the exercise of its jurisdiction: Provided, That the Board shall not decline to assert jurisdiction over any labor dispute over which it would assert jurisdiction under the standards prevailing upon August 1, 1959.

(2) Nothing in this Act shall be deemed to prevent or bar any agency or the courts of any State or Territory (including the Commonwealth of Puerto Rico, Guam, and the Virgin Islands), from assuming and asserting jurisdiction over labor disputes over which the Board declines, pursuant to paragraph (1) of this subsection, to assert jurisdiction.

Sec. 15. [Reference to repealed provisions of the Bankruptcy Act.]

Sec. 16. If any provision of this Act, or the application of such provision to any person or circumstances, shall be held invalid, the remainder of this Act, or the application of such provision to persons or circumstances other than those as to which it is held invalid, shall not be affected thereby.

Sec. 17. This Act may be cited as the "National Labor Relations Act."

Sec. 18. [This section, which refers to the now-repealed Sections 9(f), (g), (h), is omitted.]

INDIVIDUALS WITH RELIGIOUS CONVICTIONS

Sec. 19. Any employee who is a member of and adheres to established and traditional tenets or teachings of a bona fide religion, body, or sect which has historically held conscientious objections to joining or financially supporting labor organizations shall not be required to join or financially support any labor organization as a condition of employment; except that such employee may be required in a contract between such employee's employer and a labor organization in lieu of periodic dues and initiation fees, to pay sums equal to such dues and initiation fees to a nonreligious, nonlabor organization charitable fund exempt from taxation under section 501(c)(3) of title 26 of the Internal Revenue Code [section 501(c)(3) of title 26], chosen by such employee from a list of at least three such funds, designated in such contract or if the contract fails to designate such funds, then to any such fund chosen by the employee. If such employee who holds conscientious objections pursuant to this section

requests the labor organization to use the grievance-arbitration procedure on the employee's behalf, the labor organization is authorized to charge the employee for the reasonable cost of using such procedure.*

---

* This section was added by Pub.L. 93–360, July 26, 1974, 88 Stat. 397, and amended, Pub.L. 96–593, Dec. 24, 1980, 94 Stat. 3452.

LABOR MANAGEMENT RELATIONS ACT

61 Stat. 136 (1947), as amended; 29 U.S.C. §§ 141–97 (1988).

SHORT TITLE AND DECLARATION OF POLICY

Sec. 1. (a) This Act may be cited as the "Labor Management Relations Act, 1947."

(b) Industrial strife which interferes with the normal flow of commerce and with the full production of articles and commodities for commerce, can be avoided or substantially minimized if employers, employees, and labor organizations each recognize under law one another's legitimate rights in their relations with each other, and above all recognize under law that neither party has any right in its relations with any other to engage in acts or practices which jeopardize the public health, safety, or interest.

It is the purpose and policy of this Act, in order to promote the full flow of commerce, to prescribe the legitimate rights of both employees and employers in their relations affecting commerce, to provide orderly and peaceful procedures for preventing the interference by either with the legitimate rights of the other, to protect the rights of individual employees in their relations with labor organizations whose activities affect commerce, to define and proscribe practices on the part of labor and management which affect commerce and are inimical to the general welfare, and to protect the rights of the public in connection with labor disputes affecting commerce.

TITLE I

AMENDMENT OF NATIONAL LABOR RELATIONS ACT

Sec. 101.   The National Labor Relations Act is hereby amended to read as follows: [The text of the National Labor Relations Act as amended is set forth supra.]

TITLE II

CONCILIATION OF LABOR DISPUTES IN INDUSTRIES AFFECTING COMMERCE; NATIONAL EMERGENCIES

Sec. 201.   That it is the policy of the United States that—

(a) sound and stable industrial peace and the advancement of the general welfare, health, and safety of the Nation and of the best interests of employers and employees can most satisfactorily be secured by the settlement of issues between employers and employees through the processes of conference and collective bargaining between employers and the representatives of their employees;

(b) the settlement of issues between employers and employees through collective bargaining may be advanced by making available full and adequate governmental facilities for conciliation, mediation, and voluntary arbitration to aid and encourage employers and the representatives of their employees to reach and maintain agreements concerning rates of pay, hours, and working conditions, and to make all reasonable efforts to settle their differences by mutual agreement reached through conferences and collective bargaining or by such methods as may be provided for in any applicable agreement for the settlement of disputes; and

(c) certain controversies which arise between parties to collective-bargaining agreements may be avoided or minimized by making available full and adequate governmental facilities for furnishing assistance to employers and the representatives of their employees in formulating for inclusion within such agreements provision for adequate notice of any proposed changes in the terms of such agreements, for the final adjustment of grievances or questions regarding the application or interpretation of such agreements, and other provisions designed to prevent the subsequent arising of such controversies.

Sec. 202. (a) There is hereby created an independent agency to be known as the Federal Mediation and Conciliation Service (herein referred to as the "Service," except that for sixty days after the date of the enactment of this Act such term shall refer to the Conciliation Service of the Department of Labor). The Service shall be under the direction of a Federal Mediation and Conciliation Director (hereinafter referred to as the "Director"), who shall be appointed by the President by and with the advice and consent of the Senate. The Director shall not engage in any other business, vocation, or employment.

(b) The Director is authorized, subject to the civil-service laws, to appoint such clerical and other personnel as may be necessary for the execution of the functions of the Service, and shall fix their compensation in accordance with chapter 51 and subchapter III of chapter 53 of title 5, and may, without regard to the provisions of the civil-service laws, appoint such conciliators and mediators as may be necessary to carry out the functions of the Service. The Director is authorized to make such expenditures for supplies, facilities, and services as he deems necessary. Such expenditures shall be allowed and paid upon presentation of itemized vouchers therefor approved by the Director or by any employee designated by him for that purpose.

(c) The principal office of the Service shall be in the District of Columbia, but the Director may establish regional offices convenient to localities in which labor controversies are likely to arise. The Director may by order, subject to revocation at any time, delegate any authority and discretion conferred upon him by this Act to any regional director, or other officer or employee of the Service. The Director may establish suitable procedures for cooperation with State and local mediation agencies. The Director shall make an annual report in writing to Congress at the end of the fiscal year.

(d) All mediation and conciliation functions of the Secretary of Labor or the United States Conciliation Service under section 8 of the Act entitled "An Act to create a Department of Labor," approved March 4, 1913 (U.S.C., title 29, sec. 51), and all functions of the United States Conciliation Service under any other law are transferred to the Federal Mediation and Conciliation Service, together with the personnel and records of the United States Conciliation Service. Such transfer shall take effect upon the sixtieth day after June 23, 1947. Such transfer shall not affect any proceedings pending before the United States Conciliation Service or any certification, order, rule, or regulation theretofore made by it or by the Secretary of Labor. The Director and the Service shall not be subject in any way to the jurisdiction or authority of the Secretary of Labor or any official or division of the Department of Labor.

FUNCTIONS OF THE SERVICE

Sec. 203. (a) It shall be the duty of the Service, in order to prevent or minimize interruptions of the free flow of commerce growing out of labor disputes, to assist parties to labor disputes in industries affecting commerce to settle such disputes through conciliation and mediation.

(b) The Service may proffer its services in any labor dispute in any industry affecting commerce, either upon its own motion or upon the request of one or more of the parties to the dispute, whenever in its judgment such dispute threatens to cause a substantial interruption of commerce. The Director and the Service are directed to avoid attempting to mediate disputes which would have only a minor effect on interstate commerce if State or other conciliation services are available to the parties. Whenever the Service does proffer its services in any dispute, it shall be the duty of the Service promptly to put itself in communication with the parties and to use its best efforts, by mediation and conciliation, to bring them to agreement.

(c) If the Director is not able to bring the parties to agreement by conciliation within a reasonable time, he shall seek to induce the parties voluntarily to seek other means of settling the dispute without resort to strike, lock-out, or other coercion, including submission to the employees in the bargaining unit of the employer's last offer of settlement for approval or rejection in a secret ballot. The failure or refusal of either party to agree to any procedure suggested by the Director shall not be deemed a violation of any duty or obligation imposed by this Act.

(d) Final adjustment by a method agreed upon by the parties is hereby declared to be the desirable method for settlement of grievance disputes arising over the application or interpretation of an existing collective-bargaining agreement. The Service is directed to make its conciliation and mediation services available in the settlement of such grievance disputes only as a last resort and in exceptional cases.

(e)* The Service is authorized and directed to encourage and support the establishment and operation of joint labor management activities conducted by plant, area, and industrywide committees designed to improve labor management relationships, job security and organizational effectiveness, in accordance with the provisions of section 205A.

Sec. 204. (a) In order to prevent or minimize interruptions of the free flow of commerce growing out of labor disputes, employers and employees and their representatives, in any industry affecting commerce, shall—

---

* Subsection (e) was added in 1978, by Pub.L. 95–524, § 6(c)(1), 92 Stat. 2020.

(1) exert every reasonable effort to make and maintain agreements concerning rates of pay, hours, and working conditions, including provision for adequate notice of any proposed change in the terms of such agreements;

(2) whenever a dispute arises over the terms or application of a collective-bargaining agreement and a conference is requested by a party or prospective party thereto, arrange promptly for such a conference to be held and endeavor in such conference to settle such dispute expeditiously; and

(3) in case such dispute is not settled by conference, participate fully and promptly in such meetings as may be undertaken by the Service under this Act for the purpose of aiding in a settlement of the dispute.

Sec. 205.   (a) There is created a National Labor–Management Panel which shall be composed of twelve members appointed by the President, six of whom shall be selected from among persons outstanding in the field of management and six of whom shall be selected from among persons outstanding in the field of labor. Each member shall hold office for a term of three years, except that any member appointed to fill a vacancy occurring prior to the expiration of the term for which his predecessor was appointed shall be appointed for the remainder of such term, and the terms of office of the members first taking office shall expire, as designated by the President at the time of appointment, four at the end of the first year, four at the end of the second year, and four at the end of the third year after the date of appointment. Members of the panel, when serving on business of the panel, shall be paid compensation at the rate of $25 per day, and shall also be entitled to receive an allowance for actual and necessary travel and subsistence expenses while so serving away from their places of residence.

(b) It shall be the duty of the panel, at the request of the Director, to advise in the avoidance of industrial controversies and the manner in which mediation and voluntary adjustment shall be administered, particularly with reference to controversies affecting the general welfare of the country.

Sec. 205A.*   **(a)**(1) The Service is authorized and directed to provide assistance in the establishment and operation of plant, area and industrywide labor management committees which—

(A) have been organized jointly by employers and labor organizations representing employees in that plant, area, or industry; and

(B) are established for the purpose of improving labor management relationships, job security, organizational effectiveness, enhancing economic development or involving workers in decisions affecting their jobs including improving communication with respect to subjects of mutual interest and concern.

---

*   This section was added in 1978, by Pub.L. 95–524, § 6(c)(2), 92 Stat. 2020.

(2) The Service is authorized and directed to enter into contracts and to make grants, where necessary or appropriate, to fulfill its responsibilities under this section.

(b)(1) No grant may be made, no contract may be entered into and no other assistance may be provided under the provisions of this section to a plant labor management committee unless the employees in that plant are represented by a labor organization and there is in effect at that plant a collective bargaining agreement.

(2) No grant may be made, no contract may be entered into and no other assistance may be provided under the provisions of this section to an area or industrywide labor management committee unless its participants include any labor organizations certified or recognized as the representative of the employees of an employer participating in such committee. Nothing in this clause shall prohibit participation in an area or industrywide committee by an employer whose employees are not represented by a labor organization.

(3) No grant may be made under the provisions of this section to any labor management committee which the Service finds to have as one of its purposes the discouragement of the exercise of rights contained in section 7 of the National Labor Relations Act (29 U.S.C. § 157) [section 157 of this title], or the interference with collective bargaining in any plant, or industry.

(c) The Service shall carry out the provisions of this section through an office established for that purpose.

(d) There are authorized to be appropriated to carry out the provisions of this section $10,000,000 for the fiscal year 1979, and such sums as may be necessary thereafter.

NATIONAL EMERGENCIES

Sec. 206.   Whenever in the opinion of the President of the United States, a threatened or actual strike or lock-out affecting an entire industry or a substantial part thereof engaged in trade, commerce, transportation, transmission, or communication among the several States or with foreign nations, or engaged in the production of goods for commerce, will, if permitted to occur or to continue, imperil the national health or safety, he may appoint a board of inquiry to inquire into the issues involved in the dispute and to make a written report to him within such time as he shall prescribe. Such report shall include a statement of the facts with respect to the dispute, including each party's statement of its position but shall not contain any recommendations. The President shall file a copy of such report with the Service and shall make its contents available to the public.

Sec. 207.   (a) A board of inquiry shall be composed of a chairman and such other members as the President shall determine, and shall have power to sit and act in any place within the United States and to conduct such hearings either in public or in private, as it may deem necessary or proper, to ascertain the facts with respect to the causes and circumstances of the dispute.

(b) Members of a board of inquiry shall receive compensation at the rate of $50 for each day actually spent by them in the work of the board, together with necessary travel and subsistence expenses.

(c) For the purpose of any hearing or inquiry conducted by any board appointed under this title, the provisions of sections 9 and 10 (relating to the attendance of witnesses and the production of books, papers, and documents) of the Federal Trade Commission Act of September 16, 1914, as amended (U.S.C. 19, title 15, secs. 49 and 50, as amended), are made applicable to the powers and duties of such board.

Sec. 208.   (a) Upon receiving a report from a board of inquiry the President may direct the Attorney General to petition any district court of the United States having jurisdiction of the parties to enjoin such strike or lock-out or the continuing thereof, and if the court finds that such threatened or actual strike or lock-out—

(i) affects an entire industry or a substantial part thereof engaged in trade, commerce, transportation, transmission, or communication among the several States or with foreign nations, or engaged in the production of goods for commerce; and

(ii) if permitted to occur or to continue, will imperil the national health or safety, it shall have jurisdiction to enjoin any such strike or lock-out, or the continuing thereof, and to make such other orders as may be appropriate.

(b) In any case, the provisions of the Act of March 23, 1932, entitled "An Act to amend the Judicial Code and to define and limit the jurisdiction of courts sitting in equity, and for other purposes," shall not be applicable.

(c) The order or orders of the court shall be subject to review by the appropriate United States court of appeals and by the Supreme Court upon writ of certiorari or certification as provided in sections 239 and 240 of the Judicial Code, as amended (U.S.C., title 29, secs. 346 and 347).

Sec. 209.   (a) Whenever a district court has issued an order under section 208 enjoining acts or practices which imperil or threaten to imperil the national health or safety, it shall be the duty of the parties to the labor dispute giving rise to such order to make every effort to adjust and settle their differences, with the assistance of the Service created by this Act. Neither party shall be under any duty to accept, in whole or in part, any proposal of settlement made by the Service.

(b) Upon the issuance of such order, the President shall reconvene the board of inquiry which has previously reported with respect to the dispute. At the end of a sixty-day period (unless the dispute has been settled by that time), the board of inquiry shall report to the President the current position of the parties and the efforts which have been made for settlement, and shall include a statement by each party of its position and a statement of the employer's last offer of settlement. The President shall make such report available to the public. The National Labor Relations Board, within the succeeding fifteen days, shall take a secret ballot of the employees of each employer involved in the dispute on the question of whether they wish to accept the final offer of settlement made by their employer as stated by him and shall certify the results thereof to the Attorney General within five days thereafter.

Sec. 210.   Upon the certification of the results of such ballot or upon a settlement being reached, whichever happens sooner, the Attorney General shall move the court to discharge the injunction, which motion shall then be granted and the injunction discharged. When such motion is granted, the President shall submit to the Congress a full and comprehensive report of the proceedings, including the findings of the board of inquiry and the ballot taken by the National Labor Relations Board, together with such recommendations as he may see fit to make for consideration and appropriate action.

COMPILATION OF COLLECTIVE BARGAINING AGREEMENTS, ETC.

Sec. 211.   (a) For the guidance and information of interested representatives of employers, employees, and the general public, the Bureau of Labor Statistics of the Department of Labor shall maintain a file of copies of all available collective-bargaining agreements and other available agreements and actions thereunder settling or adjusting labor disputes. Such file shall be open to inspection under appropriate conditions prescribed by the Secretary of Labor, except that no specific information submitted in confidence shall be disclosed.

(b) The Bureau of Labor Statistics in the Department of Labor is authorized to furnish upon request of the Service, or employers, employees, or their representatives, all available data and factual information which may aid in the settlement of any labor dispute, except that no specific information submitted in confidence shall be disclosed.

EXEMPTION OF RAILWAY LABOR ACT

Sec. 212.   The provisions of this title shall not be applicable with respect to any matter which is subject to the provisions of the Railway Labor Act, as amended from time to time.

CONCILIATION OF LABOR DISPUTES IN THE HEALTH CARE INDUSTRY

Sec. 213.   (a) If, in the opinion of the Director of the Federal Mediation and Conciliation Service a threatened or actual strike or lockout affecting a health care institution will, if permitted to occur or to continue, substantially interrupt the delivery of health care in the locality concerned, the Director may further assist in the resolution of the impasse by establishing within 30 days after the notice to the Federal Mediation and Conciliation Service under clause (A) of the last sentence of section 8(d) (which is required by clause (3) of such section 8(d)), or within 10 days after the notice under clause (B), an impartial Board of Inquiry to investigate the issues involved in the dispute and to make a written report thereon to the parties within fifteen (15) days after the establishment of such a Board. The written report shall contain the findings of fact together with the Board's recommendations for settling the dispute, with the objective of achieving a prompt, peaceful and just settlement of the dispute. Each such Board shall be composed of such number of individuals as the Director may deem desirable. No member appointed under this section shall have any interest or involvement in the health care institutions or the employee organizations involved in the dispute.

(b)(1) Members of any board established under this section who are otherwise employed by the Federal Government shall serve without compensation but shall be reimbursed for travel, subsistence, and other necessary expenses incurred by them in carrying out its duties under this section.

(2) Members of any board established under this section who are not subject to paragraph (1) shall receive compensation at a rate prescribed by the Director but not to exceed the daily rate prescribed for GS–18 of the General Schedule under section 5332 of title 5, United States Code, including travel for each day they are engaged in the performance of their duties under this section and shall be entitled to reimbursement for travel, subsistence, and other necessary expenses incurred by them in carrying out their duties under this section.

(c) After the establishment of a board under subsection (a) of this section and for 15 days after any such board has issued its report, no change in the status quo in effect prior to the expiration of the contract in the case of negotiations for a contract renewal, or in effect prior to the time of the impasse in the case of an initial bargaining negotiation, except by agreement, shall be made by the parties to the controversy.

(d) There are authorized to be appropriated such sums as may be necessary to carry out the provisions of this section.

TITLE III

SUITS BY AND AGAINST LABOR ORGANIZATIONS

Sec. 301.   (a) Suits for violation of contracts between an employer and a labor organization representing employees in an industry affecting commerce as defined in this Act, or between any such labor organizations, may be brought in any district court of the United States having jurisdiction of the parties, without respect to the amount in controversy or without regard to the citizenship of the parties.

(b) Any labor organization which represents employees in an industry affecting commerce as defined in this Act and any employer whose activities affect commerce as defined in this Act shall be bound by the acts of its agents. Any such labor organization may sue or be sued as an entity and in behalf of the employees whom it represents in the courts of the United States. Any money judgment against a labor organization in a district court of the United States shall be enforceable only against the organization as an entity and against its assets, and shall not be enforceable against any individual member or his assets.

(c) For the purposes of actions and proceedings by or against labor organizations in the district courts of the United States, district courts shall be deemed to have jurisdiction of a labor organization (1) in the district in which such organization maintains its principal office, or (2) in any district in which its duly authorized officers or agents are engaged in representing or acting for employee members.

(d) The service of summons, subpena, or other legal process of any court of the United States upon an officer or agent of a labor organization, in his capacity as such, shall constitute service upon the labor organization.

(e) For the purposes of this section, in determining whether any person is acting as an "agent" of another person so as to make such other person responsible for his acts, the question of whether the specific acts performed were actually authorized or subsequently ratified shall not be controlling.

RESTRICTIONS ON PAYMENTS TO EMPLOYEE REPRESENTATIVES

Sec. 302. (a) It shall be unlawful for any employer or association of employers or any person who acts as a labor relations expert, adviser, or consultant to an employer or who acts in the interest of an employer to pay, lend, or deliver, or agree to pay, lend, or deliver, any money or other thing of value—

(1) to any representative of any of his employees who are employed in an industry affecting commerce; or

(2) to any labor organization, or any officer or employee thereof, which represents, seeks to represent, or would admit to membership, any of the employees of such employer who are employed in an industry affecting commerce; or

(3) to any employee or group or committee of employees of such employer employed in an industry affecting commerce in excess of their normal compensation for the purpose of causing such employee or group or committee directly or indirectly to influence any other employees in the exercise of the right to organize and bargain collectively through representatives of their own choosing; or

(4) to any officer or employee of a labor organization engaged in an industry affecting commerce with intent to influence him in respect to any of his actions, decisions, or duties as a representative of employees or as such officer or employee of such labor organization.

(b)(1) It shall be unlawful for any person to request, demand, receive, or accept, or agree to receive or accept, any payment, loan or delivery of any money or other thing of value prohibited by subsection (a).

(2) It shall be unlawful for any labor organization, or for any person acting as an officer, agent, representative, or employee of such labor organization, to demand or accept from the operator of any motor vehicle (as defined in part II of the Interstate Commerce Act) employed in the transportation of property in commerce, or the employer of any such operator, any money or other thing of value payable to such organization or to an officer, agent, representative or employee thereof as a fee or charge for the unloading, or in connection with the unloading, of the cargo of such vehicle: *Provided*, That nothing in this paragraph shall be construed to make unlawful any payment by an employer to any of his employees as compensation for their services as employees.

(c) The provisions of this section shall not be applicable (1) in respect to any money or other thing of value payable by an employer to any of his employees whose established duties include acting openly for such employer in matters of labor relations or personnel administration or to any representative of his employees, or to any officer or employee of a labor organization, who is also an employee or former employee of such employer, as compensation for, or by reason of, his service as an employee of such employer; (2) with respect to the payment or delivery of any money or other thing of value in satisfaction of a judgment of any court or a decision or award of an arbitrator or impartial chairman or in compromise, adjustment, settlement, or release of any claim, complaint, grievance, or dispute in the absence of fraud or duress; (3) with respect to the sale or purchase of an article or commodity at the prevailing market price in the regular course of business; (4) with respect to money deducted from the wages of employees in payment of membership dues in a labor organization: *Provided*, That the employer has received from each employee, on whose account such deductions are made, a written assignment which shall not be irrevocable for a period of more than one year, or beyond the termination date of the applicable collective agreement, whichever occurs sooner; (5) with respect to money or other thing of value paid to a trust fund established by such representative, for the sole and exclusive benefit of the employees of such employer, and their families and dependents (or of such employees, families, and dependents jointly with the employees of other employers making similar payments, and their families and dependents): *Provided*, That (A) such payments are held in trust for the purpose of paying, either from principal or income or both, for the benefit of employees, their families and dependents, for medical or hospital care, pensions on retirement or death of employees, compensation for injuries or illness resulting from occupational activity or insurance to provide any of the foregoing, or unemployment benefits or life insurance, disability and sickness insurance, or accident insurance; (B) the detailed basis on which such payments are to be made is specified in a written agreement with the employer, and employees and employers are equally represented in the administration of such fund, together with such neutral persons as the representatives of the employers and the representatives of employees may agree upon and in the event the employer and employee groups deadlock on the administration of such fund and there are no neutral persons empowered to break such deadlock, such agreement provides that the two groups shall agree on an impartial umpire to decide such dispute, or in event of their failure to agree within a reasonable length of time, an impartial umpire to decide such dispute shall, on petition of either group, be appointed by the district court of the United States for the district where the trust fund has its principal office, and shall also contain provisions for an annual audit of the trust fund, a statement of the results of which shall be available for inspection by interested persons at the principal office of the trust fund and at such other places as may be designated in such written agreement; and (C) such payments as are intended to be used for the purpose of providing pensions or annuities for employees are made to a separate trust which provides that the funds held therein cannot be used for any purpose other than paying such pensions or annuities; (6) with respect to money or other thing of value paid by any employer to a trust fund established by such representative for the purpose of pooled vacation, holiday, severance or similar benefits, or defraying costs of apprenticeship or other training programs: *Provided*, That the requirements of clause (B) of the proviso to clause (5) of this subsection, shall apply to such trust funds; (7) with respect to money or other thing of value paid by any employer to a pooled or individual trust fund established by such representative for the purpose of (A) scholarships for the benefit of employees, their families, and dependents for study at educational institutions, (B) child care centers for pre-school and school age dependents of employees, or (C) financial assistance for employee housing: *Provided*, That no labor organization or employer shall be required to bargain on the establishment of any such trust fund, and refusal to do so shall not constitute an unfair labor practice: *Provided further*, That the requirements of clause (B) of the proviso to clause (5) of this subsection shall apply to such trust funds; (8) with respect to money or any other thing of value paid by any employer to a trust fund established by such representative for the purpose of defraying the costs of legal services for employees, their families, and dependents for counsel or plan of their choice: *Provided*, That the requirements of clause (B) of the proviso to clause (5) of this subsection shall apply to such trust funds: *Provided further*, That no such legal services shall be furnished: (A) to initiate any proceeding directed (i) against any such employer or its officers or agents except in workman's compensation cases, or (ii) against such labor organization, or its parent or subordinate bodies, or their officers or agents, or (iii) against any other employer or labor organization, or their officers or agents, in any matter arising under the National Labor Relations Act, as amended, or this Act; and (B) in any proceeding where a labor organization would be prohibited from defraying the costs of legal services by the provisions of the Labor–Management Reporting and Disclosure Act of 1959; or (9) with respect to money or other things of value paid by an employer to a plant, area or industry-wide labor management committee established for one or more of the purposes set forth in section 5(b) of the Labor Management Cooperation Act of 1978.*

(d)(1) Any person who participates in a transaction involving a payment, loan, or delivery of money or other thing of value to a labor organization in payment of membership dues or to a joint labor-management trust fund as defined by clause (B) of the proviso to clause (5) of subsection (c) of this section or to a plant, area, or industry-wide labor-management committee that is received and used by such labor organization, trust fund, or committee, which transaction does not satisfy all the applicable requirements of subsections (c)(4) through (c)(9) of this section, and willfully and with intent to benefit himself or to benefit other persons he knows are not permitted to receive a payment, loan, money, or other thing of value under subsections (c)(4) through (c)(9) violates this subsection, shall, upon conviction thereof, be guilty of a felony and be subject to a fine of not more than $15,000, or imprisoned for not more than five years, or both; but if the value of the amount of money or thing of value involved in any violation of the provisions of this section does not exceed $1,000, such person shall be guilty of a misdemeanor and be subject to a fine of not more than $10,000, or imprisoned for not more than one year, or both.

(2) Except for violations involving transactions covered by subsection (d)(1) of this section, any person who willfully violates this

---

* Sec. 302(c)(7) was added by Pub.L. 91–86, Oct. 14, 1969, 83 Stat. 133; Sec. 302(c)(8) by Pub.L. 93–95, Aug. 15, 1973, 87 Stat. 314; and Sec. 302(c)(9) by Pub.L. 95–524, Oct. 27, 1978, 92 Stat. 2021.

section shall, upon conviction thereof, be guilty of a felony and be subject to a fine of not more than $15,000 or imprisoned for not more than five years, or both; but if the value of the amount of money or thing of value involved in any violation of the provisions of this section does not exceed $1,000, such person shall be guilty of a misdemeanor and be subject to a fine of not more than $10,000, or imprisoned for not more than one year, or both.**

(e) The district courts of the United States and the United States courts of the Territories and possessions shall have jurisdiction, for cause shown, and subject to the provisions of section 17 (relating to notice to opposite party) of the Act entitled "An Act to supplement existing laws against unlawful restraints and monopolies, and for other purposes," approved October 15, 1914, as amended (U.S.C., title 28, section 381), to restrain violations of this section, without regard to the provisions of sections 6 and 20 of such Act of October 15, 1914, as amended (U.S.C., title 15, section 17, and title 29, section 52), and the provisions of the Act entitled "An Act to amend the Judicial Code and to define and limit the jurisdiction of courts sitting in equity, and for other purposes," approved March 23, 1932 (U.S.C., title 29, sections 101–115).

(f) This section shall not apply to any contract in force on the date of enactment of this Act, until the expiration of such contract, or until July 1, 1948, whichever first occurs.

(g) Compliance with the restrictions contained in subsection (c)(5)(B) upon contributions to trust funds, otherwise lawful, shall not be applicable to contributions to such trust funds established by collective agreement prior to January 1, 1946, nor shall subsection (c)(5)(A) be construed as prohibiting contributions to such trust funds if prior to January 1, 1947, such funds contained provisions for pooled vacation benefits.

BOYCOTTS AND OTHER UNLAWFUL COMBINATIONS

Sec. 303.   (a) It shall be unlawful, for the purpose of this section only, in an industry or activity affecting commerce, for any labor organization to engage in any activity or conduct defined as an unfair labor practice in section 8(b)(4) of the National Labor Relations Act, as amended.

(b) Whoever shall be injured in his business or property by reason of any violation of subsection (a) may sue therefor in any district court of the United States subject to the limitations and provisions of section 301 hereof without respect to the amount in controversy, or in any other court having jurisdiction of the parties, and shall recover the damages by him sustained and the cost of the suit.

Sec. 304.   [Repealed.]

Sec. 305.   [Repealed.]

** Section 302(d) was amended by Pub.L. 98–473, Oct. 12, 1984, 98 Stat. 2131.

TITLE IV
CREATION OF JOINT COMMITTEE TO STUDY AND
REPORT ON BASIC PROBLEMS AFFECTING FRIENDLY
LABOR RELATIONS AND PRODUCTIVITY

*   *   *

TITLE V
DEFINITIONS

Sec. 501. When used in this Act—

(1) The term "industry affecting commerce" means any industry or activity in commerce or in which a labor dispute would burden or obstruct commerce or tend to burden or obstruct commerce or the free flow of commerce.

(2) The term "strike" includes any strike or other concerted stoppage of work by employees (including a stoppage by reason of the expiration of a collective-bargaining agreement) and any concerted slow-down or other concerted interruption of operations by employees.

(3) The terms "commerce", "labor disputes", "employer", "employee", "labor organization", "representative", "person", and "supervisor" shall have the same meaning as when used in the National Labor Relations Act as amended by this Act.

SAVING PROVISION

Sec. 502. Nothing in this Act shall be construed to require an individual employee to render labor or service without his consent, nor shall anything in this Act be construed to make the quitting of his labor by an individual employee an illegal act; nor shall any court issue any process to compel the performance by an individual employee of such labor or service, without his consent; nor shall the quitting of labor by an employee or employees in good faith because of abnormally dangerous conditions for work at the place of employment of such employee or employees be deemed a strike under this Act.

SEPARABILITY

Sec. 503. If any provision of this Act, or the application of such provision to any person or circumstance, shall be held invalid, the remainder of this Act, or the application of such provision to persons or circumstances other than those as to which it is held invalid, shall not be affected thereby.

LABOR-MANAGEMENT REPORTING AND DISCLOSURE ACT OF 1959

73 Stat. 519 (1959), as amended; 29 U.S.C. §§ 401–531 (1988).

SHORT TITLE

Sec. 1. This Act may be cited as the "Labor–Management Reporting and Disclosure Act of 1959".

DECLARATION OF FINDINGS, PURPOSES, AND POLICY

Sec. 2. (a) The Congress finds that, in the public interest, it continues to be the responsibility of the Federal Government to protect employees' rights to organize, choose their own representatives, bargain collectively, and otherwise engage in concerted activities for their mutual aid or protection; that the relations between employers and labor organizations and the millions of workers they represent have a substantial impact on the commerce of the Nation; and that in order to accomplish the objective of a free flow of commerce it is essential that labor organizations, employers, and their officials adhere to the highest standards of responsibility and ethical conduct in administering the affairs of their organizations, particularly as they affect labor-management relations.

(b) The Congress further finds, from recent investigations in the labor and management fields, that there have been a number of instances of breach of trust, corruption, disregard of the rights of individual employees, and other failures to observe high standards of responsibility and ethical conduct which require further and supplementary legislation that will afford necessary protection of the rights and interests of employees and the public generally as they relate to the activities of labor organizations, employers, labor relations consultants, and their officers and representatives.

(c) The Congress, therefore, further finds and declares that the enactment of this Act is necessary to eliminate or prevent improper practices on the part of labor organizations, employers, labor relations consultants, and their officers and representatives which distort and defeat the policies of the Labor Management Relations Act, 1947, as amended, and the Railway Labor Act, as amended, and have the tendency or necessary effect of burdening or obstructing commerce by (1) impairing the efficiency, safety, or operation of the instrumentalities of commerce; (2) occurring in the current of commerce; (3) materially affecting, restraining, or controlling the flow of raw materials or manufactured or processed goods into or from the channels of commerce, or the prices of such materials or goods in commerce; or (4) causing diminution of employment and wages in such volume as substantially to impair or disrupt the market for goods flowing into or from the channels of commerce.

DEFINITIONS

Sec. 3. For the purposes of titles I, II, III, IV, V (except section 505), and VI of this Act—

(a) "Commerce" means trade, traffic, commerce, transportation, transmission, or communication among the several States or between any State and any place outside thereof.

(b) "State" includes any State of the United States, the District of Columbia, Puerto Rico, the Virgin Islands, American Samoa, Guam, Wake Island, the Canal Zone, and Outer Continental Shelf lands defined in the Outer Continental Shelf Lands Act (43 U.S.C. §§ 1331–1343).

(c) "Industry affecting commerce" means any activity, business, or industry in commerce or in which a labor dispute would hinder or obstruct commerce or the free flow of commerce and includes any activity or industry "affecting commerce" within the meaning of the Labor Management Relations Act, 1947, as amended, or the Railway Labor Act, as amended.

(d) "Person" includes one or more individuals, labor organizations, partnerships, associations, corporations, legal representatives, mutual companies, joint-stock companies, trusts, unincorporated organizations, trustees, trustees in bankruptcy, or receivers.

(e) "Employer" means any employer or any group or association of employers engaged in an industry affecting commerce (1) which is, with respect to employees engaged in an industry affecting commerce, an employer within the meaning of any law of the United States relating to the employment of any employees or (2) which may deal with any labor organization concerning grievances, labor disputes, wages, rates of pay, hours of employment, or conditions of work, and includes any person acting directly or indirectly as an employer or as an agent of an employer in relation to an employee but does not include the United States or any corporation wholly owned by the Government of the United States or any State or political subdivision thereof.

(f) "Employee" means any individual employed by an employer, and includes any individual whose work has ceased as a consequence of, or in connection with, any current labor dispute or because of any unfair labor practice or because of exclusion or expulsion from a labor organization in any manner or for any reason inconsistent with the requirements of this Act.

(g) "Labor dispute" includes any controversy concerning terms, tenure, or conditions of employment, or concerning the association or representation of persons in negotiating, fixing, maintaining, changing or seeking to arrange terms or conditions of employment, regardless of whether the disputants stand in the proximate relation of employer and employee.

(h) "Trusteeship" means any receivership, trusteeship, or other method of supervision or control whereby a labor organization suspends the autonomy otherwise available to a subordinate body under its constitution or bylaws.

(i) "Labor organization" means a labor organization engaged in an industry affecting commerce and includes any organization of any kind, any agency, or employee representation committee, group, association, or plan so engaged in which employees participate and which exists for the purpose, in whole or in part, of dealing with employers concerning grievances, labor disputes, wages, rates of pay, hours, or other terms or conditions of employment, and any conference, general committee, joint or system board, or joint council so engaged which is subordinate to a national or international labor organization, other than a State or local central body.

(j) A labor organization shall be deemed to be engaged in an industry affecting commerce if it—

(1) is the certified representative of employees under the provisions of the National Labor Relations Act, as amended, or the Railway Labor Act, as amended; or

(2) although not certified, is a national or international labor organization or a local labor organization recognized or acting as the representative of employees of an employer or employers engaged in an industry affecting commerce; or

(3) has chartered a local labor organization or subsidiary body which is representing or actively seeking to represent employees of employers within the meaning of paragraph (1) or (2); or

(4) has been chartered by a labor organization representing or actively seeking to represent employees within the meaning of paragraph (1) or (2) as the local or subordinate body through which such employees may enjoy membership or become affiliated with such labor organization; or

(5) is a conference, general committee, joint or system board, or joint council, subordinate to a national or international labor organization, which includes a labor organization engaged in an industry affecting commerce within the meaning of any of the preceding paragraphs of this subsection, other than a State or local central body.

(k) "Secret ballot" means the expression by ballot, voting machine, or otherwise, but in no event by proxy, of a choice with respect to any election or vote taken upon any matter, which is cast in such a manner that the person expressing such choice cannot be identified with the choice expressed.

(l) "Trust in which a labor organization is interested" means a trust or other fund or organization (1) which was created or established by a labor organization, or one or more of the trustees or one or more members of the governing body of which is selected or appointed by a labor organization, and (2) a primary purpose of which is to provide benefits for the members of such labor organization or their beneficiaries.

(m) "Labor relations consultant" means any person who, for compensation, advises or represents an employer, employer organization, or labor organization concerning employee organizing, concerted activities, or collective bargaining activities.

(n) "Officer" means any constitutional officer, any person authorized to perform the functions of president, vice president, secretary, treasurer, or other executive functions of a labor organization, and any member of its executive board or similar governing body.

(*o*) "Member" or "member in good standing", when used in reference to a labor organization, includes any person who has fulfilled the requirements for membership in such organization, and who neither has voluntarily withdrawn from membership nor has been expelled or suspended from membership after appropriate proceedings consistent with lawful provisions of the constitution and bylaws of such organization.

(p) "Secretary" means the Secretary of Labor.

(q) "Officer, agent, shop steward, or other representative", when used with respect to a labor organization, includes elected officials and key administrative personnel, whether elected or appointed (such as business agents, heads of departments or major units, and organizers who exercise substantial independent authority), but does not include salaried nonsupervisory professional staff, stenographic, and service personnel.

(r) "District court of the United States" means a United States district court and a United States court of any place subject to the jurisdiction of the United States.

TITLE I—BILL OF RIGHTS OF MEMBERS OF LABOR ORGANIZATIONS

BILL OF RIGHTS

Sec. 101. (a)(1) EQUAL RIGHTS.—Every member of a labor organization shall have equal rights and privileges within such organization to nominate candidates, to vote in elections or referendums of the labor organization, to attend membership meetings, and to participate in the deliberations and voting upon the business of such meetings, subject to reasonable rules and regulations in such organization's constitution and bylaws.

(2) FREEDOM OF SPEECH AND ASSEMBLY.—Every member of any labor organization shall have the right to meet and assemble freely with other members; and to express any views, arguments, or opinions; and to express at meetings of the labor organization his views, upon candidates in an election of the labor organization or upon any business properly before the meeting, subject to the organization's established and reasonable rules pertaining to the conduct of meetings: *Provided*, That nothing herein shall be construed to impair the right of a labor organization to adopt and enforce reasonable rules as to the responsibility of every member toward the organization as an institution and to his refraining from conduct that would interfere with its performance of its legal or contractual obligations.

(3) DUES, INITIATION FEES, AND ASSESSMENTS.—Except in the case of a federation of national or international labor organizations, the rates of dues and initiation fees payable by members of any labor organization in effect on the date of enactment of this Act shall not be increased, and no general or special assessment shall be levied upon such members, except—

    (A) in a case of a local labor organization, (i) by majority vote by secret ballot of the members in good standing voting at a general or special membership meeting, after reasonable notice of the intention to vote upon such question, or (ii) by majority vote of the members in good standing voting in a membership referendum conducted by secret ballot; or

(B) in the case of a labor organization, other than a local labor organization or a federation of national or international labor organizations, (i) by majority vote of the delegates voting at a regular convention, or at a special convention of such labor organization held upon not less than thirty days' written notice to the principal office of each local or constituent labor organization entitled to such notice, or (ii) by majority vote of the members in good standing of such labor organization voting in a membership referendum conducted by secret ballot, or (iii) by majority vote of the members of the executive board or similar governing body of such labor organization, pursuant to express authority contained in the constitution and bylaws of such labor organization: *Provided*, That such action on the part of the executive board or similar governing body shall be effective only until the next regular convention of such labor organization.

(4) PROTECTION OF THE RIGHT TO SUE.—No labor organization shall limit the right of any member thereof to institute an action in any court, or in a proceeding before any administrative agency, irrespective of whether or not the labor organization or its officers are named as defendants or respondents in such action or proceeding, or the right of any member of a labor organization to appear as a witness in any judicial, administrative, or legislative proceeding, or to petition any legislature or to communicate with any legislator: *Provided*, That any such member may be required to exhaust reasonable hearing procedures (but not to exceed a four-month lapse of time) within such organization, before instituting legal or administrative proceedings against such organizations or any officer thereof: *And provided further*, That no interested employer or employer association shall directly or indirectly finance, encourage, or participate in, except as a party, any such action, proceeding, appearance, or petition.

(5) SAFEGUARDS AGAINST IMPROPER DISCIPLINARY ACTION.—No member of any labor organization may be fined, suspended, expelled, or otherwise disciplined except for nonpayment of dues by such organization or by any officer thereof unless such member has been (A) served with written specific charges; (B) given a reasonable time to prepare his defense; (C) afforded a full and fair hearing.

(b) Any provision of the constitution and bylaws of any labor organization which is inconsistent with the provisions of this section shall be of no force or effect.

CIVIL ENFORCEMENT

Sec. 102.   Any person whose rights secured by the provisions of this title have been infringed by any violation of this title may bring a civil action in a district court of the United States for such relief (including injunctions) as may be appropriate. Any such action against a labor organization shall be brought in the district court of the United

States for the district where the alleged violation occurred, or where the principal office of such labor organization is located.

RETENTION OF EXISTING RIGHTS

Sec. 103. Nothing contained in this title shall limit the rights and remedies of any member of a labor organization under any State or Federal law or before any court or other tribunal, or under the constitution and bylaws of any labor organization.

RIGHT TO COPIES OF COLLECTIVE BARGAINING AGREEMENTS

Sec. 104. It shall be the duty of the secretary or corresponding principal officer of each labor organization, in the case of a local labor organization, to forward a copy of each collective bargaining agreement made by such labor organization with any employer to any employee who requests such a copy and whose rights as such employee are directly affected by such agreement, and in the case of a labor organization other than a local labor organization, to forward a copy of any such agreement to each constituent unit which has members directly affected by such agreement; and such officer shall maintain at the principal office of the labor organization of which he is an officer copies of any such agreement made or received by such labor organization, which copies shall be available for inspection by any member or by any employee whose rights are affected by such agreement. The provisions of section 210 shall be applicable in the enforcement of this section.

INFORMATION AS TO ACT

Sec. 105. Every labor organization shall inform its members concerning the provisions of this Act.

TITLE II—REPORTING BY LABOR ORGANIZATIONS, OFFICERS AND EMPLOYEES OF LABOR ORGANIZATIONS, AND EMPLOYERS

REPORT OF LABOR ORGANIZATIONS

Sec. 201. (a) Every labor organization shall adopt a constitution and bylaws and shall file a copy thereof with the Secretary, together with a report, signed by its president and secretary or corresponding principal officers, containing the following information—

(1) the name of the labor organization, its mailing address, and any other address at which it maintains its principal office or at which it keeps the records referred to in this title;

(2) the name and title of each of its officers;

(3) the initiation fee or fees required from a new or transferred member and fees for work permits required by the reporting labor organization;

(4) the regular dues or fees or other periodic payments required to remain a member of the reporting labor organization; and

(5) detailed statements, or references to specific provisions of documents filed under this subsection which contain such statements, showing the provision made and procedures followed with respect to each of the following: (A) qualifications

for or restrictions on membership, (B) levying of assessments, (C) participation in insurance or other benefit plans, (D) authorization for disbursement of funds of the labor organization, (E) audit of financial transactions of the labor organization, (F) the calling of regular and special meetings, (G) the selection of officers and stewards and of any representatives to other bodies composed of labor organizations' representatives, with a specific statement of the manner in which each officer was elected, appointed, or otherwise selected, (H) discipline or removal of officers or agents for breaches of their trust, (I) imposition of fines, suspensions and expulsions of members, including the grounds for such action and any provision made for notice, hearing, judgment on the evidence, and appeal procedures, (J) authorization for bargaining demands, (K) ratification of contract terms, (L) authorization for strikes, and (M) issuance of work permits. Any change in the information required by this subsection shall be reported to the Secretary at the time the reporting labor organization files with the Secretary the annual financial report required by subsection (b).

(b) Every labor organization shall file annually with the Secretary a financial report signed by its president and treasurer or corresponding principal officers containing the following information in such detail as may be necessary accurately to disclose its financial condition and operations for its preceding fiscal year—

(1) assets and liabilities at the beginning and end of the fiscal year;

(2) receipts of any kind and the sources thereof;

(3) salary, allowances, and other direct or indirect disbursements (including reimbursed expenses) to each officer and also to each employee who, during such fiscal year, received more than $10,000 in the aggregate from such labor organization and any other labor organization affiliated with it or with which it is affiliated, or which is affiliated with the same national or international labor organization;

(4) direct and indirect loans made to any officer, employee, or member, which aggregated more than $250 during the fiscal year, together with a statement of the purpose, security, if any, and arrangements for repayment;

(5) direct and indirect loans to any business enterprise, together with a statement of the purpose, security, if any, and arrangements for repayment; and

(6) other disbursements made by it including the purposes thereof;

all in such categories as the Secretary may prescribe.

(c) Every labor organization required to submit a report under this title shall make available the information required to be contained in such report to all of its members, and every such labor organization and its officers shall be under a duty enforceable at the suit of any member of such organization in any State court of competent jurisdiction or in the district court of the United States for the district in which such labor organization maintains its principal office, to permit such member for just cause to examine any books, records, and accounts necessary to verify such report. The court in such action may, in its discretion, in addition to any judgment awarded to the plaintiff or plaintiffs, allow a reasonable attorney's fee to be paid by the defendant, and costs of the action.

REPORT OF OFFICERS AND EMPLOYEES OF LABOR ORGANIZATIONS

Sec. 202. (a) Every officer of a labor organization and every employee of a labor organization (other than an employee performing exclusively clerical or custodial services) shall file with the Secretary a signed report listing and describing for his preceding fiscal year—

(1) any stock, bond, security, or other interest, legal or equitable, which he or his spouse or minor child directly or indirectly held in, and any income or any other benefit with monetary value (including reimbursed expenses) which he or his spouse or minor child derived directly or indirectly from, an employer whose employees such labor organization represents or is actively seeking to represent, except payments and other benefits received as a bona fide employee of such employer;

(2) any transaction in which he or his spouse or minor child engaged, directly or indirectly, involving any stock, bond, security, or loan to or from, or other legal or equitable interest in the business of an employer whose employees such labor organization represents or is actively seeking to represent;

(3) any stock, bond, security, or other interest, legal or equitable, which he or his spouse or minor child directly or indirectly held in, and any income or any other benefit with monetary value (including reimbursed expenses) which he or his spouse or minor child directly or indirectly derived from, any business a substantial part of which consists of buying from, selling or leasing to, or otherwise dealing with, the business of an employer whose employees such labor organization represents or is actively seeking to represent;

(4) any stock, bond, security, or other interest, legal or equitable, which he or his spouse or minor child directly or indirectly held in, and any income or any other benefit with monetary value (including reimbursed expenses) which he or his spouse or minor child directly or indirectly derived from, a business any part of which consists of buying from, or selling or leasing directly or indirectly to, or otherwise dealing with such labor organization;

(5) any direct or indirect business transaction or arrangement between him or his spouse or minor child and any employer whose employees his organization represents or is actively seeking to represent, except work performed and payments and benefits received as a bona fide employee of such employer and except purchases and sales of goods or services in the regular course of business at prices generally available to any employee of such employer; and

(6) any payment of money or other thing of value (including reimbursed expenses) which he or his spouse or minor child received directly or indirectly from any employer or any person who acts as a labor relations consultant to an employer, except payments of the kinds referred to in section 302(c) of the Labor Management Relations Act, 1947, as amended.

(b) The provisions of paragraphs (1), (2), (3), (4), and (5) of subsection (a) shall not be construed to require any such officer or employee to report his bona fide investments in securities traded on a securities exchange registered as a national securities exchange under the Securities Exchange Act of 1934, in shares in an investment company registered under the Investment Company Act of 1940, or in securities of a public utility holding company registered under the Public Utility Holding Company Act of 1935, or to report any income derived therefrom.

(c) Nothing contained in this section shall be construed to require any officer or employee of a labor organization to file a report under subsection (a) unless he or his spouse or minor child holds or has held an interest, has received income or any other benefit with monetary value or a loan, or has engaged in a transaction described therein.

REPORT OF EMPLOYERS

Sec. 203.   (a) Every employer who in any fiscal year made—

(1) any payment or loan, direct or indirect, of money or other thing of value (including reimbursed expenses), or any promise or agreement therefor, to any labor organization or officer, agent, shop steward, or other representative of a labor organization, or employee of any labor organization, except (A) payments or loans made by any national or State bank, credit union, insurance company, savings and loan association or other credit institution and (B) payments of the kind referred to in section 302(c) of the Labor Management Relations Act, 1947, as amended;

(2) any payment (including reimbursed expenses) to any of his employees, or any group or committee of such employees, for the purpose of causing such employee or group or committee of employees to persuade other employees to exercise or not to exercise, or as the manner of exercising, the right to organize and bargain collectively through representatives of their own choosing unless such payments were contemporaneously or previously disclosed to such other employees;

(3) any expenditure, during the fiscal year, where an object thereof, directly or indirectly, is to interfere with, restrain, or coerce employees in the exercise of the right to organize and bargain collectively through representatives of their own choosing, or is to obtain information concerning the activities of employees or a labor organization in connection with a labor dispute involving such employer, except for use solely in conjunction with an administrative or arbitral proceeding or a criminal or civil judicial proceeding;

(4) any agreement or arrangement with a labor relations consultant or other independent contractor or organization pursuant to which such person undertakes activities where an object thereof, directly or indirectly, is to persuade employees to exercise or not to exercise, or persuade employees as to the manner of exercising, the right to organize and bargain collectively through representatives of their own choosing, or undertakes to supply such employer with information concerning the activities of employees or a labor organization in connection with a labor dispute involving such employer, except information for use solely in conjunction with an administrative or arbitral proceeding or a criminal or civil judicial proceeding; or

(5) any payment (including reimbursed expenses) pursuant to an agreement or arrangement described in subdivision (4);

shall file with the Secretary a report, in a form prescribed by him, signed by its president and treasurer or corresponding principal officers showing in detail the date and amount of each such payment, loan, promise, agreement, or arrangement and the name, address, and position, if any, in any firm or labor organization of the person to whom it was made and a full explanation of the circumstances of all such payments, including the terms of any agreement or understanding pursuant to which they were made.

(b) Every person who pursuant to any agreement or arrangement with an employer undertakes activities where an object thereof is, directly or indirectly—

(1) to persuade employees to exercise or not to exercise, or persuade employees as to the manner of exercising, the right to organize and bargain collectively through representatives of their own choosing; or

(2) to supply an employer with information concerning the activities of employees or a labor organization in connection with a labor dispute involving such employer, except information for use solely in conjunction with an administrative or arbitral proceeding or a criminal or civil judicial proceeding;

shall file within thirty days after entering into such agreement or arrangement a report with the Secretary, signed by its president and treasurer or corresponding principal officers, containing the name under which such person is engaged in doing business and the address of its principal office, and a detailed statement of the terms and conditions of such agreement or arrangement. Every such person shall file annually, with respect to each fiscal year during which payments were made as a result of such an agreement or arrangement, a report with the Secretary, signed by its president and treasurer or corresponding principal officers, containing a statement (A) of its receipts of any kind from employers on account of labor relations advice or services, designating the sources thereof, and (B) of its disbursements of any kind, in connection with such services and the purposes thereof. In each such case such information shall be set forth in such categories as the Secretary may prescribe.

(c) Nothing in this section shall be construed to require any employer or other person to file a report covering the services of such person by reason of his giving or agreeing to give advice to such employer or representing or agreeing to represent such employer before any court, administrative agency, or tribunal of arbitration or engaging or agreeing to engage in collective bargaining on behalf of such employer with respect to wages, hours, or other terms or conditions of employment or the negotiation of an agreement or any question arising thereunder.

(d) Nothing contained in this section shall be construed to require an employer to file a report under subsection (a) unless he has made an expenditure, payment, loan, agreement, or arrangement of the kind described therein. Nothing contained in this section shall be construed to require any other person to file a report under subsection (b) unless he was a party to an agreement or arrangement of the kind described therein.

(e) Nothing contained in this section shall be construed to require any regular officer, supervisor, or employee of an employer to file a report in connection with services rendered to such employer nor shall any employer be required to file a report covering expenditures made to any regular officer, supervisor, or employee of an employer as compensation for service as a regular officer, supervisor, or employee of such employer.

(f) Nothing contained in this section shall be construed as an amendment to, or modification of the rights protected by, section 8(c) of the National Labor Relations Act, as amended.

(g) The term "interfere with, restrain, or coerce" as used in this section means interference, restraint, and coercion which, if done with respect to the exercise of rights guaranteed in section 7 of the National Labor Relations Act, as amended, would, under section 8(a) of such Act, constitute an unfair labor practice.

ATTORNEY–CLIENT COMMUNICATIONS EXEMPTED

Sec. 204.   Nothing contained in this Act shall be construed to require an attorney who is a member in good standing of the bar of any State, to include in any report required to be filed pursuant to the provisions of this Act any information which was lawfully communicated to such attorney by any of his clients in the course of a legitimate attorney-client relationship.

REPORTS MADE PUBLIC INFORMATION

Sec. 205.   (a) The contents of the reports and documents filed with the Secretary pursuant to sections 201, 202, 203, and 211 shall be public information, and the Secretary may publish any information and data which he obtains pursuant to the provisions of this title. The Secretary may use the information and data for statistical and research purposes, and compile and publish such studies, analyses, reports, and surveys based thereon as he may deem appropriate.

(b) The Secretary shall by regulation make reasonable provision for the inspection and examination, on the request of any person, of the information and data contained in any report or other document filed with him pursuant to section 201, 202, 203, or 211.

(c) The Secretary shall by regulation provide for the furnishing by the Department of Labor of copies of reports or other documents filed with the Secretary pursuant to this title, upon payment of a charge based upon the cost of the service. The Secretary shall make available without payment of a charge, or require any person to furnish, to such State agency as is designated by law or by the Governor of the State in which such person has his principal place of business or headquarters, upon request of the Governor of such State, copies of any reports and documents filed by such person with the Secretary pursuant to section 201, 202, 203, or 211, or of information and data contained therein. No person shall be required by reason of any law of any State to furnish to any officer or agency of such State any information included in a report filed by such person with the Secretary pursuant to the provisions of this title, if a copy of such report, or of the portion thereof containing such information, is furnished to such officer or agency. All moneys received in payment of such charges fixed by the Secretary pursuant to this subsection shall be deposited in the general fund of the Treasury.

RETENTION OF RECORDS

Sec. 206.   Every person required to file any report under this title shall maintain records on the matters required to be reported which will provide in sufficient detail the necessary basic information and data from which the documents filed with the Secretary may be verified, explained or clarified, and checked for accuracy and completeness, and shall include vouchers, worksheets, receipts, and applicable resolutions, and shall keep such records available for examination for a period of not less than five years after the filing of the documents based on the information which they contain.

EFFECTIVE DATE

Sec. 207.   (a) Each labor organization shall file the initial report required under section 201(a) within ninety days after the date on which it first becomes subject to this Act.

(b) Each person required to file a report under section 201(b), 202, 203(a), or the second sentence of 203(b), or section 211 shall file such report within ninety days after the end of each of its fiscal years; except that where such person is subject to section 201(b), 202, 203(a), the second sentence of 203(b), or section 211, as the case may be, for only a portion of such a fiscal year (because the date of enactment of this Act occurs during such person's fiscal year or such person becomes subject to this Act during its fiscal year) such person may consider that portion as the entire fiscal year in making such report.

RULES AND REGULATIONS

Sec. 208.   The Secretary shall have authority to issue, amend, and rescind rules and regulations prescribing the form and publication of reports required to be filed under this title and such other reasonable rules and regulations (including rules prescribing reports concerning trusts in which a labor organization is interested) as he may find necessary to prevent the circumvention or evasion of such reporting requirements. In exercising his power under this section the Secretary shall prescribe by general rule simplified reports for labor organizations or employers for whom he finds that by virtue of their size a detailed report would be unduly burdensome, but the Secretary may revoke such provision for simplified forms of any labor organization or employer if he determines, after such investigation as he deems proper and due notice and opportunity for a hearing, that the purposes of this section would be served thereby.

CRIMINAL PROVISIONS

Sec. 209. (a) Any person who willfully violates this title shall be fined not more than $10,000 or imprisoned for not more than one year, or both.

(b) Any person who makes a false statement or representation of a material fact, knowing it to be false, or who knowingly fails to disclose a material fact, in any document, report, or other information required under the provisions of this title shall be fined not more than $10,000 or imprisoned for not more than one year, or both.

(c) Any person who willfully makes a false entry in or willfully conceals, withholds, or destroys any books, records, reports, or statements required to be kept by any provision of this title shall be fined not more than $10,000 or imprisoned for not more than one year, or both.

(d) Each individual required to sign reports under sections 201 and 203 shall be personally responsible for the filing of such reports and for any statement contained therein which he knows to be false.

CIVIL ENFORCEMENT

Sec. 210. Whenever it shall appear that any person has violated or is about to violate any of the provisions of this title, the Secretary may bring a civil action for such relief (including injunctions) as may be appropriate. Any such action may be brought in the district court of the United States where the violation occurred or, at the option of the parties, in the United States District Court for the District of Columbia.

SURETY COMPANY REPORTS

Sec. 211. Each surety company which issues any bond required by this Act or the Employee Retirement Income Security Act of 1974 shall file annually with the Secretary, with respect to each fiscal year during which any such bond was in force, a report, in such form and detail as he may prescribe by regulation, filed by the president and treasurer or corresponding principal officers of the surety company, describing its bond experience under each such Act, including information as to the premiums received, total claims paid, amounts recovered by way of subrogation, administrative and legal expenses and such related data and information as the Secretary shall determine to be necessary in the public interest and to carry out the policy of the Act. Notwithstanding the foregoing, if the Secretary finds that any such specific information cannot be practicably ascertained or would be uninformative, the Secretary may modify or waive the requirement for such information.

TITLE III—TRUSTEESHIPS
REPORTS

Sec. 301.   (a) Every labor organization which has or assumes trusteeship over any subordinate labor organization shall file with the Secretary within thirty days after the date of the enactment of this Act or the imposition of any such trusteeship, and semiannually thereafter, a report, signed by its president and treasurer or corresponding principal officers, as well as by the trustees of such subordinate labor organization, containing the following information: (1) the name and address of the subordinate organization; (2) the date of establishing the trusteeship; (3) a detailed statement of the reason or reasons for establishing or continuing the trusteeship; and (4) the nature and extent of participation by the membership of the subordinate organization in the selection of delegates to represent such organization in regular or special conventions or other policy-determining bodies and in the election of officers of the labor organization which has assumed trusteeship over such subordinate organization. The initial report shall also include a full and complete account of the financial condition of such subordinate organization as of the time trusteeship was assumed over it. During the continuance of a trusteeship the labor organization which has assumed trusteeship over a subordinate labor organization shall file on behalf of the subordinate labor organization the annual financial report required by section 201(b) signed by the president and treasurer or corresponding principal officers of the labor organization which has assumed such trusteeship and the trustees of the subordinate labor organization.

(b) The provisions of sections 201(c), 205, 206, 208, and 210 shall be applicable to reports filed under this title.

(c) Any person who willfully violates this section shall be fined not more than $10,000 or imprisoned for not more than one year, or both.

(d) Any person who makes a false statement or representation of a material fact, knowing it to be false, or who knowingly fails to disclose a material fact, in any report required under the provisions of this section or willfully makes any false entry in or willfully withholds, conceals, or destroys any documents, books, records, reports, or statements upon which such report is based, shall be fined not more than $10,000 or imprisoned for not more than one year, or both.

(e) Each individual required to sign a report under this section shall be personally responsible for the filing of such report and for any statement contained therein which he knows to be false.

PURPOSES FOR WHICH A TRUSTEESHIP
MAY BE ESTABLISHED

Sec. 302.   Trusteeships shall be established and administered by a labor organization over a subordinate body only in accordance with the constitution and bylaws of the organization which has assumed trusteeship over the subordinate body and for the purpose of correcting corruption or financial malpractice, assuring the performance of collective bargaining agreements or other duties of a bargaining representative, restoring democratic procedures, or otherwise carrying out the legitimate objects of such labor organization.

UNLAWFUL ACTS RELATING TO LABOR ORGANIZATION UNDER TRUSTEESHIP

Sec. 303. (a) During any period when a subordinate body of a labor organization is in trusteeship, it shall be unlawful (1) to count the vote of delegates from such body in any convention or election of officers of the labor organization unless the delegates have been chosen by secret ballot in an election in which all the members in good standing of such subordinate body were eligible to participate, or (2) to transfer to such organization any current receipts or other funds of the subordinate body except the normal per capita tax and assessments payable by subordinate bodies not in trusteeship: *Provided*, That nothing herein contained shall prevent the distribution of the assets of a labor organization in accordance with its constitution and bylaws upon the bona fide dissolution thereof.

(b) Any person who willfully violates this section shall be fined not more than $10,000 or imprisoned for not more than one year, or both.

ENFORCEMENT

Sec. 304. (a) Upon the written complaint of any member or subordinate body of a labor organization alleging that such organization has violated the provisions of this title (except section 301) the Secretary shall investigate the complaint and if the Secretary finds probable cause to believe that such violation has occurred and has not been remedied he shall, without disclosing the identity of the complainant, bring a civil action in any district court of the United States having jurisdiction of the labor organization for such relief (including injunctions) as may be appropriate. Any member or subordinate body of a labor organization affected by any violation of this title (except section 301) may bring a civil action in any district court of the United States having jurisdiction of the labor organization for such relief (including injunctions) as may be appropriate.

(b) For the purpose of actions under this section, district courts of the United States shall be deemed to have jurisdiction of a labor organization (1) in the district in which the principal office of such labor organization is located, or (2) in any district in which its duly authorized officers or agents are engaged in conducting the affairs of the trusteeship.

(c) In any proceeding pursuant to this section a trusteeship established by a labor organization in conformity with the procedural requirements of its constitution and bylaws and authorized or ratified after a fair hearing either before the executive board or before such other body as may be provided in accordance with its constitution or bylaws shall be presumed valid for a period of eighteen months from the date of its establishment and shall not be subject to attack during such period except upon clear and convincing proof that the trusteeship was not established or maintained in good faith for a purpose allowable under section 302. After the expiration of eighteen months the trusteeship shall be presumed invalid in any such proceeding and its discontinuance shall be decreed unless the labor organization shall show by clear and convincing proof that the continuation of the trusteeship is necessary for a purpose allowable under section 302. In the latter event the court may dismiss the complaint or retain jurisdiction of the cause on such conditions and for such period as it deems appropriate.

REPORT TO CONGRESS

Sec. 305. The Secretary shall submit to the Congress at the expiration of three years from the date of enactment of this Act a report upon the operation of this title.

COMPLAINT BY SECRETARY

Sec. 306. The rights and remedies provided by this title shall be in addition to any and all other rights and remedies at law or in equity: *Provided*, That upon the filing of a complaint by the Secretary the jurisdiction of the district court over such trusteeship shall be exclusive and the final judgment shall be res judicata.

TITLE IV—ELECTIONS

TERMS OF OFFICE; ELECTION PROCEDURES

Sec. 401. (a) Every national or international labor organization, except a federation of national or international labor organizations, shall elect its officers not less often than once every five years either by secret ballot among the members in good standing or at a convention of delegates chosen by secret ballot.

(b) Every local labor organization shall elect its officers not less often than once every three years by secret ballot among the members in good standing.

(c) Every national or international labor organization, except a federation of national or international labor organizations, and every local labor organization, and its officers, shall be under a duty, enforceable at the suit of any bona fide candidate for office in such labor organization in the district court of the United States in which such labor organization maintains its principal office, to comply with all reasonable requests of any candidate to distribute by mail or otherwise at the candidate's expense campaign literature in aid of such person's candidacy to all members in good standing of such labor organization and to refrain from discrimination in favor of or against any candidate with respect to the use of lists of members, and whenever such labor organizations or its officers authorize the distribution by mail or otherwise to members of campaign literature on behalf of any candidate or of the labor organization itself with reference to such election, similar distribution at the request of any other bona fide candidate shall be made by such labor organization and its officers, with equal treatment as to the expense of such distribution. Every bona fide candidate shall have the right, once within 30 days prior to an election of a labor organization in which he is a candidate, to inspect a list containing the names and last known addresses of all members of the labor organization who are subject to a collective bargaining agreement requiring membership therein as a condition of employment, which list shall be maintained and kept at the principal office of such labor organization by a designated official thereof. Adequate safeguards to insure a fair election shall be provided, including the right of any candidate to have an observer at the polls and at the counting of the ballots.

(d) Officers of intermediate bodies, such as general committees, system boards, joint boards, or joint councils, shall be elected not less often than once every four years by secret ballot among the members in good standing or by labor organization officers representative of such members who have been elected by secret ballot.

(e) In any election required by this section which is to be held by secret ballot a reasonable opportunity shall be given for the nomination of candidates and every member in good standing shall be eligible to be a candidate and to hold office (subject to section 504 and to reasonable qualifications uniformly imposed) and shall have the right to vote for or otherwise support the candidate or candidates of his choice, without being subject to penalty, discipline, or improper interference or reprisal of any kind by such organization or any member thereof. Not less than fifteen days prior to the election notice thereof shall be mailed to each member at his last known home address. Each member in good standing shall be entitled to one vote. No member whose dues have been withheld by his employer for payment to such organization pursuant to his voluntary authorization provided for in a collective bargaining agreement, shall be declared ineligible to vote or be a candidate for office in such organization by reason of alleged delay or default in the payment of dues. The votes cast by members of each local labor organization shall be counted, and the results published, separately. The election officials designated in the constitution and bylaws or the secretary, if no other official is designated, shall preserve for one year the ballots and all other records pertaining to the election. The election shall be conducted in accordance with the constitution and bylaws of such organization insofar as they are not inconsistent with the provisions of this title.

(f) When officers are chosen by a convention of delegates elected by secret ballot, the convention shall be conducted in accordance with the constitution and bylaws of the labor organization insofar as they are not inconsistent with the provisions of this title. The officials designated in the constitution and bylaws or the secretary, if no other is designated, shall preserve for one year the credentials of the delegates and all minutes and other records of the convention pertaining to the election of officers.

(g) No moneys received by any labor organization by way of dues, assessment, or similar levy, and no moneys of an employer shall be contributed or applied to promote the candidacy of any person in an election subject to the provisions of this title. Such moneys of a labor organization may be utilized for notices, factual statements of issues not involving candidates, and other expenses necessary for the holding of an election.

(h) If the Secretary, upon application of any member of a local labor organization, finds after hearing in accordance with the Administrative Procedure Act that the constitution and bylaws of such labor organization do not provide an adequate procedure for the removal of an elected officer guilty of serious misconduct, such officer may be removed, for cause shown and after notice and hearing, by the members in good standing voting in a secret ballot conducted by the officers of such labor organization in accordance with its constitution and bylaws insofar as they are not inconsistent with the provisions of this title.

(i) The Secretary shall promulgate rules and regulations prescribing minimum standards and procedures for determining the adequacy of the removal procedures to which reference is made in subsection (h).

ENFORCEMENT

Sec. 402.   (a) A member of a labor organization—

(1) who has exhausted the remedies available under the constitution and bylaws of such organization and of any parent body or

(2) who has invoked such available remedies without obtaining a final decision within three calendar months after their invocation,

may file a complaint with the Secretary within one calendar month thereafter alleging the violation of any provision of section 401 (including violation of the constitution and bylaws of the labor organization pertaining to the election and removal of officers). The challenged election shall be presumed valid pending a final decision thereon (as hereinafter provided) and in the interim the affairs of the organization shall be conducted by the officers elected or in such other manner as its constitution and bylaws may provide.

(b) The Secretary shall investigate such complaint and, if he finds probable cause to believe that a violation of this title has occurred and has not been remedied, he shall, within sixty days after the filing of such complaint, bring a civil action against the labor organization as an entity in the district court of the United States in which such labor organization maintains its principal office to set aside the invalid election, if any, and to direct the conduct of an election or hearing and vote upon the removal of officers under the supervision of the Secretary and in accordance with the provisions of this title and such rules and regulations as the Secretary may prescribe. The court shall have power to take such action as it deems proper to preserve the assets of the labor organization.

(c) If, upon a preponderance of the evidence after a trial upon the merits, the court finds—

(1) that an election has not been held within the time prescribed by section 401, or

(2) that the violation of section 401 may have affected the outcome of an election

the court shall declare the election, if any, to be void and direct the conduct of a new election under supervision of the Secretary and, so far as lawful and practicable, in conformity with the constitution and bylaws of the labor organization. The Secretary shall promptly certify to the court the names of the persons elected, and the court shall thereupon enter a decree declaring such persons to be the officers of the labor organization. If the proceeding is for the removal of officers pursuant to subsection (h) of section 401, the Secretary shall certify the results of the vote and the court shall enter a decree declaring whether such persons have been removed as officers of the labor organization.

(d) An order directing an election, dismissing a complaint, or designating elected officers of a labor organization shall be appealable in the same manner as the final judgment in a civil action, but an order directing an election shall not be stayed pending appeal.

APPLICATION OF OTHER LAWS

Sec. 403.   No labor organization shall be required by law to conduct elections of officers with greater frequency or in a different form or manner than is required by its own constitution or bylaws, except as otherwise provided by this title. Existing rights and remedies to enforce the constitution and bylaws of a labor organization with respect to elections prior to the conduct thereof shall not be affected by the provisions of this title. The remedy provided by this title for challenging an election already conducted shall be exclusive.

EFFECTIVE DATE

Sec. 404.   The provisions of this title shall become applicable—

(1) ninety days after the date of enactment of this Act in the case of a labor organization whose constitution and bylaws can lawfully be modified or amended by action of its constitutional officers or governing body, or

(2) where such modification can only be made by a constitutional convention of the labor organization, not later than the next constitutional convention of such labor organization after the date of enactment of this Act, or one year after such date, whichever is sooner. If no such convention is held within such one-year period, the executive board or similar governing body empowered to act for such labor organization between conventions is empowered to make such interim constitutional changes as are necessary to carry out the provisions of this title.

TITLE V—SAFEGUARDS FOR LABOR ORGANIZATIONS

FIDUCIARY RESPONSIBILITY OF OFFICERS OF LABOR ORGANIZATIONS

Sec. 501.   (a) The officers, agents, shop stewards, and other representatives of a labor organization occupy positions of trust in relation to such organization and its members as a group. It is, therefore, the duty of each such person, taking into account the special problems and functions of a labor organization, to hold its money and property solely for the benefit of the organization and its members and to manage, invest, and expend the same in accordance with its constitution and bylaws and any resolutions of the governing bodies adopted thereunder, to refrain from dealing with such organization as an adverse party or in behalf of an adverse party in any matter connected with his duties and from holding or acquiring any pecuniary or personal interest which conflicts with the interests of such organization, and to account to the organization for any profit received by him in whatever capacity in connection with transactions conducted by him or under his direction on behalf of the organization. A general exculpatory provision in the constitution and bylaws of such a labor organization or a general exculpatory resolution of a governing body purporting to relieve any such person of liability for breach of the duties declared by this section shall be void as against public policy.

(b) When any officer, agent, shop steward, or representative of any labor organization is alleged to have violated the duties declared in subsection (a) and the labor organization or its governing board or officers refuse or fail to sue or recover damages or secure an accounting or other appropriate relief within a reasonable time after being requested to do so by any member of the labor organization, such member may sue such officer, agent, shop steward, or representative in any district court of the United States or in any State court of competent jurisdiction to recover damages or secure an accounting or other appropriate relief for the benefit of the labor organization. No such proceeding shall be brought except upon leave of the court obtained upon verified application and for good cause shown which application may be made ex parte. The trial judge may allot a reasonable part of the recovery in any action under this subsection to pay the fees of counsel prosecuting the suit at the instance of the member of the labor organization and to compensate such member for any expenses necessarily paid or incurred by him in connection with the litigation.

(c) Any person who embezzles, steals, or unlawfully and willfully abstracts or converts to his own use, or the use of another, any of the moneys, funds, securities, property, or other assets of a labor organization of which he is an officer, or by which he is employed, directly or indirectly, shall be fined not more than $10,000 or imprisoned for not more than five years, or both.

BONDING

Sec. 502.   (a) Every officer, agent, shop steward, or other representative or employee of any labor organization (other than a labor organization whose property and annual financial receipts do not exceed $5,000 in value), or of a trust in which a labor organization is interested, who handles funds or other property thereof shall be bonded to provide protection against loss by reason of acts of fraud or dishonesty on his part directly or through connivance with others. The bond of each such person shall be fixed at the beginning of the organization's fiscal year and shall be in an amount not less than 10 per centum of the funds handled by him and his predecessor or predecessors, if any, during the preceding fiscal year, but in no case more than $500,000. If the labor organization or the trust in which a labor organization is interested does not have a preceding fiscal year, the amount of the bond shall be, in the case of a local labor organization, not less than $1,000, and in the case of any other labor organization or of a trust in which a labor organization is interested, not less than $10,000. Such bonds shall be individual or schedule in form, and shall have a corporate surety company as surety thereon. Any person who is not covered by such bonds shall not be permitted to receive, handle, disburse, or otherwise exercise custody or control of the funds or other property of a labor organization or of a trust in which a labor organization is interested. No such bond shall be placed through an agent or broker or with a surety company in which any labor organization or any officer, agent, shop steward, or other representative of a labor organization has any direct or indirect interest. Such surety company shall be a corporate surety which holds a grant of authority from the Secretary of the Treasury under the Act of July 30, 1947 (6

U.S.C. 6–13), as an acceptable surety on Federal bonds: *Provided*, That when in the opinion of the Secretary a labor organization has made other bonding arrangements which would provide the protection required by this section at comparable cost or less, he may exempt such labor organization from placing a bond through a surety company holding such grant of authority.

(b) Any person who willfully violates this section shall be fined not more than $10,000 or imprisoned for not more than one year, or both.

MAKING OF LOANS; PAYMENT OF FINES

Sec. 503.   (a) No labor organization shall make directly or indirectly any loan or loans to any officer or employee of such organization which results in a total indebtedness on the part of such officer or employee to the labor organization in excess of $2,000.

(b) No labor organization or employer shall directly or indirectly pay the fine of any officer or employee convicted of any willful violation of this Act.

(c) Any person who willfully violates this section shall be fined not more than $5,000 or imprisoned for not more than one year, or both.

PROHIBITION AGAINST CERTAIN PERSONS HOLDING OFFICE

Sec. 504.*   (a) No person who is or has been a member of the Communist Party or who has been convicted of, or served any part of a prison term resulting from his conviction of, robbery, bribery, extortion, embezzlement, grand larceny, burglary, arson, violation of narcotics laws, murder, rape, assault with intent to kill, assault which inflicts grievous bodily injury, or a violation of subchapter III or IV of this chapter, any felony involving abuse or misuse of such person's position or employment in a labor organization or employee benefit plan to seek or obtain an illegal gain at the expense of the members of the labor organization or the beneficiaries of the employee benefit plan, or conspiracy to commit any such crimes or attempt to commit any such crimes, or a crime in which any of the foregoing crimes is an element, shall serve or be permitted to serve—

(1) as a consultant or adviser to any labor organization,

(2) as an officer, director, trustee, member of any executive board or similar governing body, business agent, manager, organizer, employee, or representative in any capacity of any labor organization,

(3) as a labor relations consultant or adviser to a person engaged in an industry or activity affecting commerce, or as an officer, director, agent, or employee of any group or association of employers dealing with any labor organization, or in a position having specific collective bargaining authority or direct responsibility in the area of labor-management relations in any corporation or association engaged in an industry or activity affecting commerce, or

---

*   This section was amended by Pub.L. 98–473, Title II, § 803, Oct. 12, 1984, 98 Stat. 2133.

(4) in a position which entitles its occupant to a share of the proceeds of, or as an officer or executive or administrative employee of, any entity whose activities are in whole or substantial part devoted to providing goods or services to any labor organization, or

(5) in any capacity, other than in his capacity as a member of such labor organization, that involves decisionmaking authority concerning, or decisionmaking authority over, or custody of, or control of the moneys, funds, assets, or property of any labor organization,

during or for the period of thirteen years after such conviction or after the end of such imprisonment, whichever is later, unless the sentencing court on the motion of the person convicted sets a lesser period of at least three years after such conviction or after the end of such imprisonment, whichever is later, or unless prior to the end of such period, in the case of a person so convicted or imprisoned, (A) his citizenship rights, having been revoked as a result of such conviction, have been fully restored, or (B) the United States Parole Commission determines that such person's service in any capacity referred to in clauses (1) through (5) would not be contrary to the purposes of this chapter. Prior to making any such determination the Commission shall hold an administrative hearing and shall give notice of such proceeding by certified mail to the Secretary of Labor and to State, county, and Federal prosecuting officials in the jurisdiction or jurisdictions in which such person was convicted. The Commission's determination in any such proceeding shall be final. No person shall knowingly hire, retain, employ, or otherwise place any other person to serve in any capacity in violation of this subsection.

(b) Any person who willfully violates this section shall be fined not more than $10,000 or imprisoned for not more than five years, or both.

(c) For the purpose of this section—

(1) A person shall be deemed to have been "convicted" and under the disability of "conviction" from the date of the judgment of the trial court, regardless of whether that judgment remains under appeal.

(2) A period of parole shall not be considered as part of a period of imprisonment.

(d) Whenever any person—

(1) by operation of this section, has been barred from office or other position in a labor organization as a result of a conviction, and

(2) has filed an appeal of that conviction,

any salary which would be otherwise due such person by virtue of such office or position, shall be placed in escrow by the individual employer or organization responsible for payment of such salary. Payment of such salary into escrow shall continue for the duration of the appeal or for the period of time during which such salary would be otherwise due, whichever period is shorter. Upon the final reversal of such person's conviction on appeal, the amounts in escrow shall be paid to such person. Upon the final sustaining of such person's conviction on appeal, the amounts in escrow shall be returned to the individual employer or organization responsible for payments of those amounts. Upon final reversal of such person's conviction, such person shall no longer be barred by this statute from assuming any position from which such person was previously barred.

TITLE VI—MISCELLANEOUS PROVISIONS
INVESTIGATIONS

Sec. 601.   (a) The Secretary shall have power when he believes it necessary in order to determine whether any person has violated or is about to violate any provision of this Act (except title I or amendments made by this Act to other statutes) to make an investigation and in connection therewith he may enter such places and inspect such records and accounts and question such persons as he may deem necessary to enable him to determine the facts relative thereto. The Secretary may report to interested persons or officials concerning the facts required to be shown in any report required by this Act and concerning the reasons for failure or refusal to file such a report or any other matter which he deems to be appropriate as a result of such an investigation.

(b) For the purpose of any investigation provided for in this Act, the provisions of sections 9 and 10 (relating to the attendance of witnesses and the production of books, papers, and documents) of the Federal Trade Commission Act of September 16, 1914, as amended (15 U.S.C. 49, 50), are hereby made applicable to the jurisdiction, powers, and duties of the Secretary or any officers designated by him.

EXTORTIONATE PICKETING

Sec. 602.   (a) It shall be unlawful to carry on picketing on or about the premises of any employer for the purpose of, or as part of any conspiracy or in furtherance of any plan or purpose for, the personal profit or enrichment of any individual (except a bona fide increase in wages or other employee benefits) by taking or obtaining any money or other thing of value from such employer against his will or with his consent.

(b) Any person who willfully violates this section shall be fined not more than $10,000 or imprisoned not more than twenty years, or both.

RETENTION OF RIGHTS UNDER OTHER FEDERAL AND STATE LAWS

Sec. 603.   (a) Except as explicitly provided to the contrary, nothing in this Act shall reduce or limit the responsibilities of any labor organization or any officer, agent, shop steward, or other representative of a labor organization, or of any trust in which a labor organization is interested, under any other Federal law or under the laws of any State, and, except as explicitly provided to the contrary, nothing in this Act shall take away any right or bar any remedy to which members of a labor organization are entitled under such other Federal law or law of any State.

(b) Nothing contained in titles I, II, III, IV, V, or VI of this Act shall be construed to supersede or impair or otherwise affect the provisions of the Railway Labor Act, as amended, or any of the obligations, rights, benefits, privileges, or immunities of any carrier, employee, organization, representative, or person subject thereto; nor shall anything contained in said titles (except section 505) of this Act be construed to confer any rights, privileges, immunities, or defenses upon employers, or to impair or otherwise affect the rights of any person under the National Labor Relations Act, as amended.

EFFECT ON STATE LAWS

Sec. 604.   Nothing in this Act shall be construed to impair or diminish the authority of any State to enact and enforce general criminal laws with respect to robbery, bribery, extortion, embezzlement, grand larceny, burglary, arson, violation of narcotics laws, murder, rape, assault with intent to kill, or assault which inflicts grievous bodily injury, or conspiracy to commit any of such crimes.

STATE AUTHORITY TO ENACT AND ENFORCE LEGISLATION

Sec. 604a.   Notwithstanding this or any other Act regulating labor-management relations, each State shall have the authority to enact and enforce, as part of a comprehensive statutory system to eliminate the threat of pervasive racketeering activity in an industry that is, or over time has been, affected by such activity, a provision of law that applies equally to employers, employees, and collective bargaining representatives, which provision of law governs service in any position in a local labor organization which acts or seeks to act in that State as a collective bargaining representative pursuant to the National Labor Relations Act [29 U.S.C.A. § 151 et seq.], in the industry that is subject to that program.*

SERVICE OF PROCESS

Sec. 605.   For the purposes of this Act, service of summons, subpena, or other legal process of a court of the United States upon an officer or agent of a labor organization in his capacity as such shall constitute service upon the labor organization.

ADMINISTRATIVE PROCEDURE ACT

Sec. 606.   The provisions of the Administrative Procedure Act shall be applicable to the issuance, amendment, or rescission of any rules or regulations, or any adjudication, authorized or required pursuant to the provisions of this Act.

OTHER AGENCIES AND DEPARTMENTS

Sec. 607.   In order to avoid unnecessary expense and duplication of functions among Government agencies, the Secretary may make such arrangements or agreements for cooperation or mutual assistance in the performance of his functions under this Act and the functions of any such agency as he may find to be practicable and consistent with law. The Secretary may utilize the facilities or services of any department, agency, or establishment of the United States or of any State or political subdivision of a State, including the services of any of its employees, with the lawful consent of such department, agency, or establishment; and each department, agency, or establishment of the United States is authorized and directed to cooperate with the Secretary and, to the extent permitted by law, to provide such information and facilities as he may request for his assistance in the performance of his functions under

---

*   Pub.L. 98–473, Title II, § 2201, Oct. 12, 1984, 98 Stat. 2192.

this Act. The Attorney General or his representative shall receive from the Secretary for appropriate action such evidence developed in the performance of his functions under this Act as may be found to warrant consideration for criminal prosecution under the provisions of this Act or other Federal law.

CRIMINAL CONTEMPT

Sec. 608.   No person shall be punished for any criminal contempt allegedly committed outside the immediate presence of the court in connection with any civil action prosecuted by the Secretary or any other person in any court of the United States under the provisions of this Act unless the facts constituting such criminal contempt are established by the verdict of the jury in a proceeding in the district court of the United States, which jury shall be chosen and empaneled in the manner prescribed by the law governing trial juries in criminal prosecutions in the district courts of the United States.

PROHIBITION ON CERTAIN DISCIPLINE
BY LABOR ORGANIZATION

Sec. 609.   It shall be unlawful for any labor organization, or any officer, agent, shop steward, or other representative of a labor organization, or any employee thereof to fine, suspend, expel, or otherwise discipline any of its members for exercising any right to which he is entitled under the provisions of this Act. The provisions of section 102 shall be applicable in the enforcement of this section.

DEPRIVATION OF RIGHTS UNDER ACT BY VIOLENCE

Sec. 610.   It shall be unlawful for any person through the use of force or violence, or threat of the use of force or violence, to restrain, coerce, or intimidate, or attempt to restrain, coerce, or intimidate any member of a labor organization for the purpose of interfering with or preventing the exercise of any right to which he is entitled under the provisions of this Act. Any person who willfully violates this section shall be fined not more than $1,000 or imprisoned for not more than one year, or both.

SEPARABILITY PROVISIONS

Sec. 611.   If any provision of this Act, or the application of such provision to any person or circumstances, shall be held invalid, the remainder of this Act or the application of such provision to persons or circumstances other than those as to which it is held invalid, shall not be affected thereby.

CIVIL RIGHTS ACT OF 1964

78 Stat. 253 (1964), as amended; 42 U.S.C. § 2000e et seq. (1988); as amended Pub.L. 102–166 (Nov. 21, 1991).

TITLE VII—EQUAL EMPLOYMENT OPPORTUNITY
DEFINITIONS

Sec. 701.   (§ 2000e) For the purposes of this title—

(a) The term "person" includes one or more individuals, governments, governmental agencies, political subdivisions, labor unions, partnerships, associations, corporations, legal representatives, mutual companies, joint-stock companies, trusts, unincorporated organizations, trustees, trustees in bankruptcy, or receivers.

(b) The term "employer" means a person engaged in an industry affecting commerce who has fifteen or more employees for each working day in each of twenty or more calendar weeks in the current or preceding calendar year, and any agent of such a person, but such term does not include (1) the United States, a corporation wholly owned by the Government of the United States, an Indian tribe, or any department or agency of the District of Columbia subject by statute to procedures of the competitive service (as defined in section 2102 of Title 5), or (2) a bona fide private membership club (other than a labor organization) which is exempt from taxation under section 501(c) of Title 26, except that during the first year after March 24, 1972, persons having fewer than twenty-five employees (and their agents) shall not be considered employers.

(c) The term "employment agency" means any person regularly undertaking with or without compensation to procure employees for an employer or to procure for employees opportunities to work for an employer and includes an agent of such a person.

(d) The term "labor organization" means a labor organization engaged in an industry affecting commerce, and any agent of such an organization, and includes any organization of any kind, any agency, or employee representation committee, group, association, or plan so engaged in which employees participate and which exists for the purpose, in whole or in part, of dealing with employers concerning grievances, labor disputes, wages, rates of pay, hours, or other terms or conditions of employment, and any conference, general committee, joint or system board, or joint council so engaged which is subordinate to a national or international labor organization.

(e) A labor organization shall be deemed to be engaged in an industry affecting commerce if (1) it maintains or operates a hiring hall or hiring office which procures employees for an employer or procures for employees opportunities to work for an employer, or (2) the number of its members (or, where it is a labor organization composed of other labor organizations or their representatives, if the aggregate number of the members of such other labor organization) is (A) twenty-five or more during the first year after March 24, 1972, or (B) fifteen or more thereafter, and such labor organization—

(1) is the certified representative of employees under the provisions of the National Labor Relations Act, as amended, or the Railway Labor Act, as amended;

(2) although not certified, is a national or international labor organization or a local labor organization recognized or acting as the representative of employees of an employer or employers engaged in an industry affecting commerce; or

(3) has chartered a local labor organization or subsidiary body which is representing or actively seeking to represent employees of employers within the meaning of paragraph (1) or (2); or

(4) has been chartered by a labor organization representing or actively seeking to represent employees within the meaning of paragraph (1) or (2) as the local or subordinate body through which such employees may enjoy membership or become affiliated with such labor organization; or

(5) is a conference, general committee, joint or system board, or joint council subordinate to a national or international labor organization, which includes a labor organization engaged in an industry affecting commerce within the meaning of any of the preceding paragraphs of this subsection.

(f) The term "employee" means an individual employed by an employer, except that the term "employee" shall not include any person elected to public office in any State or political subdivision of any State by the qualified voters thereof, or any person chosen by such officer to be on such officer's personal staff, or an appointee on the policy making level or an immediate adviser with respect to the exercise of the constitutional or legal powers of the office. The exemption set forth in the preceding sentence shall not include employees subject to the civil service laws of a State government, governmental agency or political subdivision. With respect to employment in a foreign country, such term includes an individual who is a citizen of the United States.

(g) The term "commerce" means trade, traffic, commerce, transportation, transmission, or communication among the several States; or between a State and any place outside thereof; or within the District of Columbia, or a possession of the United States; or between points in the same State but through a point outside thereof.

(h) The term "industry affecting commerce" means any activity, business, or industry in commerce or in which a labor dispute would hinder or obstruct commerce or the free flow of commerce and includes any activity or industry "affecting commerce" within the meaning of the Labor–Management Reporting and Disclosure Act of 1959, and further includes any governmental industry, business, or activity.

(i) The term "State" includes a State of the United States, the District of Columbia, Puerto Rico, the Virgin Islands, American Samoa, Guam, Wake Island, the Canal Zone, and Outer Continental Shelf lands defined in the Outer Continental Shelf Lands Act.

(j) The term "religion" includes all aspects of religious observance and practice, as well as belief, unless an employer demonstrates that he is unable to reasonably accommodate to an employee's or prospective employee's religious observance or practice without undue hardship on the conduct of the employer's business.

(k) The terms "because of sex" or "on the basis of sex" include, but are not limited to, because of or on the basis of pregnancy, childbirth, or related medical conditions; and women affected by pregnancy, childbirth, or related medical conditions shall be treated the same for all employment-related purposes, including receipt of benefits under fringe benefit programs, as other persons not so affected but similar in their ability or inability to work, and nothing in section 2(h) of this Act shall be interpreted to permit otherwise. This subsection shall not require an employer to pay for health insurance benefits for abortion, except where the life of the mother would be endangered if the fetus were carried to term, or except where medical complications have arisen from an abortion: *Provided*, That nothing herein shall preclude an employer from providing abortion benefits or otherwise affect bargaining agreements in regard to abortion.

(*l*) The term "complaining party" means the Commission, the Attorney General, or a person who may bring an action or proceeding under this subchapter.

(m) The term "demonstrates" means meets the burdens of production and persuasion.

(n) The term "respondent" means an employer, employment agency, labor organization, joint labor-management committee controlling apprenticeship or other training or retraining program, including an on-the-job training program, or Federal entity subject to section 2000e–16 of this title.

FOREIGN AND RELIGIOUS EMPLOYMENT

Sec. 702. (§ 2000e–1) (a) This Subchapter shall not apply to an employer with respect to the employment of aliens outside any State, or to a religious corporation, association, educational institution, or society with respect to the employment of individuals of a particular religion to perform work connected with the carrying on by such corporation, association, educational institution, or society of its activities.

(b) It shall not be unlawful under section 2000e–2 or 2000e–3 of this title for an employer (or a corporation controlled by an employer), labor organization, employment agency, or joint labor-management committee controlling apprenticeship or other training or retraining (including on-the-job training programs) to take any action otherwise prohibited by such section, with respect to an employee in a workplace in a foreign country if compliance with such section would cause such employer (or such corporation), such organization, such agency, or such committee to violate the law of the foreign country in which such workplace is located.

(c)(1) If an employer controls a corporation whose place of incorporation is a foreign country, any practice prohibited by section 2000e–2 or 2000e–3 of this title engaged in by such corporation shall be presumed to be engaged in by such employer.

(2) Sections 2000e–2 and 2000e–3 of this title shall not apply with respect to the foreign operations of an employer that is a foreign person not controlled by an American employer.

(3) For purposes of this subsection, the determination of whether an employer controls a corporation shall be based on—

(A) the interrelation of operations;

(B) the common management;

(C) the centralized control of labor relations; and

(D) the common ownership or financial control,

of the employer and the corporation.

DISCRIMINATION BECAUSE OF RACE, COLOR, RELIGION, SEX, OR NATIONAL ORIGIN

Sec. 703.   (§ 2000e–2) (a) It shall be an unlawful employment practice for an employer—

(1) to fail or refuse to hire or to discharge any individual, or otherwise to discriminate against any individual with respect to his compensation, terms, conditions, or privileges of employment, because of such individual's race, color, religion, sex, or national origin; or

(2) to limit, segregate, or classify his employees or applicants for employment in any way which would deprive or tend to deprive any individual of employment opportunities or otherwise adversely affect his status as an employee, because of such individual's race, color, religion, sex, or national origin.

(b) It shall be an unlawful employment practice for an employment agency to fail or refuse to refer for employment, or otherwise to discriminate against, any individual because of his race, color, religion, sex, or national origin, or to classify or refer for employment any individual on the basis of his race, color, religion, sex, or national origin.

(c) It shall be an unlawful employment practice for a labor organization—

(1) to exclude or to expel from its membership, or otherwise to discriminate against, any individual because of his race, color, religion, sex, or national origin;

(2) to limit, segregate, or classify its membership or applicants for membership, or to classify or fail or refuse to refer for employment any individual, in any way which would deprive or tend to deprive any individual of employment opportunities, or would limit such employment opportunities or otherwise adversely affect his status as an employee or as an applicant for employment, because of such individual's race, color, religion, sex, or national origin; or

(3) to cause or attempt to cause an employer to discriminate against an individual in violation of this section.

(d) It shall be an unlawful employment practice for any employer, labor organization, or joint labor-management committee controlling apprenticeship or other training or retraining, including on-the-job training programs to discriminate against any individual because of his race, color, religion, sex, or national origin in admission to, or employment in, any program established to provide apprenticeship or other training.

(e) Notwithstanding any other provision of this Subchapter (1) it shall not be an unlawful employment practice for an employer to hire and employ employees, for an employment agency to classify, or refer for employment any individual, for a labor organization to classify its membership or to classify or refer for employment any individual, or for an employer, labor organization, or joint labor-management committee controlling apprenticeship or other training or retraining programs to admit or employ any individual in any such program, on the basis of his religion, sex, or national origin in those certain instances where religion, sex, or national origin is a bona fide occupational qualification reasonably necessary to the normal operation of that particular business or enterprise, and (2) it shall not be an unlawful employment practice for a school, college, university, or other educational institution or institution of learning to hire and employ employees of a particular religion if such school, college, university, or other educational institution or institution of learning is, in whole or in substantial part, owned, supported, controlled, or managed by a particular religion or by a particular religious corporation, association, or society, or if the curriculum of such school, college, university, or other educational institution or institution of learning is directed toward the propagation of a particular religion.

(f) As used in this Subchapter, the phrase "unlawful employment practice" shall not be deemed to include any action or measure taken by an employer, labor organization, joint labor-management committee, or employment agency with respect to an individual who is a member of the Communist Party of the United States or of any other organization required to register as a Communist-action or Communist-front organization by final order of the Subversive Activities Control Board pursuant to the Subversive Activities Control Act of 1950.

(g) Notwithstanding any other provision of this Subchapter, it shall not be an unlawful employment practice for an employer to fail or refuse to hire and employ any individual for any position, for an employer to discharge any individual from any position, or for an employment agency to fail or refuse to refer any individual for employment in any position, or for a labor organization to fail or refuse to refer any individual for employment in any position, if—

(1) the occupancy of such position, or access to the premises in or upon which any part of the duties of such position is performed or is to be performed, is subject to any requirement imposed in the interest of the national security of the United States under any security program in effect pursuant to or administered under any statute of the United States or any Executive order of the President; and

(2) such individual has not fulfilled or has ceased to fulfill that requirement.

(h) Notwithstanding any other provision of this Subchapter, it shall not be an unlawful employment practice for an employer to apply different standards of compensation, or different terms, conditions, or privileges of employment pursuant to a bona fide seniority or merit system, or a system which measures earnings by quantity or quality of production or to employees who work in different locations, provided that such differences are not the result of an intention to discriminate because of race, color, religion, sex, or national origin, nor shall it be an unlawful employment practice for an employer to give and to act upon the results of any professionally developed ability test provided that such test, its administration or action upon the results is not designed, intended or used to discriminate because of race, color, religion, sex or national origin. It shall not be an unlawful employment practice under this subchapter for any employer to differentiate upon the basis of sex in determining the amount of the wages or compensation paid or to be paid to employees of such employer if such differentiation is authorized by the provisions of section 206(d) of Title 29.

(i) Nothing contained in this Subchapter shall apply to any business or enterprise on or near an Indian reservation with respect to any publicly announced employment practice of such business or enterprise under which a preferential treatment is given to any individual because he is an Indian living on or near a reservation.

(j) Nothing contained in this Subchapter shall be interpreted to require any employer, employment agency, labor organization, or joint labor-management committee subject to this subchapter to grant preferential treatment to any individual or to any group because of the race, color, religion, sex, or national origin of such individual or group on account of an imbalance which may exist with respect to the total number of percentage of persons of any race, color, religion, sex, or national origin employed by any employer, referred or classified for employment by any employment agency or labor organization, admitted to membership or classified by any labor organization, or admitted to, or employed in, any apprenticeship or other training program, in comparison with the total number or percentage of persons of such race, color, religion, sex, or national origin in any community, State, section, or other area, or in the available work force in any community, State, section, or other area.

(k)(1)**(A)** An unlawful employment practice based on disparate impact is established under this subchapter only if—

(i) a complaining party demonstrates that a respondent uses a particular employment practice that causes a disparate impact on the basis of race, color, religion, sex, or national origin and the respondent fails to demonstrate that the challenged practice is job related for the position in question and consistent with business necessity; or

(ii) the complaining party makes the demonstration described in subparagraph (C) with respect to an alternative employment practice and the respondent refuses to adopt such alternative employment practice.

(B)(i) With respect to demonstrating that a particular employment practice causes a disparate impact as described in subparagraph (A)(i), the complaining party shall demonstrate that each particular challenged employment practice causes a disparate impact, except that if the complaining party can demonstrate to the court that the elements of a respondent's decisionmaking process are not capable of separation for analysis, the decisionmaking process may be analyzed as one employment practice.

(ii) If the respondent demonstrates that a specific employment practice does not cause the disparate impact, the respondent shall not be required to demonstrate that such practice is required by business necessity.

(C) The demonstration referred to by subparagraph (A)(ii) shall be in accordance with the law as it existed on June 4, 1989, with respect to the concept of "alternative employment practice".

(2) A demonstration that an employment practice is required by business necessity may not be used as a defense against a claim of intentional discrimination under this subchapter.

(3) Notwithstanding any other provision of this subchapter, a rule barring the employment of an individual who currently and knowingly uses or possesses a controlled substance, as defined in schedules I and II of section 102(6) of the Controlled Substances Act (21 U.S.C. 802(6)), other than the use or possession of a drug taken under the supervision of a licensed health care professional, or any other use or possession authorized by the Controlled Substances Act or any other provision of Federal law, shall be considered an unlawful employment practice under this subchapter only if such rule is adopted or applied with an intent to discriminate because of race, color, religion, sex, or national origin.

(*l*) It shall be an unlawful employment practice for a respondent, in connection with the selection or referral of applicants or candidates for employment or promotion, to adjust the scores of, use different cutoff scores for, or otherwise alter the results of, employment related tests on the basis of race, color, religion, sex, or national origin.

(m) Except as otherwise provided in this subchapter, an unlawful employment practice is established when the complaining party demonstrates that race, color, religion, sex, or national origin was a motivating factor for any employment practice, even though other factors also motivated the practice.

(n)(1)**(A)** Notwithstanding any other provision of law, and except as provided in paragraph (2), an employment practice that implements and is within the scope of a litigated or consent judgment or order that resolves a claim of employment discrimination under the Constitution or Federal civil rights laws may not be challenged under the circumstances described in subparagraph (B).

(B) A practice described in subparagraph (A) may not be challenged in a claim under the Constitution or Federal civil rights laws—

(i) by a person who, prior to the entry of the judgment or order described in subparagraph (A), had—

(I) actual notice of the proposed judgment or order sufficient to apprise such person that such judgment or order might adversely affect the interests and legal rights of such person and that an opportunity was available to present objections to such judgment or order by a future date certain; and

(II) a reasonable opportunity to present objections to such judgment or order; or

(ii) by a person whose interests were adequately represented by another person who had previously challenged the judgment or order on the same legal grounds and with a similar factual situation, unless there has been an intervening change in law or fact.

(2) Nothing in this subsection shall be construed to—

(A) alter the standards for intervention under rule 24 of the Federal Rules of Civil Procedure or apply to the rights of parties who have successfully intervened pursuant to such rule in the proceeding in which the parties intervened;

(B) apply to the rights of parties to the action in which a litigated or consent judgment or order was entered, or of members of a class represented or sought to be represented in such action, or of members of a group on whose behalf relief was sought in such action by the Federal Government;

(C) prevent challenges to a litigated or consent judgment or order on the ground that such judgment or order was obtained through collusion or fraud, or is transparently invalid or was entered by a court lacking subject matter jurisdiction; or

(D) authorize or permit the denial to any person of the due process of law required by the Constitution.

(3) Any action not precluded under this subsection that challenges an employment consent judgment or order described in paragraph (1) shall be brought in the court, and if possible before the judge, that entered such judgment or order. Nothing in this subsection shall preclude a transfer of such action pursuant to section 1404 of Title 28.

OTHER UNLAWFUL EMPLOYMENT PRACTICES

Sec. 704.   (§ 2000e–3) (a) It shall be an unlawful employment practice for an employer to discriminate against any of his employees or applicants for employment, for an employment agency, or joint labor-management committee controlling apprenticeship or other training or retraining, including on-the-job training programs, to discriminate against any individual, or for a labor organization to discriminate against any member thereof or applicant for membership, because he has opposed any practice made an unlawful employment practice by this subchapter, or because he has made a charge, testified, assisted, or participated in any manner in an investigation, proceeding, or hearing under this subchapter.

(b) It shall be an unlawful employment practice for an employer, labor organization, employment agency, or joint labor-management committee controlling apprenticeship or other training or retraining; including on-the-job training programs, to print or publish or cause to be printed or published any notice or advertisement relating to employment by such an employer or membership in or any classification or referral for employment by such a labor organization, or relating to any classification or referral for employment by such an employment agency, or relating to admission to, or employment in, any program established to provide apprenticeship or other training by such a joint labor management committee, indicating any preference, limitation, specification, or discrimination, based on race, color, religion, sex, or national origin, except that such a notice or advertisement may indicate a preference, limitation, specification, or discrimination based on religion, sex, or national origin when religion, sex, or national origin is a bona fide occupational qualification for employment.

* * *

WORKER ADJUSTMENT AND RETRAINING NOTIFICATION ACT

102 Stat. 890 (1988), 29 U.S.C. §§ 2101–2109 (1988).

§ 2101. Definitions; exclusions from definition of loss of employment

(a) Definitions.—As used in this chapter—

(1) the term "employer" means any business enterprise that employs—

    (A) 100 or more employees, excluding part-time employees; or

(B) 100 or more employees who in the aggregate work at least 4,000 hours per week (exclusive of hours of overtime);

(2) the term "plant closing" means the permanent or temporary shutdown of a single site of employment, or one or more facilities or operating units within a single site of employment, if the shutdown results in an employment loss at the single site of employment during any 30–day period for 50 or more employees excluding any part-time employees;

(3) the term "mass layoff" means a reduction in force which—

    (A) is not the result of a plant closing; and

    (B) results in an employment loss at the single site of employment during any 30–day period for—

        (i)(I) at least 33 percent of the employees (excluding any part-time employees); and

        (II) at least 50 employees (excluding any part-time employees); or

        (ii) at least 500 employees (excluding any part-time employees);

(4) the term "representative" means an exclusive representative of employees within the meaning of section 158(f) or 159(a) of this title or section 152 of Title 45;

(5) the term "affected employees" means employees who may reasonably be expected to experience an employment loss as a consequence of a proposed plant closing or mass layoff by their employer;

(6) subject to subsection (b) of this section the term "employment loss" means (A) an employment termination, other than a discharge for cause, voluntary departure, or retirement, (B) a layoff exceeding 6 months, or (C) a reduction in hours of work of more than 50 percent during each month of any 6–month period;

(7) the term "unit of local government" means any general purpose political subdivision of a State which has the power to levy taxes and spend funds, as well as general corporate and police powers; and

(8) the term "part-time employee" means an employee who is employed for an average of fewer than 20 hours per week or who has been employed for fewer than 6 of the 12 months preceding the date on which notice is required.

(b) Exclusions from definition of employment loss.—(1) In the case of a sale of part or all of an employer's business, the seller shall be responsible for providing notice for any plant closing or mass layoff in accordance with section 2102 of this title, up to and including the effective date of the sale. After the effective date of the sale of part or all of an employer's business, the purchaser shall be responsible for providing notice for any plant closing or mass layoff in accordance with section 2102 of this title. Notwithstanding any other provision of this chapter, any person who is an employee of the seller (other than a part-time employee) as of the effective date of the sale shall be considered an employee of the purchaser immediately after the effective date of the sale.

(2) Notwithstanding subsection (a)(6) of this section, an employee may not be considered to have experienced an employment loss if the closing or layoff is the result of the relocation or consolidation of part or all of the employer's business and, prior to the closing or layoff—

(A) the employer offers to transfer the employee to a different site of employment within a reasonable commuting distance with no more than a 6–month break in employment; or

(B) the employer offers to transfer the employee to any other site of employment regardless of distance with no more than a 6–month break in employment, and the employee accepts within 30 days of the offer or of the closing or layoff, whichever is later.

§ 2102. Notice required before plant closings and mass layoffs

(a) Notice to employees, state dislocated worker units, and local governments.—An employer shall not order a plant closing or mass layoff until the end of a 60–day period after the employer serves written notice of such an order—

(1) to each representative of the affected employees as of the time of the notice or, if there is no such representative at that time, to each affected employee; and

(2) to the State dislocated worker unit (designated or created under title III of the Job Training Partnership Act [29 U.S.C.A. § 1651 et seq.]), and the chief elected official of the unit of local government within which such closing or layoff is to occur.

If there is more than one such unit, the unit of local government which the employer shall notify is the unit of local government to which the employer pays the highest taxes for the year preceding the year for which the determination is made.

(b) Reduction of notification period.—**(1)** An employer may order the shutdown of a single site of employment before the conclusion of the 60–day period if as of the time that notice would have been required the employer was actively seeking capital or business which, if obtained, would have enabled the employer to avoid or postpone the shutdown and the employer reasonably and in good faith believed that giving the notice required would have precluded the employer from obtaining the needed capital or business.

(2)(A) An employer may order a plant closing or mass layoff before the conclusion of the 60–day period if the closing or mass layoff is caused by business circumstances that were not reasonably foreseeable as of the time that notice would have been required.

(B) No notice under this chapter shall be required if the plant closing or mass layoff is due to any form of natural disaster, such as a flood, earthquake, or the drought currently ravaging the farmlands of the United States.

(3) An employer relying on this subsection shall give as much notice as is practicable and at that time shall give a brief statement of the basis for reducing the notification period.

(c) Extension of layoff period.—A layoff of more than 6 months which, at its outset, was announced to be a layoff of 6 months or less, shall be treated as an employment loss under this chapter unless—

(1) the extension beyond 6 months is caused by business circumstances (including unforeseeable changes in price or cost) not reasonably foreseeable at the time of the initial layoff; and

(2) notice is given at the time it becomes reasonably foreseeable, that the extension beyond 6 months will be required.

(d) Determinations with respect to employment loss.—For purposes of this section, in determining whether a plant closing or mass layoff has occurred or will occur, employment losses for 2 or more groups at a single site of employment, each of which is less than the minimum number of employees specified in section 2101(a)(2) or (3) of this title but which in the aggregate exceed that minimum number, and which occur within any 90–day period shall be considered to be a plant closing or mass layoff unless the employer demonstrates that the employment losses are the result of separate and distinct actions and causes and are not an attempt by the employer to evade the requirements of this chapter.

§ 2103. Exemptions

This chapter shall not apply to a plant closing or mass layoff if—

(1) the closing is of a temporary facility or the closing or layoff is the result of the completion of a particular project or undertaking, and the affected employees were hired with the understanding that their employment was limited to the duration of the facility or the project or undertaking; or

(2) the closing or layoff constitutes a strike or constitutes a lockout not intended to evade the requirements of this chapter. Nothing in this chapter shall require an employer to serve written notice pursuant to section 2102(a) of this title when permanently replacing a person who is deemed to be an economic striker under the National Labor Relations Act [29 U.S.C.A. § 151 et seq.]: *Provided*, That nothing in this chapter shall be deemed to validate or invalidate any judicial or administrative ruling relating to the hiring of permanent replacements for economic strikers under the National Labor Relations Act.

§ 2104. Administration and enforcement of requirements

(a) Civil actions against employers.—(1) Any employer who orders a plant closing or mass layoff in violation of section 2102 of this title shall be liable to each aggrieved employee who suffers an employment loss as a result of such closing or layoff for—

(A) back pay for each day of violation at a rate of compensation not less than the higher of—

(i) the average regular rate received by such employee during the last 3 years of the employee's employment; or

(ii) the final regular rate received by such employee; and

(B) benefits under an employee benefit plan described in section 1002(3) of this title, including the cost of medical expenses incurred during the employment loss which would have been covered under an employee benefit plan if the employment loss had not occurred.

Such liability shall be calculated for the period of the violation, up to a maximum of 60 days, but in no event for more than one-half the number of days the employee was employed by the employer.

(2) The amount for which an employer is liable under paragraph (1) shall be reduced by—

(A) any wages paid by the employer to the employee for the period of the violation;

(B) any voluntary and unconditional payment by the employer to the employee that is not required by any legal obligation; and

(C) any payment by the employer to a third party or trustee (such as premiums for health benefits or payments to a defined contribution pension plan) on behalf of and attributable to the employee for the period of the violation.

In addition, any liability incurred under paragraph (1) with respect to a defined benefit pension plan may be reduced by crediting the employee with service for all purposes under such a plan for the period of the violation.

(3) Any employer who violates the provisions of section 2102 of this title with respect to a unit of local government shall be subject to a civil penalty of not more than $500 for each day of such violation, except that such penalty shall not apply if the employer pays to each aggrieved employee the amount for which the employer is liable to that employee within 3 weeks from the date the employer orders the shutdown or layoff.

(4) If an employer which has violated this chapter proves to the satisfaction of the court that the act or omission that violated this chapter was in good faith and that the employer had reasonable grounds for believing that the act or omission was not a violation of this chapter the court may, in its discretion, reduce the amount of the liability or penalty provided for in this section.

(5) A person seeking to enforce such liability, including a representative of employees or a unit of local government aggrieved under paragraph (1) or (3), may sue either for such person or for other persons similarly situated, or both, in any district court of the United States for any district in which the violation is alleged to have occurred, or in which the employer transacts business.

(6) In any such suit, the court, in its discretion, may allow the prevailing party a reasonable attorney's fee as part of the costs.

(7) For purposes of this subsection, the term, "aggrieved employee" means an employee who has worked for the employer ordering the plant closing or mass layoff and who, as a result of the failure by the employer to comply with section 2102 of this title, did not receive timely notice either directly or through his or her representative as required by section 2102 of this title.

(b) Exclusivity of remedies.—The remedies provided for in this section shall be the exclusive remedies for any violation of this chapter. Under this chapter, a Federal court shall not have authority to enjoin a plant closing or mass layoff.

§ 2105. Procedures in addition to other rights of employees

The rights and remedies provided to employees by this chapter are in addition to, and not in lieu of, any other contractual or statutory rights and remedies of the employees, and are not intended to alter or affect such rights and remedies, except that the period of notification required by this chapter shall run concurrently with any period of notification required by contract or by any other statute.

§ 2106. Procedures encouraged where not required

It is the sense of Congress that an employer who is not required to comply with the notice requirements of section 2102 of this title should, to the extent possible, provide notice to its employees about a proposal to close a plant or permanently reduce its workforce.

§ 2107. Authority to prescribe regulations

(a) The Secretary of Labor shall prescribe such regulations as may be necessary to carry out this chapter. Such regulations shall, at a minimum, include interpretative regulations describing the methods by which employers may provide for appropriate service of notice as required by this chapter.

(b) The mailing of notice to an employee's last known address or inclusion of notice in the employee's paycheck will be considered acceptable methods for fulfillment of the employer's obligation to give notice to each affected employee under this chapter.

§ 2108. Effect on other laws

The giving of notice pursuant to this chapter, if done in good faith compliance with this chapter, shall not constitute a violation of the National Labor Relations Act [29 U.S.C.A. § 151 et seq.] or the Railway Labor Act [45 U.S.C.A. 151 et seq.].

§ 2109. Report on employment and international competitiveness

Two years after Aug. 4, 1988, the Comptroller General shall submit to the Committee on Small Business of both the House and Senate, the Committee on Labor and Human Resources, and the Committee on Education and Labor a report containing a detailed and objective analysis of the effect of this chapter on employers (especially small- and medium-sized businesses), the economy (international competitiveness), and employees (in terms of levels and conditions of employment). The Comptroller General shall assess both costs and benefits, including the effect on productivity, competitiveness, unemployment rates and compensation, and worker retraining and readjustment.

Montana Wrongful Discharge from Employment Act

Montana Code §§ 39–2–901 to 39–2–915 (1987), as amended.

Sec. 39–2–902. Purpose. This part sets forth certain rights and remedies with respect to wrongful discharge. Except as limited in this part, employment having no specified term may be terminated at the will of either the employer or the employee on notice to the other for any reason considered sufficient by the terminating party. Except as provided in Sec. 39–2–912, this part provides the exclusive remedy for a wrongful discharge from employment.

Sec. 39–2–903. Definitions.

* * *

(2) "Discharge" includes a constructive discharge as defined in subsection (1) and any other termination of employment, including resignation, elimination of the job, layoff for lack of work, failure to recall or rehire, and any other cutback in the number of employees for a legitimate business reason.

* * *

(5) "Good cause" means reasonable job-related grounds for dismissal based on a failure to satisfactorily perform job duties, disruption of the employer's operation, or other legitimate business reason.

* * *

(7) "Public policy" means a policy in effect at the time of the discharge concerning the public health, safety, or welfare established by constitutional provision, statute, or administrative rule.

Sec. 39–2–904. Elements of wrongful discharge. A discharge is wrongful only if: (1) it was in retaliation for the employee's refusal to violate public policy or for reporting a violation of public policy; or

(2) The discharge was not for good cause and the employee had completed the employer's probationary period of employment; or

(3) The employer violated the express provisions of its own written personnel policy.

Sec. 34–2–905. Remedies. (1) If an employer has committed a wrongful discharge, the employee may be awarded lost wages and fringe benefits for a period not to exceed 4 years from the date of discharge, together with interest thereon. Interim earnings, including amounts the employee could have earned with reasonable diligence, must be deducted from the amount awarded for lost wages.

(2) The employee may recover punitive damages otherwise allowed by law if it is established by clear and convincing evidence that the employer engaged in actual fraud or actual malice in the discharge of the employee in violation of 39–2–904(1).

(3) There is no right under any legal theory to damages for wrongful discharge under this part for pain and suffering, emotional distress, compensatory damages, punitive damages, or any other form of damages, except as provided for in subsections (1) and (2).

Sec. 39–2–911.   Limitation of actions. (1) An action under this part must be filed within 1 year after the date of discharge.

(2) If an employer maintains written internal procedures, other than those specified in 39–2–912, under which an employee may appeal a discharge within the organizational structure of the employer, the employee shall first exhaust those procedures prior to filing an action under this part. The employee's failure to initiate or exhaust available internal procedures is a defense to an action brought under this part. If the employer's internal procedures are not completed within 90 days from the date the employee initiates the internal procedures, the employee may file an action under this part and for purposes of this subsection the employer's internal procedures are considered exhausted. The limitation period in subsection (1) is tolled until the procedures are exhausted. In no case may the provisions of the employer's internal procedures extend the limitation period in subsection (1) more than 120 days.

(3) If the employer maintains written internal procedures under which an employee may appeal a discharge within the organizational structure of the employer, the employer shall within 7 days of the date of the discharge notify the discharged employee of the existence of such procedures and shall supply the discharged employee with a copy of them. If the employer fails to comply with this subsection, the discharged employee need not comply with subsection (2).

Sec. 39–2–912.   Exemptions. This part does not apply to a discharge

(1) that is subject to any other state or federal statute that provides a procedure or remedy for contesting the dispute. The statutes include those that prohibit discharge for filing complaints, charges, or claims with administrative bodies or that prohibit unlawful discrimination based on race, national origin, sex, age, disability, creed, religion, political belief, color, marital status, and other similar grounds.

(2) of an employee covered by a written collective bargaining agreement or a written contract of employment for a specific term.

Sec. 39–2–913.   Preemption of common-law remedies. Except as provided in this part, no claim for discharge may arise from tort or express or implied contract.

Sec. 39–2–914.   Arbitration. (1) A party may make a written offer to arbitrate a dispute that otherwise could be adjudicated under this part.

(2) An offer to arbitrate must be in writing and contain the following provisions:

(a) A neutral arbitrator must be selected by mutual agreement or, in the absence of agreement, as provided in 27–5–211.

(b) The arbitration must be governed by the Uniform Arbitration Act, Title 27, chapter 5. If there is a conflict between the Uniform Arbitration Act and this part, this part applies.

(c) The arbitrator is bound by this part.

(3) If complaint is filed under this part, the offer to arbitrate must be made within 60 days after service of the complaint and must be accepted in writing within 30 days after the date the offer is made.

(4) A discharged employee who makes a valid offer to arbitrate that is accepted by the employer and who prevails in such arbitration is entitled to have the arbitrator's fee and all costs of arbitration paid by the employer.

(5) If a valid offer to arbitrate is made and accepted, arbitration is the exclusive remedy for the wrongful discharge dispute and there is no right to bring or continue a lawsuit under this part. The arbitrator's award is final and binding, subject to review of the arbitrator's decision under the provisions of the Uniform Arbitration Act.

Sec. 39–2–915.   Effect of rejection of offer to arbitrate. A party who makes a valid offer to arbitrate that is not accepted by the other party and who prevails in an action under this part is entitled as an element of costs to reasonable attorney fees incurred subsequent to the date of the offer.

COLLECTIVE BARGAINING AGREEMENT

PREAMBLE

This Agreement is made and entered into by and between the MAJOR CONTAINER COMPANY ("Company"), their successors or assigns, and the UNITED PAPERWORKERS INTERNATIONAL UNION, AFL–CIO ("Union").

I.   PURPOSE

Section 1.   WITNESSETH, whereas the parties hereto have reached agreement as a result of collective bargaining for the purpose of facilitating the peaceful adjustment of differences which may arise from time to time between this Company and the Union, and to promote harmony and efficiency and to the end that the employees and the Company and the general public may mutually benefit, the parties hereto contract and agree with each other as follows:

II.   RECOGNITION AND UNION SECURITY

Section 1. The Company recognizes the Union as the sole agency for collective bargaining on behalf of all employees, with the exception of timekeepers, clerks, office employees, watchmen and non-working foremen and non-working supervisors, in charge of any classes of labor.

Section 2. This recognition is interpreted by the parties to apply to any transfer or relocation of the Company's present facility to another location within or outside of the metropolitan area, which are an accretion to the existing bargaining unit, where the jobs performed are substantially the same as are covered by the present Agreement.

Section 3. All employees with the exceptions noted in Section 1 who are members of the Union in good standing on the effective date of this Agreement, shall as a condition of continued employment, maintain their membership in good standing in the Union. All employees, who on the effective date of this Agreement, are not as yet members in good standing of the Union, shall become members of the Union in good standing by no later than thirty (30) days following the effective date of this Agreement and shall maintain membership in good standing in the Union in order to continue in employment. All new employees, shall as a condition of continued employment, become members and maintain membership in good standing in the Union by no later than thirty (30) days following the date of their employment or the effective date of this Agreement, whichever is the later.

Section 4. The Company agrees to discharge any employee who does not join or maintain his membership in good standing in the Union within seven (7) calendar days after receipt of written notice from the Union that such employee is delinquent in initiation fee or dues. The Union will indemnify and save harmless the Company against any and all claims, demands, or suits that may arise out of the discharge of any employee under this section.

Section 5. During the term of this Agreement, and at the written request of the Union, the Company will deduct from their wages and remit promptly to the Union the regular monthly membership dues and/or initiation fees established by the Union in accordance with the

Constitution and By–Laws of the Union for all employees who have executed and caused to be delivered to the Company a written authorization for such deductions, on a form in conformity with the applicable statutes, which shall not be irrevocable for a period of more than one (1) year, or the termination date of this Agreement, whichever occurs sooner.

III. MANAGEMENT RIGHTS

Section 1.   It is understood and agreed that the management of the Plant and the direction of the work force, including but not limited to the right to hire, suspend, transfer or discharge for proper cause and the right to relieve employees from duty because of lack of work, the right to establish, determine, and maintain reasonable standards of production, to introduce new and improved methods, materials, equipment or facilities and change or eliminate methods, materials, equipment or facilities are vested exclusively in the Company, subject to the provisions of this Agreement.

IV. DISCRIMINATION

Section 1. No employee shall be discriminated against by the Company for activity in or on behalf of the Union, but shall not be exempted from discipline that is not discriminatory.

Section 2. The Company and the Union agree that there shall be no discrimination in regard to hiring, tenure of employment or any condition of employment, or in regard to membership in the Union, because of race, color, religion, sex, age, disability, national origin, marital status, sexual orientation, veteran status, or any other classification protected by law.

Section 3. The parties recognize that in complying with this Article they are subject to the specific provisions and exemptions of Title VII of the Civil Rights Act of 1964, the Age Discrimination in Employment Act of 1967, the Americans with Disabilities Act, as well as the specific statutes of the various states and pertinent Executive Orders issued by the President of the United States.

V. WAGES

Section 1.   The schedule of rates attached hereto as "Exhibit A" shall become a part of this Agreement and they shall be the minimum rates of pay to be paid by the Company to its employees for the duration of this Agreement.

Section 2.   All employees shall receive their pay weekly.

VI. HOURS OF WORK; OVERTIME

Section 1.   Eight (8) consecutive hours, shall constitute a normal day's work; five (5) days, shall constitute a normal work week. Employees assigned to work days will be granted an unpaid lunch period of thirty (30) minutes. Shift employees will be granted a paid twenty (20) minutes lunch period during the shift, when operating requirements permit. Any employee who works over eight (8) hours in any twenty-four (24) hour period, or forty (40) hours (for which overtime has not previously been paid) in any one work week, shall be paid at the rate of time and a half. This provision shall not be construed to guarantee any specific hours or days of work.

Any employee who works over sixty (60) hours (for which double-time has not previously been paid) in any one work week shall be paid at the rate of double-time.

Section 2.   Overtime shall be distributed as equitably as possible among the employees who can perform the work. The Company shall maintain open overtime records for the purpose of distributing over time equitably.

Section 3.   All work performed on Sundays and holidays shall be paid for at the rate of double time.

Section 4.   All work performed on Saturdays shall be paid for at the rate of time and one-half.

Section 5.   Employees working on second shift shall receive a shift premium of fifteen (15) cents per hour.

Section 6.   Employees working on third shift shall receive a shift premium of twenty-five (25) cents per hour.

VII. HOLIDAYS

Section 1.   The following holidays or days celebrated in place thereof shall be observed and shall be paid for even though not worked at eight hours of the regular hourly rate of pay for all employees who have worked sixty (60) days or more in the Company. Holidays falling on Sunday shall be observed on the following Monday.

New Year's Day.

Decoration Day

Fourth of July

Good Friday

Labor Day

Employee's Birthday

Thanksgiving Day

Day after Thanksgiving

Christmas Day

Christmas Eve Day

New Year's Eve Day

Section 2.   Any employee entitled to a holiday with pay shall not be required to work on said holiday.

Section 3.   It is agreed that to qualify for such holiday pay an employee shall have worked the regular scheduled work day immediately preceding and succeeding said holiday, provided work is available unless excused from such work by the plant management.

VIII.   VACATIONS

Section 1.   Vacation pay shall be computed on the basis of regular hourly rates of pay.

Section 2.   The following schedule shall be the method of application of vacation periods and vacation pay.

Length of Service	Vacation Periods	Vacation Pay at Regular Hourly Rates of Pay
1 Year	1	42 Hours Pay
3 Years	2	84 Hours Pay
8 Years	3	126 Hours Pay
15 Years	4	168 Hours Pay
20 Years	5	210 Hours Pay
25 Years	6	252 Hours Pay

Section 3.   The Company may shut down the plant completely or partially to grant vacations to all or part of the employees at one time provided it shall notify the employees of such a plan at least sixty (60) days before a vacation commences. Otherwise, vacations will be scheduled according to employees' desires, subject to the exclusive right of the Company to change vacation periods to assure orderly and efficient operation of the Plant. In the event of a dispute between two or more employees as to the time of their vacations, the employee with the greatest seniority with the Company shall receive the preference.

Section 4.   Any employee eligible for a vacation, who is severed from the payroll of the Company in any calendar year before having taken his or her vacation, except one who is discharged for cause or who quits without two weeks' notice, shall receive vacation pay.

IX. SENIORITY

Section 1.   Seniority is defined as the length of an employee's service with the Company within the bargaining unit; it shall apply plant-wide.

Section 2.   The Company agrees to draw up a plant-wide Seniority list as of June 1st of each year, which shall be posted in a location available to all employees.

Section 3.   The Union may select from the employees covered by this Agreement a Steward who has been employed by the Company for a period of at least one (1) year, whose duty it is to see that this contract is not broken by either the employees or the Employer. The Union shall notify the Company, in writing, of the name of the Shop Steward.

Section 4.   In the event of layoff, all Union officers, shop stewards, and shop committee members shall have seniority during their terms of office only, over other employees of the Company provided they have at least one (1) year service with the Company.

Section 5.   Production foremen, or other non-bargaining unit employees, shall not do any work, the performance of which, would cause any employee to suffer lay-off or loss of overtime.

Section 6.   An employee shall be terminated and shall lose all accumulated seniority when he or she:

a) quits

b) is discharged

c) is laid off for lack of work for a continuous period of 15 calendar months or a period of time equal to the employee's plant seniority, whichever comes first.

d) fails to return to work within four (4) days of notice to return to work, unless such failure to return is for reason satisfactory to the Company

e) engages in gainful employment during a leave of absence except in cases where such leave of absence is expressly granted for this purpose

f) fails to return to work within three (3) working days from the date of expiration of his leave of absence

g) is absent due to non-industrial accident or illness for a period of two (2) years

h) is retired under the Company's Pension Plan.

X.   PERMANENT VACANCIES

Section 1.   Each permanent job vacancy and each permanent new job which falls within the scope of the Union's certification shall be filled as follows:

(a) Notice of such job shall be posted in the plant for two (2) days. Such job postings shall include the job classification, department, and the shift on which the new job or vacancy exists. Any employee who wishes to bid for such jobs shall sign the posting. Job postings shall be placed in three locations throughout the plant for official signing in the presence of a member of management, who will initial the posting. Two postings will be provided in the supervisory offices assigned in the plant; a third posting will be placed in the Human Resources office for signing. At all posting locations, job descriptions for all jobs will be available for review. At the end of the two (2) days, the Company shall remove the posting.

(b) Where skill and ability are relatively equal, seniority shall prevail, providing the employee is physically able to perform the work without endangering his or her health or safety. The most senior qualified employee will be awarded the job and be notified by the Human Resources office within five (5) days after removal of the posting. The Company will transfer the employee awarded the vacancy hereunder to the new job within fifteen (15) calendar days, provided the release of the employee does not interfere with the efficient operations of the department. Multiple postings will be awarded from the highest pay grade posting to the lowest pay grade posting.

(c) An employee awarded the vacancy hereunder shall be given up to sixteen (16) working days in which to demonstrate his or her ability to perform the work involved. In some circumstances, extensions may be required, not to exceed sixteen (16) additional workdays. During the qualifying period, employees are unable to bid. During this period, the Company may remove the employee from the job if the Company considers the employee's work to be unsatisfactory. The employee may then bid on any other vacancy. An employee disqualified from a job will be unable to bid that job for a period of three (3) months.

Section 2.   The Union and the Company may, by mutual agreement, provide rules whereby disabled employees may be assigned to jobs which they are able to satisfactorily perform without regard to this Article. When the Union and the Company agree to placement of an employee hereunder, the conditions pertaining to that placement shall be reduced to writing and signed by the parties.

XI. LAYOFF AND RECALL

Section 1.   If the Company decides to reduce the number of employees in a job classification in a department, and the reduction is expected to continue for more than four (4) days, the reduction shall be made as follows:

(a) The least senior employee or employees shall be removed from the classification provided the skill and ability of the employees in the classification are relatively equal.

(b) An employee removed from his or her classification and/or shift pursuant to (a) shall be afforded the opportunity to move into a job classification in an equal or lower labor grade on any shift provided he or she has the proven skill and ability to perform such work which is held by an employee with less seniority. An employee displaced from his job classification by the exercise of the seniority rights granted in this paragraph shall also be afforded the opportunity to displace other employees in accordance with this paragraph and the exercise of seniority hereunder.

(c) In the operation of (a) and (b) above, a senior employee has the prerogative of accepting layoff instead of displacing a junior employee, if he or she so desires.

(d) The Company will post a notice of layoff expected to last more than four (4) days at least ten (10) days in advance of such layoff, unless the conditions leading to such layoff resulted from an Act of God, labor dispute, or other condition beyond the control of the Company.

Section 2.   (a) Employees affected by a reduction of forces shall be recalled to their regular job classification and department in the inverse order of the force reduction. If the employee refuses such recall, he will be terminated as a voluntary quit. Employees recalled to their regular job classification and department, but not to their regular shift, shall be returned to their regular shift in order of seniority as openings occur.

(b) When a vacancy exists after exhausting paragraph (a), the job will be posted for bid according to the bidding procedure. If no employee is awarded such job vacancy, the most senior employee on layoff shall be afforded the vacancy providing he or she has the skill and ability to perform the work.

Section 3.   Nothing in this Agreement shall prohibit the Company's laying off the employees for the purpose of taking inventory and offering the work available during such period to the senior qualified employees in the department.

XII. EMPLOYEE SAFETY

Section 1.   The Company agrees to provide a place of employment which shall be safe for the employees therein, shall furnish and use safety devices and safeguards, and shall adopt and use methods and processes adequate to render such places of employment safe. The term "safe" or "safety" as applied to employment or place of employment shall include conditions and methods of sanitation and hygiene necessary for the protection of life, health and safety of the employees.

Section 2.   The Company agrees that all machinery, equipment and facilities the Company furnishes shall meet with all required legal standards of safety and sanitation. Accident records shall be kept and maintained by the Company and shall be made available on request to the Safety Committee

Section 3.   The Company agrees to maintain a Joint Labor–Management Safety Committee. The Safety Committee shall be composed of at least two (2) representatives of Management and at least two (2) representatives of the Union. The Union representatives shall be selected by the local Union. The Safety Committee shall be able to sit in on any safety investigation when any employee is questioned and shall:

Meet at least once every month on definitely established dates;

Make inspections of the plant at least once every month;

Make recommendations for the correction of unsafe or harmful work practices;

Review and analyze all reports of industrial injury and illness, investigate causes of same and recommend rules and procedures for the prevention of accidents and disease and for the promotion of health and safety of employees;

Promote health and safety education.

Section 4.   All disputes and disagreements brought to the attention of the Safety Committee, arising under the Safety clause of this contract, if not disposed of by the Safety Committee, shall be subject to the Grievance Procedure.

Section 5.   In the event of special circumstances, the Safety Committee may seek advice, opinion and suggestions of experts and authorities on safety matters. Such experts shall have access to the plant for the purpose of applying this article at any time upon providing reasonable notice. The Personnel Manager or his/her designee and a Union designee shall accompany the Safety representative.

Section 6.   Employees injured in the plant shall be furnished medical aid or treatment on Company time, and shall receive full pay for the shift on which they were working when injured.

Section 7.   The Union agrees to participate on the Safety Committee and will endeavor to have its members observe all safety rules and use all equipment and safeguards provided. The Union representative on the Safety Committee, upon request, shall be allowed to leave his or her work during working hours for the purpose of performing his or duties as outlined in this Article without loss of time or pay.

XIII.   DISCIPLINE

Section 1.   The Employer may not discipline or discharge except for just cause and only after due regard for principles of progressive discipline, except as specified otherwise herein.

Section 2.   The following shall be causes for immediate discharge:

(a) Bringing intoxicants, narcotics or other dangerous drugs into or consuming intoxicants or such narcotics or drugs in the plant or on the plant premises.

(b) Reporting for duty under the influence of liquor, narcotics or drugs.

(c) Smoking while on duty or in prohibited areas.

(d) Deliberate destruction or removal of Company's or another employee's property.

(e) Refusal to comply with Company rules, provided that such rules shall be posted in a conspicuous place where they may be read by all employees; and further provided that no changes in present rules or no additional rules shall be made that are inconsistent with this Agreement.

(f) Disorderly conduct.

(g) Sleeping on duty.

(h) Giving or taking a bribe of any nature, as an inducement to obtaining work or retaining a position.

(i) Failure to report for duty without bona fide reasons.

(j) Reading of books, magazines or newspapers while on duty except where required in line of duty.

(k) Unsanitary practice endangering the health of others.

(*l*) Gambling during working hours.

Section 3.   Except for the infractions noted in Section 2, above, the Employer shall not discharge or suspend an employee without first having discussed such action with the employee and Shop Steward or, in absence of both, having given notice to the Union. Such notice may be by telephone, telegram, or letter, and such notice must include the reason or reasons for an employee's discharge or suspension.

Section 4.   No employee in the bargaining unit shall be required to take any polygraph test, but an employee may, of his own volition, take such a test.

XIV.   GRIEVANCE PROCEDURE

Section 1.   Should grievances arise, a diligent effort shall be made to settle all grievances as soon as possible after they have been presented either by the Union or an employee.

Any employee having a grievance shall submit same in writing as promptly as possible after its occurrence but no grievance shall be valid if not presented within fifteen (15) days from the time the cause for complaint became known to the employee.

If at any time a grievance remains at any step below Step 4 for more than seven (7) working days, the Local Union may, by written notice to local management, request that such grievance be heard at the next step.

Section 2.   When grievances arise, the following steps shall be followed, each to be exhausted before resorting to the next:

Step 1. Between the immediate supervisor and the aggrieved employee; the appropriate Union representative shall be given an opportunity to be present.

Step 2. Between the Production Superintendent and the Union Committee.

Step 3. Between the Operations Manager and the Union Committee.

Step 4. Between the Divisional Vice President of the Company, or his representative, and the President of the International Union, or his representative.

XV. ARBITRATION

Section 1. In the event that a grievance based upon the interpretation, application or compliance with the terms of this Agreement shall not have been satisfactorily settled, the Union within thirty (30) days after the Company's answer to the last step in the grievance procedure may submit the matter to the American Arbitration Association under their rules then in effect. Expenses of the arbitrator shall be shared equally by the Company and the Union. The decision of the arbitrator shall be binding upon both parties to this Agreement. Such decision shall be within the scope and terms of this Agreement, but shall not change any of its terms or conditions.

XVI.   STRIKES AND LOCKOUTS

Section 1. The Union and the Company agree that there shall be no strikes, sympathy strikes, boycotts, lockouts or general slowing down of production by employees, during the life of this Agreement, and that in the event differences should arise between the Company and the Union or its members employed by the Company, as to the meaning and application of this Agreement, or should any local trouble of any kind arise in the plant, there shall be no suspension of work by the employees on account of such differences.

XVII.   EMPLOYEE BENEFITS

The benefits as shown in this section shall continue in effect during the life of this Agreement.

Medical Insurance: Blue Cross Preferred Comprehensive; Blue Shield, 100; and Major Medical Insurance shall continue to be provided at Company expense for employees until age 70. The Major Medical Insurance referred to herein shall be provided on the basis of $10,000 maximum; $100 deductible per person, and 80/20 participation.

A Blue Shield Eye Examination and Refraction Program shall be provided for employees and certain of their dependents at Company expense as promptly as arrangements can be made.

Dental Insurance: A dental insurance plan to be agreed upon by the parties shall be effective April 1, 2012. This plan shall provide dental benefits for employees and their covered dependents. Company shall contribute $20.00 per month per covered employee toward the cost of this coverage and any excess cost shall be made up by employee contributions.

Death in Family: Should death occur to the Mother, Father, Stepmother, Stepfather, Wife, Children, Stepchildren, Sister or Brother of any employee, he or she shall be entitled to a three-day leave of absence and should death occur to the Grandparent of any employee he or she shall be entitled to a one-day leave of absence. For all such leaves of absence the employee will be paid at his or her straight-time rate provided the leave is taken during the normal week, i.e., Monday through Friday.

Jury Duty: The Company agrees to pay to any employee who shall serve on a bona fide jury panel an amount equal to the difference between the employee's earnings from such service and his or her regular eight (8) hours straight time pay for the days, not in excess of fifteen days for any single period of jury service, during which the employee shall be absent and on jury service.

Sick Benefits: Provision is made for the payment of Sick Benefits to hourly paid employees who have been on the payroll for not less than one year immediately prior to the event of sickness.

On presentation of a licensed physician's, dentist's, chiropodist's, or chiropractor's certificate, an employee who has been ill seven (7) or more consecutive days is entitled to an amount equal to fifty (50) percent of his or her forty-hour weekly wages or the amount to which the employee would be entitled under the State Temporary Disability Law, whichever is greater, from the day he became ill, for a period not in excess of twenty-six weeks in any twelve-month period.

Sick benefits have no connection with illness due to injury in the plant. Disabilities due to injuries in the plant are compensated for under Employers' Liability Insurance in accordance with State regulations.

Retirement: All employees covered by this Agreement are also covered by the Pension Plan which went into operation July 1, 1985, as amended: This is a funded pension plan.

A copy of the Summary Plan Description will be regularly furnished to each new employee. Additional copies may be obtained upon request at the Personnel Office.

Life Insurance: A group life insurance policy will be purchased by the Company so that each employee with one or more years of continuous service with the Company shall have life insurance protection in the amount of $10,000 in the event such employee shall die while employed by the Company and before such employee's retirement. Beneficiary designations shall be made by each such employee in accordance with the provisions of such group policy.

XVIII.   NEW EMPLOYEES

Section 1.   New employees shall be considered probationary employees and shall not rank for seniority until they shall have been in the employ of the Company for sixty (60) calendar days, unless otherwise extended by mutual agreement. After the expiration of the sixty (60) day period, they shall cease to be probationary employees and rates of pay and all other provisions of this Agreement shall be applicable to them. They shall then rank for seniority from the date of original hiring in the plant. During the probationary period the Company may pay the employee the regular job wage rate.

XIX.   SCOPE OF WORK; NEW TECHNOLOGIES

Section 1. It is the intent of the parties to permit the Company to remain technologically competitive and to meet its customer's needs so long as work opportunities now and in the future are preserved for the employees within the bargaining unit identified in Article II. As new technologies develop, the parties pledge their best efforts to fully train and include bargaining unit employees in the implementation of such technologies.

Section 2. In furtherance of the parties' intent, a technology committee consisting of two (2) Union and two (2) Company representatives shall be established and shall meet at the request of either the Union or the Company. The committee shall be empowered to investigate and discuss all issues involving the impact of new technology on bargaining unit work. The committee shall reach agreement on issues investigated and discussed.

Section 3. The Company shall provide training, if required, on any new technology used to perform bargaining unit work. The Company will not permit its proprietary or licensed software, data, hardware, equipment or facilities to be used by others to perform work or functions that replace work or functions being performed by bargaining unit employees.

XX.   COMPLETE AGREEMENT

Section 1. The parties hereto acknowledge that, during the negotiations which resulted in this Agreement, each had the unlimited right and opportunity to make demands and proposals with respect to any subject or matter not removed by law from the area of collective bargaining, and that the understandings and Agreements arrived at by the parties after the exercise of the right and opportunity are set forth in this Agreement. Therefore, the parties hereto, for the life of this Agreement, each voluntarily and unqualifiedly waives the right, and each expressly agrees that the other shall not be obligated, to bargain collectively with respect to any subject or matter referred to, or covered or not specifically referred to or covered in the Agreement, even though such subject or matter may not have been within the knowledge or contemplation of either or both of the parties at the time that they negotiated or signed this Agreement.

Section 2. The parties hereto expressly agree that this contract is the sole and complete Agreement between them and that any other previous understandings or Agreements, oral or written (inconsistent with the provisions of this Agreement), are superseded and are of no effect during the term of this Agreement (except as elsewhere provided in the Agreement).

XXI.   TERM OF AGREEMENT

Section 1. This Agreement shall be effective April 1, 2011, and shall continue in full force and effect to and including March 31, 2014, and from year to year after the latter date, unless and until either of the parties hereto shall give to the other three (3) months' written notice prior to the end of the original term, or three (3) months' written notice prior to the end of any subsequent year, of an intention to modify or terminate at the end of the original term or of the then current year.

XXII.   SUCCESSORS AND ASSIGNS

Section 1. This Agreement shall be binding upon the successors, purchasers, transferees and assignees of the Company.

Section 2. The Company shall give notice of the existence of this Agreement to any successor, purchaser, transferee or assignee. Such notice shall be in writing, with a copy to the Union, at least sixty (60) days in advance of the effective date of transfer. After such notice is given, upon the request of either party, the parties shall bargain in good faith about any matter not covered by this Agreement.

Exhibit A

All incumbent employees shall receive the following wages:

Effective June 1, 2011

Work Level A	Start	$10.71	--$14.06
Work Level B	Start	$11.64	--$15.02
Work Level C	Start	$12.53	--$16.48
Work Level D	Start	$13.01	--$16.96
Work Level E	Start	$15.15	--$19.10

Effective June 1, 2012

Work Level A	Start	$10.88	--$14.34
Work Level B	Start	$11.83	--$15.32
Work Level C	Start	$12.74	--$16.81
Work Level D	Start	$13.23	--$17.30
Work Level E	Start	$15.41	--$19.48

Effective June 1, 2013

Work Level A	Start	$11.20	--$14.84
Work Level B	Start	$12.18	--$15.86
Work Level C	Start	$13.12	--$17.40
Work Level D	Start	$13.62	--$17.91
Work Level E	Start	$15.88	--$20.16

MEMORANDUM OF UNDERSTANDING #1 ABSENTEE CONTROL PROGRAM

Executed by Company and Union on June 1, 1998

The Company shall have the sole option of placing an employee on the absentee watch list by issuing a written notice to the employee, with a copy to the Union. The Company's decision to place an employee on the absentee watch list shall not be subject to the grievance or arbitration provisions of the contract.

Once an employee is placed on the absentee watch list, termination will take place in the event there are two (2) unexcused absences or four (4) tardinesses, or any combination thereof in any rolling 90–calendar day period. An unexcused absence is defined as *any* absence that is not approved by the Company in writing and signed by the Company President or a designee. In the event a termination based upon absenteeism or tardiness is processed to arbitration, the arbitrator shall be limited to determining whether or not an individual had two (2) or more unexcused absences or four (4) or more tardinesses, or any combination thereof, in the rolling 90–day period. It is further understood that an individual placed on the absentee watch list shall remain on that list for 300 calendar days provided there is no intervening unexcused absence or tardiness and otherwise for 365 calendar days from the date of written notice provided for above.

MEMORANDUM OF UNDERSTANDING #2
CHEMICAL SUBSTANCE ABUSE POLICY
Executed by Company and Union on October 15, 2010

1.   An employee who is found or reasonable believed to be under the influence of alcohol, drugs or an intoxicant in the employee's system during the course of business on Company premises or when conducting Company business *at any time* will be subject to discipline including discharge, or may be referred to the Employee Assistance Program. Being "under the influence" of alcohol is defined as a blood alcohol content of .04 or higher; and being "under the influence" of an unauthorized controlled substance, illegal drug, prescription, or non-prescription drug is defined as testing positive at specified ng/ml levels.

2.   It is the responsibility of each employee to report promptly to the Medical Department the use or possession of any prescribed medication which may affect judgment, performance, or behavior. No prescription drug will be brought on the Company premises or business in any manner, combination, or quantity other than that prescribed by a licensed physician. Failure to comply may result in discipline, including discharge, or the employee may be referred to the Employee Assistance Program.

3.   All new hires will be tested for the use of drugs, alcohol, and intoxicating substances. Refusal to submit to testing, or testing positive, will result in rejection of employment by the Company. Applicants who are denied employment because of a positive test result may reapply for employment and be re-tested after one year from the time of initial rejection.

4.   If Management has reasonable suspicion (as herein defined) that an employee is under the influence or, impaired by, or unfit for work due to a chemical substance, including but not limited to a drug, alcohol, or intoxicating substance, or in the event of an accident when the cause may be human error, the subject employee shall be required to submit to medical chemical screening, which may include breath, saliva, urine, and/or blood specimen testing. Positive test results may result in the employee being disciplined, up to and including discharge, or the employee may be referred to the Employee Assistance Program.

5. "Reasonable suspicion" means objective belief based upon reasonable, individualized suspicion that can be described with particularity that a specific employee may be under the influence of alcohol, drugs, or other intoxicating substances based on direct observation by a supervisor or management representative.

NATIONAL LABOR RELATIONS BOARD FORMS

(1) Petition for Election.

(2) Stipulated Election Agreement, and

(3) Unfair Labor Practice Charge Against Employer.

(4) Unfair Labor Practice Charge Against Union.

(5) Remedial Notice.

INTERNET FORM NLRB-502 (2-08)	UNITED STATES GOVERNMENT NATIONAL LABOR RELATIONS BOARD **PETITION**	FORM EXEMPT UNDER 44 U.S.C.
		DO NOT WRITE IN THIS SPACE
		Case No. / Date Filed

INSTRUCTIONS: Submit an original of this Petition to the NLRB Regional Office in the Region in which the employer concerned is located.

The Petitioner alleges that the following circumstances exist and requests that the NLRB proceed under its proper authority pursuant to Section 9 of the NLRA.

1. PURPOSE OF THIS PETITION (if box RC, RM, or RD is checked and a charge under Section 8(b)7 of the Act has been filed involving the Employer named herein, the statement following the description of the type of petition shall not be deemed made.) (Check One)

☐ **RC-CERTIFICATION OF REPRESENTATIVE** - A substantial number of employees wish to be represented for purposes of collective bargaining by Petitioner and Petitioner desires to be certified as representative of the employees.

☐ **RM-REPRESENTATION (EMPLOYER PETITION)** - One or more individuals or labor organizations have presented a claim to Petitioner to be recognized as the representative of employees of Petitioner.

☐ **RD-DECERTIFICATION (REMOVAL OF REPRESENTATIVE)** - A substantial number of employees assert that the certified or currently recognized bargaining representative is no longer their representative.

☐ **UD-WITHDRAWAL OF UNION SHOP AUTHORITY (REMOVAL OF OBLIGATION TO PAY DUES)** - Thirty percent (30%) or more of employees in a bargaining unit covered by an agreement between their employer and a labor organization desire that such authority be rescinded.

☐ **UC-UNIT CLARIFICATION** - A labor organization is currently recognized by Employer, but Petitioner seeks clarification of placement of certain employees: (Check one) ☐ In unit not previously certified. ☐ In unit previously certified in Case No. _____

☐ **AC-AMENDMENT OF CERTIFICATION** - Petitioner seeks amendment of certification issued in Case No. _____ Attach statement describing the specific amendment sought.

2. Name of Employer	Employer Representative to contact	Tel. No.
3. Address(es) of Establishment(s) involved (Street and number, city, State, ZIP code)		Fax No.
4a. Type of Establishment (Factory, mine, wholesaler, etc.)	4b. Identify principal product or service	Cell No. / e-Mail

5. Unit Involved (In UC petition, describe present bargaining unit and attach description of proposed clarification.)	6a. Number of Employees in Unit:
Included	Present
Excluded	Proposed (By UC/AC)
	6b. Is this petition supported by 30% or more of the employees in the unit?* ☐ Yes ☐ No *Not applicable in RM, UC, and AC

(If you have checked box RC in 1 above, check and complete EITHER item 7a or 7b, whichever is applicable)

7a. ☐ Request for recognition as Bargaining Representative was made on (Date) _____ and Employer declined recognition on or about (Date) _____ (If no reply received, so state).

7b. ☐ Petitioner is currently recognized as Bargaining Representative and desires certification under the Act.

8. Name of Recognized or Certified Bargaining Agent (If none, so state.)	Affiliation
Address	Tel. No. / Cell No.	Date of Recognition or Certification / Fax No. / e-Mail

9. Expiration Date of Current Contract. If any (Month, Day, Year) _____

10. If you have checked box UD in 1 above, show here the date of execution of agreement granting union shop (Month, Day and Year) _____

11a. Is there now a strike or picketing at the Employer's establishment(s) Involved? Yes ☐ No ☐

11b. If so, approximately how many employees are participating? _____

11c. The Employer has been picketed by or on behalf of (Insert Name) _____ , a labor organization, of (Insert Address) _____ Since (Month, Day, Year) _____

12. Organizations or individuals other than Petitioner (and other than those named in items 8 and 11c), which have claimed recognition as representatives and other organizations and individuals known to have a representative interest in any employees in unit described in item 5 above. (If none, so state)

Name	Address	Tel. No.	Fax No.
		Cell No.	e-Mail

13. Full name of party filing petition (If labor organization, give full name, including local name and number)

14a. Address (street and number, city, state, and ZIP code)	14b. Tel. No. EXT	14c. Fax No.
	14d. Cell No.	14e. e-Mail

15. Full name of national or international labor organization of which Petitioner is an affiliate or constituent (to be filled in when petition is filed by a labor organization)

I declare that I have read the above petition and that the statements are true to the best of my knowledge and belief.

Name (Print)	Signature	Title (if any)
Address (street and number, city, state, and ZIP code)	Tel. No. / Cell No.	Fax No. / eMail

WILLFUL FALSE STATEMENTS ON THIS PETITION CAN BE PUNISHED BY FINE AND IMPRISONMENT (U.S. CODE, TITLE 18, SECTION 1001)

PRIVACY ACT STATEMENT

Solicitation of the information on this form is authorized by the National Labor Relations Act (NLRA), 29 U.S.C. § 151 *et seq.* The principal use of the information is to assist the National Labor Relations Board (NLRB) in processing unfair labor practice and related proceedings or litigation. The routine uses for the information are fully set forth in the Federal Register, 71 Fed. Reg. 74942-43 (Dec. 13, 2006). The NLRB will further explain these uses upon request. Disclosure of this information to the NLRB is voluntary; however, failure to supply the information will cause the NLRB to decline to invoke its processes.

FORM NLRB-652
(4-95)

UNITED STATES OF AMERICA
NATIONAL LABOR RELATIONS BOARD
STIPULATED ELECTION AGREEMENT

The parties agree that a hearing is waived, that approval of this Agreement constitutes withdrawal of any notice of hearing previously issued in this matter, that the petition is amended to conform to this Agreement, and further **AGREE AS FOLLOWS:**

1. **SECRET BALLOT.** A secret-ballot election shall be held under the supervision of the Regional Director in the unit defined below at the agreed time and place, under the Board's Rules and Regulations.

2. **ELIGIBLE VOTERS.** The eligible voters shall be unit employees employed during the payroll period for eligibility, including employees who did not work during that period because they were ill, on vacation, or temporarily laid off, employees engaged in an economic strike which commenced less than 12 months before the election date and who retained their status as such during the eligibility period and their replacements, and employees in the military services of the United States who appear in person at the polls. Ineligible to vote are employees who have quit or been discharged for cause since the payroll period for eligibility, employees engaged in a strike who have been discharged for cause since the commencement thereof and who have not been rehired or reinstated before the election date, and employees engaged in an economic strike which commenced more than 12 months before the election date and who have been permanently replaced. The Employer shall provide to the Regional Director, within 7 days after the Regional Director has approved this Agreement, an election eligibility list containing the full names and addresses of all eligible voters. *Excelsior Underwear, Inc.*, 156 NLRB 1236 (1966). *North Macon Health Care Facility*, 315 NLRB 359 (1994).

3. **NOTICE OF ELECTION.** Copies of the Notice of Election shall be posted by the Employer in conspicuous places and usual posting places easily accessible to the voters at least three (3) full working days prior to 12:01 a.m. of the day of the election. As soon as the election arrangements are finalized, the Employer will be informed when the Notices must be posted in order to comply with the posting requirement. Failure to post the Election Notices as required shall be grounds for setting aside the election whenever proper and timely objections are filed.

4. **ACCOMMODATIONS REQUIRED.** All parties should notify the Regional Director as soon as possible of any voters, potential voters, or other participants in this election who have handicaps falling within the provisions of Section 504 of the Rehabilitation Act of 1973, as amended, and 29 C.F.R. 100.603, and who in order to participate in this election need appropriate auxiliary aids, as defined in 29 C.F.R. 100.603, and request the necessary assistance.

5. **OBSERVERS.** Each party may station an equal number of authorized, nonsupervisory-employee observers at the polling places to assist in the election, to challenge the eligibility of voters, and to verify the tally.

6. **TALLY OF BALLOTS.** Upon conclusion of the election, the ballots will be counted and a tally of ballots prepared and immediately made available to the parties.

7. **POSTELECTION AND RUNOFF PROCEDURES.** All procedures after the ballots are counted shall conform with the Board's Rules and Regulations.

8. **RECORD.** The record in this case shall include this Agreement and be governed by the Board's Rules and Regulations.

¡Over)

9. **COMMERCE.** The Employer is engaged in commerce within the meaning of Section 2(6) and (7) of the National Labor Relations Act and a question affecting commerce has arisen concerning the representation of employees within the meaning of Section 9(c). (Insert commerce facts.)

10. **WORDING ON THE BALLOT.** When only one labor organization is on the ballot, the choice shall be "Yes" or "No." If more than one labor organization is on the ballot, the choices shall appear as follows, reading left to right or top to bottom. (If more than one labor organization is on the ballot, any labor organization may have its name removed by the approval of the Regional Director of a timely written request.)

First.

Second.

Third.

11. **PAYROLL PERIOD FOR ELIGIBILITY - THE PERIOD ENDING** _____

12. **DATE, HOURS, AND PLACE OF ELECTION.**

13. **THE APPROPRIATE COLLECTIVE-BARGAINING UNIT.**

_____
(Employer)

By _____
(Name)   (Date)

_____
(Title)

Recommended:

_____
(Board Agent)   (Date)

Date approved _____

_____
Regional Director
National Labor Relations Board

Case _____

_____
(Labor Organization)

By _____
(Name)   (Date)

_____
(Title)

_____
(Labor Organization)

By _____
(Name)   (Date)

_____
(Title)

FORM EXEMPT UNDER 44 U.S.C. 3512

INTERNET FORM NLRB-501 (2-08)	UNITED STATES OF AMERICA NATIONAL LABOR RELATIONS BOARD CHARGE AGAINST EMPLOYER	DO NOT WRITE IN THIS SPACE	
		Case	Date Filed

INSTRUCTIONS:
File an original with NLRB Regional Director for the region in which the alleged unfair labor practice occurred or is occurring.

1. EMPLOYER AGAINST WHOM CHARGE IS BROUGHT

a. Name of Employer	b. Tel. No.
	c. Cell No.
	f. Fax No
d. Address (Street, city, state, and ZIP code) e. Employer Representative	g. e-Mail
	h. Number of workers employed
i. Type of Establishment (factory, mine, wholesaler, etc.) j. Identify principal product or service	

k. The above-named employer has engaged in and is engaging in unfair labor practices within the meaning of section 8(a), subsections (1) and (list

subsections)   of the National Labor Relations Act, and these unfair labor

practices are practices affecting commerce within the meaning of the Act, or these unfair labor practices are unfair practices affecting commerce within the meaning of the Act and the Postal Reorganization Act.

2. Basis of the Charge (set forth a clear and concise statement of the facts constituting the alleged unfair labor practices)

3. Full name of party filing charge (if labor organization, give full name, including local name and number)

4a. Address (Street and number, city, state, and ZIP code)	4b. Tel. No.
	4c. Cell No.
	4d. Fax No.
	4e. e-Mail

5. Full name of national or international labor organization of which it is an affiliate or constituent unit (to be filled in when charge is filed by a labor organization)

6. DECLARATION	Tel. No.
I declare that I have read the above charge and that the statements are true to the best of my knowledge and belief.	Office, if any, Cell No.
By _____ (signature of representative or person making charge) (Print/type name and title or office, if any)	Fax No.
	e-Mail
Address _____ (date)	

WILLFUL FALSE STATEMENTS ON THIS CHARGE CAN BE PUNISHED BY FINE AND IMPRISONMENT (U.S. CODE, TITLE 18, SECTION 1001)

PRIVACY ACT STATEMENT

Solicitation of the information on this form is authorized by the National Labor Relations Act (NLRA), 29 U.S.C. § 151 et seq. The principal use of the information is to assist the National Labor Relations Board (NLRB) in processing unfair labor practice and related proceedings or litigation. The routine uses for the information are fully set forth in the Federal Register, 71 Fed. Reg. 74942-43 (Dec. 13, 2006). The NLRB will further explain these uses upon request. Disclosure of this information to the NLRB is voluntary; however, failure to supply the information will cause the NLRB to decline to invoke its processes.

INTERNET
FORM NLRB-508
(2-08)

UNITED STATES OF AMERICA
NATIONAL LABOR RELATIONS BOARD
**CHARGE AGAINST LABOR ORGANIZATION
OR ITS AGENTS**

FORM EXEMPT UNDER 44 U.S.C 3512

DO NOT WRITE IN THIS SPACE	
Case	Date Filed

INSTRUCTIONS: File an original with NLRB Regional Director for the region in which the alleged unfair labor practice occurred or is occurring.

1. LABOR ORGANIZATION OR ITS AGENTS AGAINST WHICH CHARGE IS BROUGHT

a. Name	b. Union Representative to contact	
c. Address (Street, city, state, and ZIP code)	d. Tel. No.	e. Cell No.
	f. Fax No.	g. e-Mail

h. The above-named organization(s) or its agents has (have) engaged in and is (are) engaging in unfair labor practices within the meaning of section 8(b), subsection(s) (list subsections) _____ of the National Labor Relations Act, and these unfair labor practices are unfair practices affecting commerce within the meaning of the Act, or these unfair labor practices are unfair practices affecting commerce within the meaning of the Act: and the Postal Reorganization Act.

2. Basis of the Charge (set forth a clear and concise statement of the facts constituting the alleged unfair labor practices)

3. Name of Employer	4a. Tel. No.	b. Cell No.
	c. Fax No.	d. e-Mail

5. Location of plant involved (street, city, state and ZIP code)	6. Employer representative to contact

7. Type of establishment (factory, mine, wholesaler, etc.)	8. Identify principal product or service	9. Number of workers employed

10. Full name of party filing charge	11a. Tel. No.	b. Cell No.
	c. Fax No.	d. e-Mail

11. Address of party filing charge (street, city, state and ZIP code.)

12. DECLARATION

I declare that I have read the above charge and that the statements therein are true to the best of my knowledge and belief.

By _____
(signature of representative or person making charge)   (Print/type name and title or office, if any)

Address _____ (date)_____

Tel. No.
Cell No.
Fax No.
e-Mail

WILLFUL FALSE STATEMENTS ON THIS CHARGE CAN BE PUNISHED BY FINE AND IMPRISONMENT (U.S. CODE, TITLE 18, SECTION 1001)
PRIVACY ACT STATEMENT

Solicitation of the information on this form is authorized by the National Labor Relations Act (NLRA), 29 L.S.C. § 151 et seq. The principal use of the information is to assist the National Labor Relations Board (NLRB) in processing unfair labor practice and related proceedings or litigation. The routine uses for the information are fully set forth in the Federal Register, 71 Fed. Reg. 74942-43 (Dec. 13, 2006). The NLRB will further explain these uses upon request. Disclosure of this information to the NLRB is voluntary, however, failure to supply the information will cause the NLRB to decline to invoke its processes.

NATIONAL LABOR RELATIONS BOARD
AN AGENCY OF THE UNITED STATES GOVERNMENT

The National Labor Relations Act gives employees these rights:

To engage in self-organization;

To form, join, or help unions;

To bargain collectively through a representative of their own choosing

To act together for collective bargaining or other mutual aid or protection;

To refrain from all of these things.

WE WILL NOT promulgate, maintain or enforce a rule which prohibits employees from posting pro-Union literature on Company bulletin boards without permission.

WE WILL NOT threaten employees with discipline for violating such a rule.

WE WILL NOT promulgate, maintain or enforce a rule which prohibits the distribution of materials related to union or other activity by Section 7 of the National Labor Relations Act in nonwork areas without prior approval.

WE WILL NOT interrogate job applicants about their union affiliation, their feelings about working for a non-union employer or whether their past employers were unionized.

WE WILL NOT request employees to report to management if they are harassed by employees who support [Union], or any other labor organization.

WE WILL NOT refer to employees interested in or engaged in union activity as "trouble" and **WE WILL NOT** threaten to discharge such employees because of their union activities.

WE WILL NOT in any other manner interfere with, restrain or coerce employees in the exercise of the rights guaranteed by Section 7 of the Act.

WE WILL notify our employees, in writing, by memorandum or letter separate from this document, that the rules referred to above are no longer in effect.

WE WILL allow our employees to wear union and/or other buttons, insignia, stickers, writings or other markings on their clothing. We will not allow our employees to put union or other buttons, insignia, stickers, writings or other markings on their hard hats, except for safety and security items specifically required by the Company.

WE WILL amend our rule with respect to hard hats to specify that the only items permitted to be put on the hard hats are safety and security items specifically required by the Company. **WE WILL NOT** promulgate, maintain or enforce a rule which allows any other items.

<u>XYZ COMPANY, INC.</u>
(Employer)

Dated: _____   By _____

                                          (Representative)   (Title)

THIS IS AN OFFICIAL NOTICE AND MUST NOT BE DEFACED BY ANYONE

This notice must remain posted for 60 consecutive days from the date of posting and must not be altered, defaced, or covered by any other material. Any questions concerning this notice or compliance with its provisions may be directed to the Board's Office.

615 Chestnut Street, One Independence Mall, 7th Floor,
Philadelphia, Pennsylvania 19106 (215) 597-7601

Notice may be posted in a language other than English when commonly spoken by the workforce. In Durham School Services, 360 N.L.R.B. No. 85 (2014), a unanimous five-member Board ordered that in all future cases the notice will include a hyperlink to a copy of the decision on the Board's website. Even if employees cannot use the hyperlink, it will give them an electronic address where they can obtain a copy of the decision for those employees who do not have access to or do not wish to use a computer to obtain an electronic copy of the decision, the notice also will provide an address to which they may write, and a telephone number which they may call, to obtain a printed copy of the decision from the Board's Executive Secretary.

PART ONE

THE EVOLUTION OF LABOR RELATIONS LAWS

I. FREE LABOR, LABOR ORGANIZATION, AND THE LAW

C. RECOGNITION: THE WAGNER ACT

2. THE WAGNER ACT

Page 47.   Add to the end of "2. THE WAGNER ACT":

The Members of the National Labor Relations Board are appointed by the President with the advice and consent of the Senate. This applies to the Board's General Counsel as well. Art. II, § 2, cl. 3, of the Constitution provides that the President shall have the power to fill vacancies "that may happen during the Recess of the Senate" effective until the expiry of the next session. It has become the practice of Presidents to make such "recess appointments" to vacancies not only at periods between the Senate's stated sessions, but also during recesses of more than brief periods that have occurred during the stated session— or "intra-session" recesses. *See* Memorandum of the Congressional Research Service, The *Noel Canning* Decision and Recess Appointments Made From 1981–2013 (Feb. 4, 2013). In Noel Canning, Inc. v. NLRB, 705 F.3d 490 (D.C. Cir. 2013), the United States Court of Appeals for the District of Columbia Circuit held that only intersession recesses permit recess appointments. Thus, it concluded that the three intra-session appointments to the Board made by President Obama during a short intra-session adjournment in January 2012 were invalid, and, as a result, the Board lacked a quorum under *New Process Steel* at the time it issued an order against Noel Canning in the underlying unfair labor practice proceeding. Two judges also opined that in order for a position to be filled constitutionally the vacancy must "happen" —that is, "occur"—during that period of time. (The Eleventh Circuit had held the opposite). Thereafter, the Third Circuit agreed with the D.C. Circuit without reaching the latter issue. NLRB v. New Vista Nursing and Rehabilitation, 719 F.3d 203 (3d Cir. 2013). Later that year, the Supreme Court granted certiorari in *Noel Canning*. 133 S.Ct. 2861 (2013).

On June 26, 2014, the Court unanimously affirmed the D.C. Circuit. NLRB v. Noel Canning, Inc., 573 U.S. ___, 2014 WL 2882090 (June 26, 2014). However, the five justice majority did so on far narrower grounds. The majority held that the Recess Appointments Clause empowers the President to fill vacancies that occur during any intra-session or intersession recess of sufficient length, whether or not the vacancy occurred during the recess. The Court invalidated the January 2012 appointments to the Board because they occurred during a pro forma intra-session adjournment of less than three days, which is too short to constitute a recess for Recess Appointments Clause purposes. Indeed, the majority concluded that periods of intra-session adjournment shorter than ten days are presumptively too short to trigger the President's recess appointments power. The four concurring justices would have affirmed on broader grounds akin to those the D.C. Circuit had articulated.

The legal and practical implications of *Noel Canning* are mixed. The narrow grounds on which the majority relied limit the impact of the decision to the Board on which the January 2012 recess appointees served, which lasted until August 2013. Earlier recess appointments to the Board—including that of Member Craig Becker, whose appointment was at issue in *New Vista*—did not occur during such a short adjournment and, thus, appear safe from invalidation. Still, hundreds of Board decisions issued during the relevant period may be subject to further litigation. In addition to the approximately 100 matters pending in federal courts, challenges may include new appeals, since, as some observers have noted, there is no statute of limitations governing a party's ability to seek review of a final order of the NLRB in a court of appeals. A number of Board decisions discussed in this Supplement therefore may be subject to reconsideration. Nevertheless, as of August 2013, the Board has been fully constituted with five Senate-confirmed members, three from the President's party. This Board may very well reach the same results upon reconsideration of these matters and reaffirm many of the principles on which the now-invalidated Board relied.

In light of the Senate's new filibuster rules, the President's potential resort to recess appointment power arguably is not as significant as it was when the Court granted review in *Noel Canning*. Going forward, what matters tremendously is who controls Congress. The decision invites one or both houses controlled by the party opposed to the President to seek to prevent recess appointments by avoiding qualifying adjournments. Even this control is not absolute; for example, the Court indicated that the Senate's simply saying it is in session is not necessarily enough. But, undoubtedly, most recesses triggering recess appointment power now can be avoided.

II. JURISDICTION, ORGANIZATION AND PROCEDURE OF THE NLRB

A. NLRB JURISDICTION

2. EXCLUDED EMPLOYERS

Page 56.   Add to the end of "2. EXCLUDED EMPLOYERS":

In Chicago Mathematics & Science Academy Charter School, Inc., 359 NLRB No. 41 (2012), the Board declined to adopt a "bright-line rule that the Board has jurisdiction over entities that operate charter schools" per se. The Board turned to the test approved by the United States Supreme Court in NLRB v. Natural Gas Utility Dist. of Hawkins County, 402 U.S. 600, 604–605 (1971), that excepts entities that are (1) "created directly by the states" so as to constitute an arm of government; or (2) are "administered by individuals who are responsible to public officials or to the general electorate." In this case, involving Illinois law, no law directed that charter schools be created; it allowed for their establishment by private initiative. Neither were those who administered the school, its governing board, responsible to public officials or the electorate in the matter of selection. One Board Member dissented in part. He did not disagree with the majority's legal analysis, but argued that the Board should exercise its discretion to decline jurisdiction because the school is integrated with and highly regulated by the local school system and is "fundamentally local in nature."

3. EXCLUDED EMPLOYEES

Page 56.   Add under "3. EXCLUDED EMPLOYEES" after reference to Hoffman Plastics:

On June 7, 2011, the NLRB's Office of General Counsel issued Memorandum OM 11–62 on NLRB Procedures in Addressing Immigration Status Issues that Arise During NLRB Proceedings. It canvasses rather comprehensively the interconnection of the immigration law with Board proceedings.

In Mezonos Maven Bakery, Inc., 357 NLRB No. 47 (2011), a three-member panel of the Board held that it was not relevant to the unavailability of backpay that it was the employer, not the employees, who was responsible for the immigration violation, by offering undocumented workers fraudulent work-authorization documents. Two members of the panel wrote separately to lament the Supreme Court's decision in *Hoffman Plastics* and to suggest the possibility of other remedies.

Page 62.   Add to the end of Problem 1:

Compare Frenchtown Acquisition Co., Inc. v. NLRB, 683 F.3d 298 (6th Cir. 2012) (charge nurses), *with* Lakeland Health Care Assoc., LLC

v. NLRB, 696 F.3d 1332 (11th Cir. 2012) (licensed practical nurses) (one judge dissenting).

Page 65.   Add following the discussion of Yeshiva University:

In Point Park University v. NLRB, 457 F.3d 42 (D.C. Cir. 2006), the Court of Appeals remanded the case to the Labor Board with instructions to identify more precisely what the relevant factors are that determine whether faculty members or other professional employees are managerial—their significance and weight. In May 2012, the Board took up the remand and called for amicus briefs to address eight questions. These include whether the Board should distinguish university faculty or align the law with managerial determination in the non-academic setting. On February 10, 2014, the Board reiterated many of the same issues in an Invitation to File Briefs in Pacific Lutheran University, Case 19–RC–102521, adding an additional request for briefs addressed to the consequences of religious affiliation under NLRB v. Catholic Bishop, 440 U.S. 490 (1979).

Though both of these cases are primarily concerned with the status of faculty, and secondarily with that of professional employees, an *amicus* brief in the *Point Park* case was submitted by a group of prominent academics in industrial and employment relations. They called upon the Board to consider the situation of non-professional employees engaged in "high performance" workplace practices that flatten the managerial pyramid and devolve decision-making authority to work groups. They argue that to exempt employees in such workplaces from statutory coverage, as managers, would discourage the adoption of those practices by dampening union support for them. It remains to be seen whether the Board will take on issues of managerial status that transcend college and university faculty or professional employment.

Page 65.   Add after entry on *"Medical residents and graduate assistants"*:

Students on athletic scholarships. On petition by the College Athletes Players Association (CAPA), the Board's Regional Director in Chicago held that students who were on athletic scholarships to play football for Northwestern University were employees within the meaning of the Act. *Northwestern University*, Case 13–RC–121359, 2014 WL 1246914 (N.L.R.B.) (March 26, 2014). (Non-scholarship "walk-on" players were not petitioned-for; because they were not compensated they were not considered to be employees.) He noted that these athletes received significant sums for playing; the University received substantial economic benefit from their services—the football team generated $235 million in revenue whilst incurring total expenses of $159 million between 2002 and 2012; the athletes devoted a considerable amount of time to their athletic training and performance—at times a good deal more than was devoted to academic work; and they were subject to extensive control by the coaching staff who could terminate their grants-in-aid. Though the Regional Director did not consider *Brown University* to be applicable, he analyzed the decision and found it distinguishable nevertheless: playing football had no analogous connection to academic continuance, degree requirements, or faculty supervision.

The Board has granted review of the decision, but the representation election was held. Subsequently, the Board invited briefing on a number of issues, including whether it should adhere to, modify, or overrule the test it articulated in *Brown University*. *See* Notice and Invitation to File Briefs, *Northwestern University*, Case 13–RC–121359 (May 12, 2014).

The ballots will be counted if the Board decides that the players are employees. If the Board decides they are not, that decision will not be reviewable. *See* Casebook at pp. 267–273. If the ballots are counted and CAPA lost, then the matter will rest until some other petition is filed. If CAPA won, it may be that the University will refuse to bargain on the ground of the lack of statutory employee status. Should CAPA file a refusal to bargain charge under § 8(a)(5), the Board's order to bargain, on the basis of its prior disposition, would be reviewable in a U.S. Court of Appeals having venue, either the Seventh Circuit or the D.C. Circuit.

Assume that when all the dust settles these collegiate athletes will be employees. Consider the potential implications of such a result, first for scholarship athletes and college athletics in general, and, second for the dealings between the Northwestern players and the university if the players voted to unionize.

As for college athletes and athletics in general, the implications are uncertain. One might expect the same result with regard to other Division I football programs with similar financial structures and control attributes. But, of course, only a small percentage of Division I football schools are private; the remaining institutions are public universities not covered by the NLRA. *See* Casebook at pp. 55–56 (discussing public employers). Moreover, in response to such an outcome in the Northwestern case, might the other private universities alter their football programs—say, by abandoning some of the strict controls over player time and activities that animated the Regional Director's analysis—in an attempt to avoid a similar result? As for scholarship athletes in other sports, key differences in both the financial realities (in most other Division I universities, only basketball generates significant revenue, and often far less than football) and the type and amount of control exercised over the athletes might lead to a different conclusion on the question of employment status. Does differing labor law treatment of scholarship athletes in different sports raise any unique concerns?

Next, think about what would lie ahead for the Northwestern players if they voted to unionize. As you proceed through this course, it might be interesting to return to their situation:

1. *Scope of bargaining.* The Regional Director's decision discusses the extensive controls the coaching staff exercises over the players' private lives: they monitor off-campus housing, outside jobs, vehicle ownership, and even social media. Can the union demand to bargain about these restrictions, possibly to abandon them? Some of these policies, drug testing, for example, are set out in rules of the National Collegiate Athletic Association (NCAA), a membership organization of the schools that sponsor these sports. May the employer refuse to bargain on the ground that they may not depart from NCAA rules?

2. *Economic conflict.* If the players strike or are locked out what happens to their status as students? To their scholarship and other economic subventions, *e.g.* for living expenses? May they be temporarily or permanently replaced? Would a player on an economic strike have a right to return to his job after his replacement graduates?

B. NLRB ORGANIZATION AND PROCEDURE

Page 76.   Add to the conclusion of "REPRESENTATION CASES":

In a Notice of Proposed Rulemaking published on June 22, 2011, the NLRB proposed significant revisions to its electoral rules. 76 FR 36812. The principal thrust of most of the changes was to expedite elections. As summarized by the Board in its June 21, 2011 press release, the proposed amendments would:

- Allow for electronic filing of election petitions and other documents.

- Ensure that employees, employers and unions receive and exchange timely information they need to understand and participate in the representation case process.

- Standardize timeframes for parties to resolve or litigate issues before and after elections.

- Require parties to identify issues and describe evidence soon after an election petition is filed to facilitate resolution and eliminate unnecessary litigation.

- Defer litigation of most voter eligibility issues until after the election.

- Require employers to provide a final voter list in electronic form soon after the scheduling of an election, including voters' telephone numbers and email addresses when available.

- Consolidate all election-related appeals to the Board into a single post-election appeals process and thereby eliminate delay in holding elections currently attributable to the possibility of pre-election appeals.

- Make Board review of post-election decisions discretionary rather than mandatory.

News Release, Board Proposes Rules to Reform Pre- and Post-Election Representation Case Procedures (June 21, 2011), available at http://www.nlrb.gov/news-outreach/news-story/board-proposes-rules-reform-pre-and-post-election-representation-case.

Perhaps the most significant of these changes in terms of expediting the election process would be the elimination of the parties' right to file a pre-election request for review by the NLRB of a regional director's decision and direction of election, thereby deferring most requests for Board review until after the election. As a direct consequence, the prior recommendation that a regional director ordinarily should not schedule an election sooner than 25 days after the decision in order to give the Board an opportunity to rule would be abandoned. The voter list provision also sparked controversy. For each eligible employee, the employer would be required to include the employee's name, work location, shift, and job classification, as well as home address, phone number, and (where available) e-mail address. Such a requirement would not only codify, but also significantly expand the voter list mandate first recognized in *Excelsior Underwear, Inc.*, 156 N.L.R.B. 1236 (1966). *See* Casebook, pp. 121–24.

After a rulemaking proceeding, the Board adopted a revised version of the proposed rules, effective April 30, 2012. 76 Fed. Reg.80,138 (Dec. 21, 2011). The final rules adopted some of the originally proposed amendments and deferred the remainder for further consideration. The provision eliminating the right to file pre-election requests for review was adopted; the expanded voter list mandate was among the deferred provisions.

On April 24, 2012, a resolution disapproving the rule under the Congressional Review Act failed to pass in the U.S. Senate on a straight party-line vote: 45 for, 54 against. Meanwhile, the Chamber of Commerce challenged the rule in federal court. On May 14, 2012, the U.S. District Court for the District of Columbia held the rule to have been impermissibly adopted for want of a statutory quorum: although three members of the Board were in office, Member Hayes declined to participate and that declination was held to deny the necessary quorum. Chamber of Commerce v. NLRB, 879 F. Supp.2d 18 (D.D.C. 2012). The court made plain that the Board as currently constituted, with five members, was free to re-issue the rules whereupon the substantive arguments made by the Chamber might be reached. Pursuant to a joint stipulation, the Board's appeal of that ruling was dismissed on December 9, 2013.

On February 5, 2014, the fully constituted Board announced that it was issuing new proposed rules amending representation election procedures. *See* News Release, The National Labor Relations Board Proposes Amendments to Improve Representation Case Procedures, *available at* http://www.nlrb.gov/news-outreach/news-story/national-labor-relations-board-proposes-amendments-improve-representation. The newly proposed amendments are identical in substance to the *original* proposed rules noticed in June of 2011. *See* Notice of Proposed Rulemaking, 79 FR 7317 (February 6, 2014). The announcement explained the return to the original version as follows:

> ... The proposals are intended to enable the Board to more effectively administer the National Labor Relations Act. Specifically, the NPRM presents a number of changes to the Board's representation case procedures aimed at modernizing processes, enhancing transparency and eliminating unnecessary litigation and delay. Issuance of the proposed rule was approved by Board Chairman Mark Gaston Pearce and Members Kent Y. Hirozawa and Nancy Schiffer. Board Members Philip A. Miscimarra and Harry I. Johnson III dissented.
>
> In announcing the proposals, Pearce said: "The Board is unanimous in its support for effective representation case procedures. I am pleased that all Members share a commitment to constructive dialogue, and we all agree that important issues are involved in this proposed rulemaking. With a Senate-confirmed five-member Board, I feel it is important for the Board to fully consider public comment on

these proposed amendments, along with the comments we previously received in 2011. These amendments would modernize the representation case process and fulfill the promise of the National Labor Relations Act."

"I believe that the NPRM first proposed in June of 2011 continues to best frame the issues and raises the appropriate concerns for public comment," Pearce said. He stressed that the Board is reviewing the proposed changes with an open mind: "No final decisions have been made. We will review all of the comments filed in response to the original proposals, so the public will not have to duplicate its prior efforts in order to have those earlier comments considered. Re-issuing the 2011 proposals is the most efficient and effective rulemaking process at this time."

"Unnecessary delay and inefficiencies hurt both employees and employers. These proposals are intended to improve the process for all parties, in all cases, whether non-union employees are seeking a union to represent them or unionized employees are seeking to decertify a union," Pearce said. "We look forward to further exchanges of ideas to improve the processes in a way that will benefit workers, employers and all of the American people." . . .

In April 2014, the Board heard public comments on the proposed changes. At this supplement goes to press, the Board has not issued final rules.

PROBLEMS FOR DISCUSSION

1. The voting list requirements were in the original proposed rule, were eliminated from the final rule published in December 2011, and are now included in the present proposals. Why—that is, what is all the fuss about? Should they have been re-introduced?

2. Currently, the median number of days from petition to election has been 38. The new rules would reduce this. Would a median time of 15 or 20 days—a probable consequence if the new proposed rules become final—be untoward? Why?

C. A CONCLUDING REFLECTION ON THE CONTEMPORARY SITUATION OF THE NLRB

Page 77.   Add to the end of "C. A CONCLUDING REFLECTION ON THE CONTEMPORARY SITUATION OF THE NLRB":

PROBLEM FOR DISCUSSION

Return to the "recess appointment" decisions discussed at p. 129, *supra.* A proposal under discussion is to abolish the NLRB, giving adjudicative authority for unfair labor practices to the federal courts and the authority over representation cases to the Department of Labor. You are a legislative assistant to a Member of Congress. What would you advise? In making your recommendation how would you have employees represented in unfair labor practice complaints?

PART TWO

THE ESTABLISHMENT OF THE COLLECTIVE BARGAINING RELATIONSHIP

I. PROTECTION OF THE RIGHT OF SELF-ORGANIZATION

A. INTERFERENCE, RESTRAINT AND COERCION

1. RESTRICTIONS ON SOLICITATION AND DISTRIBUTION

Page 86.   Add to Problems for Discussion to Question 4:

Is it enough that supervisors encourage union support in order to "taint" employee free choice, and so to set the election aside if the union wins, or must more be shown? If more, what more? *See* Veritas Health Services, Inc. v. NLRB, 671 F.3d 1267 (D.C. Cir. 2012).

Page 87.   Add to Problems for Discussion:

6.   The Communication Workers Union is bargaining with a telephone company, an affiliate of AT&T, for a bargaining unit that includes a number of service representatives who respond to calls from customers' homes. The union, dissatisfied with the company's "hard line" in bargaining, has decided to mount an appeal for public support. Part of the campaign includes providing service representatives with "prisoner shirts." These shirts are white with black lettering. On the front of the shirt is the word "INMATE #," with a black box underneath it. On the back of the shirt there are some vertical stripes and bars surrounding the following words: "PRISONER OF AT&T." The company has ordered the service representatives not to wear the shirt. Has the company violated § 8 (a)(1)? Southern New England Tel. Co., 356 NLRB No. 118 (2011).

7.   May a coffee house limit its servers to the display of only one pro-union button on their uniforms? NLRB v. Starbucks Corp, 679 F.3d 70 (2d Cir. 2012).

8.   May an employer adopt the following policy?

Certain activities are prohibited at all times on Target premises. Soliciting, distributing literature, selling merchandise or conducting monetary transactions, whether through face-to-face encounters, telephone, company mail or e-mail, are always off limits (even during meal and break periods) if they are:

For personal profit

For commercial purposes

For a charitable organization that isn't part of the Target Community Relations program and isn't designed to enhance the company's goodwill and business.

Target Corp., 359 NLRB No. 103 (2013).

Page 87.   Add before Cintas Corp:

On August 30, 2011, the NLRB adopted a rule requiring the posting of a notice, set out below, in all workplaces within the jurisdiction of the NLRB, whether unionized or not, and by electronic display by those employers who regularly communicate to their employees by that means. The Board explained that as many employees are unaware of their NLRA rights they cannot effectively exercise them. It based that conclusion on the following:

- The comparatively small percentage of private sector employees who are represented by unions and thus have ready access to information about the NLRA;

- The high percentage of immigrants in the labor force who are likely to be unfamiliar with workplace rights in the United States;

- Studies indicating that employees and high school students about to enter the workforce are generally uninformed about labor law; and

- The absence of a requirement that, except in very limited circumstances, employers or anyone else inform employees about their NLRA rights.

76 Fed. Reg. at 54014–18.

The rule was to be enforced by (1) making the failure to post a potential violation of § 8 (a)(1); and, (2) tolling the statute of limitation for unfair labor practice complaints at jobsites where the notice was not posted. The rule set out the notice to be posted:

Employee Rights
Under the National Labor Relations Act

The National Labor Relations Act (NLRA) guarantees the right of employees to organize and bargain collectively with their employers, and to engage in other protected concerted activity or to refrain from engaging in any of the above activity. Employees covered by the NLRA* are protected from certain types of employer and union misconduct. This Notice gives you general information about your rights, and about the obligations of employers and unions under the NLRA. Contact the National Labor Relations Board (NLRB), the Federal agency that investigates and resolves complaints under the NLRA, using the contact information supplied below, if you have any questions about specific rights that may apply in your particular workplace.

Under the NLRA, you have the right to:

- Organize a union to negotiate with your employer concerning your wages, hours, and other terms and conditions of employment.
- Form, join or assist a union.
- Bargain collectively through representatives of employees' own choosing for a contract with your employer setting your wages, benefits, hours, and other working conditions.
- Discuss your wages and benefits and other terms and conditions of employment or union organizing with your co-workers or a union.
- Take action with one or more co-workers to improve your working conditions by, among other means, raising work-related complaints directly with your employer or with a government agency, and seeking help from a union.
- Strike and picket, depending on the purpose or means of the strike or the picketing.
- Choose not to do any of these activities, including joining or remaining a member of a union.

Under the NLRA, it is illegal for your employer to:

- Prohibit you from talking about or soliciting for a union during non-work time, such as before or after work or during break times; or from distributing union literature during non-work time, in non-work areas, such as parking lots or break rooms.
- Question you about your union support or activities in a manner that discourages you from engaging in that activity.
- Fire, demote, or transfer you, or reduce your hours or change your shift, or otherwise take adverse action against you, or threaten to take any of these actions, because you join or support a union, or because you engage in concerted activity for mutual aid and protection, or because you choose not to engage in any such activity.
- Threaten to close your workplace if workers choose a union to represent them.
- Promise or grant promotions, pay raises, or other benefits to discourage or encourage union support.
- Prohibit you from wearing union hats, buttons, t-shirts, and pins in the workplace except under special circumstances.
- Spy on or videotape peaceful union activities and gatherings or pretend to do so.

Under the NLRA, it is illegal for a union or for the union that represents you in bargaining with your employer to:

- Threaten or coerce you in order to gain your support for the union.
- Refuse to process a grievance because you have criticized union officials or because you are not a member of the union.
- Use or maintain discriminatory standards or procedures in making job referrals from a hiring hall.
- Cause or attempt to cause an employer to discriminate against you because of your union-related activity.
- Take adverse action against you because you have not joined or do not support the union.

If you and your co-workers select a union to act as your collective bargaining representative, your employer and the union are required to bargain in good faith in a genuine effort to reach a written, binding agreement setting your terms and conditions of employment. The union is required to fairly represent you in bargaining and enforcing the agreement.

Illegal conduct will not be permitted. If you believe your rights or the rights of others have been violated, you should contact the NLRB promptly to protect your rights, generally within six months of the unlawful activity. You may inquire about possible violations without your employer or anyone else being informed of the inquiry. Charges may be filed by any person and need not be filed by the employee directly affected by the violation. The NLRB may order an employer to rehire a worker fired in violation of the law and to pay lost wages and benefits, and may order an employer or union to cease violating the law. Employees should seek assistance from the nearest regional NLRB office, which can be found on the Agency's Web site: **http://www.nlrb.gov.**

You can also contact the NLRB by calling toll-free: **1-866-667-NLRB (6572)** or **(TTY) 1-866-315-NLRB (1-866-315-6572)** for hearing impaired.

If you do not speak or understand English well, you may obtain a translation of this notice from the NLRB's Web site or by calling the toll-free numbers listed above.

*The National Labor Relations Act covers most private-sector employers. Excluded from coverage under the NLRA are public-sector employees, agricultural and domestic workers, independent contractors, workers employed by a parent or spouse, employees of air and rail carriers covered by the Railway Labor Act, and supervisors (although supervisors that have been discriminated against for refusing to violate the NLRA may be covered).

This is an official Government Notice and must not be defaced by anyone.

SEPTEMBER 2011

http://nlrb.gov/sites/default/files/documents/1562/employeerightsposter-8-5x11.pdf.

    The rule was denied enforcement by a federal district court in South Carolina. The Fourth Circuit affirmed. It held as a matter of statutory construction and of administrative law that the Labor Act did not authorize the Board to require the posting of the notice. Chamber of Commerce v. NLRB, 721 F.3d.152, (4th Cir. 2013). The United States Court of Appeals for the District of Columbia Circuit took a broader view.

National Association of Manufacturers v. National Labor Relations Board

717 F.3d 947, 2013 WL 1876234 (D.C. Cir. May 7, 2013).

■ RANDOLPH, SENIOR CIRCUIT JUDGE:

* * *

[The Court put aside the question of Member Becker's status as a recess appointee and opined that it would not address § 6, the Board rulemaking authority, but rather § 8(c) which states:

The expressing of any views, argument, or opinion, or the dissemination thereof, whether in written, printed, graphic, or visual form, shall not constitute or be evidence of an unfair labor practice under any of the provisions of this [Act], if such expression contains no threat of reprisal or force or promise of benefit.]

Although § 8(c) precludes the Board from finding noncoercive employer speech to be an unfair labor practice, or evidence of an unfair labor practice, the Board's rule does both. Under the rule an employer's failure to post the required notice constitutes an unfair labor practice. *See* 20 C.F.R. §§ 104.210, 104.212. And the Board may consider an employer's "knowing and willful" noncompliance to be "evidence of antiunion animus in cases in which unlawful motive [is] an element of an unfair labor practice. 76 Fed. Reg. at 54,035–36; *see also* 20 C.F.R. § 104.21(b). The Board, in other words, will use an employer's failure to post the notice as evidence of another unfair labor practice.

In the preamble to its rule, and in its argument to this court, the Board responds that it has not violated § 8(c) because the poster is the Board's speech, not the speech of any employer. After all, the Board says, the words on the poster are the Board's, and the last line of the poster warns: "This is an official Government Notice and must not be defaced by anyone." 29 C.F.R. pt. 104, subpt. A, app.

It is obviously correct that the poster contains the Board's speech. It is also without question that the Board is free to post the same message on its website, as it has done under the heading "Rights We Protect." *See* NLRB, http://www.nlrb.gov/rights-we-protect (last visited Apr. 25, 2013). We also assume that the Board may deliver its message directly to employees working for businesses over which the Board has jurisdiction. But we doubt whether calling the poster "Board speech" answers the question whether the rule violates § 8(c).

Our doubt stems, in part, from a comparison of § 8(c) with the law established under the First Amendment. We approach the question by considering some firmly established principles of First Amendment free-speech law. The first is that the "dissemination" of messages others have created is entitled to the same level of protection as the "creation" of messages. . . .

That § 8(c) embraces this principle is certain. The language of § 8(c) explicitly covers more than just the "expressing" of the speaker's views. It covers as well the "dissemination" of "any views, argument, or opinion," as long as the "written, printed, graphic, or visual" material disseminated is not coercive. 29 U.S.C. § 158(c).

Of course we are not faced with a regulation *forbidding* employers from disseminating information someone else has created. Instead, the Board's rule requires employers to disseminate such information, upon pain of being held to have committed an unfair labor practice. But that difference hardly ends the matter. The right to disseminate another's speech necessarily includes the right to decide not to disseminate it. First Amendment law acknowledges this apparent truth: "*all* speech inherently involves choices of what to say and what to leave unsaid." *Pac. Gas & Electric Co. v. Pub. Utils. Comm'n*, 475 U.S. 1, 11 (1986) (plurality opinion).

Chief Justice Roberts, writing for a unanimous Court, put it this way in *Rumsfeld v. Forum for Academic & Institutional Rights, Inc.*: "Some of [the] Court's leading First Amendment precedents have established the principle that freedom of speech prohibits the government from telling people what they must say." 547 U.S. 47, 61 (2006). As examples, the Chief Justice cited *West Virginia State Board of Education v. Barnette*, 319 U.S. 624 (1943), and *Wooley v. Maynard*, 430 U.S. 705 (1977).

In *Barnette* the Court held that "[t]o sustain the compulsory flag salute" and pledge of allegiance in public schools would be to conclude "that a bill of Rights which guards the individual's right to speak his own mind, left it open to public authorities to compel him to utter what is not in his mind." 319 U.S. at 634.

Wooley held much the same: the First Amendment freedom of speech "includes both the right to speak freely and the right to refrain from speaking at all." 430 U.S. at 714. New Hampshire therefore could not coerce its citizens to display the State motto "Live Free or Die" on their automobile license plates, although presumably citizens could display it voluntarily. As the Supreme Court put it in *United States v. United Foods, Inc.*: "Just as the First Amendment may prevent government from prohibiting speech, the Amendment may prevent the government from compelling individuals to express certain views. . . ." 533 U.S., 405, 410 (2001); *see also Johanns v. Livestock Mktg. Ass'n*, 544 U.S. 550, 568 (2005) (Thomas J. concurring); *R.J. Reynolds Tobacco Co. v. Food & Drug Admin.*, 696 F.3d 1205, 1211 (D.C. Cir. 2012).

We do not think these, and other such cases, may be distinguished from this one on the Board's terms. In *Barnette* and in *Wooley*, as in this case, the government selected the message and ordered its citizens to convey that message. The Supreme Court's opinions do not suggest that because the messages were, to that extent, "government speech," the First Amendment did not apply. And we do not think it matters that the Board has regulatory authority over the six million employers subject to its rule. In *Barnette* and *Wooley*, the state and local governments had regulatory authority over those (public school children and automobile drivers) it ordered to spread the message it selected. *See also United Foods*, 533 U.S. at 410; *R.J. Reynolds*, 696 F.3d at 1211.

The Board—in its Brief, but not in the rulemaking—argues that this case is significantly different in light of the content of the poster. The poster, the Board's acting general counsel tells us, merely recites the employee rights set forth in the National Labor Relations Act (and in court and Board interpretations of the Act). And so, the argument goes, this case is unlike *Barnette* or *Wooley* because the Board's message is "non-ideological." NLRB Br. 66. Even if we accepted the premise, the conclusion would not follow.

The right against compelled speech is not, and cannot be, restricted to ideological messages. Take for instance *Riley v. National Federation of the Blind of North Carolina, Inc.*, 487 U.S. 781 (1988). After recognizing that the First Amendment protects "the decision of both what to say and what *not* to say," the Court cited *Barnette* and *Wooley* in holding that these and other cases "cannot be distinguished simply because they involved compelled statements of opinion while here we deal with compelled statements of 'fact.'" *Riley*, 487 U.S. at 797.[13] Yet that distinction, rejected in *Riley*, is precisely the distinction the Board's acting general counsel urges us to adopt.

Plaintiffs here, like those in other compelled-speech cases, object to the message the government has ordered them to publish on their premises. They see the poster as one-sided, as favoring unionization, because it "fails to notify employees, *inter alia*, of their rights to decertify a union, to refuse to pay dues to a union in a right-to-work state, and to object to payment of dues in excess of the amounts required for representational purposes." Nat'l Ass'n of Mfrs. Br. 38; *see also* 76 Fed. Reg. at 54,022 (discussing comments). The Board responds that it was entitled to make "editorial judgments" about what to put in and what to leave out, NLRB Br. 68, and that "if an employer is concerned that employees will get the wrong impression, it may legally express its opinion regarding unionization as long as it does so in a noncoercive manner," 76 Fed. Reg. at 54,022.[15] Yet even in cases in which the message was other than one the government had devised, a "compelled-speech violation" occurred when "the complaining speaker's own message was affected by the speech it was forced to accommodate." *Forum for Academic & Institutional Rights*, 547 U.S. at 63.

This brings us to what the Board considers its strongest precedent—*UAW-Labor Employment & Training Corp. v. Chao*, 325 F.3d 360 (D.C. Cir. 2003). President Bush had issued an Executive Order requiring government contractors to post notices at their workplaces informing employees of their rights not to be forced to join a union or to pay union dues for non-representational activities. Three unions and the UAW brought suit (the UAW was a government

---

[13] In addition to Barnette and Wooley, the Court cited *Pacific Gas*, 475 U.S. 1 (plurality opinion), and *Miami Herald Publishing Co. v. Tornillo*, 418 U.S. 241 (1974). The Supreme Court has thus far recognized that its "compelled-speech cases" apply to situations "in which an individual must personally speak the government's message," as well as those in which one must "host or accommodate another speaker's message." Forum for Academic & Institutional Rights, 547 U.S. at 63; see also *Hurley v. Irish-Am. Gay, Lesbian & Bisexual Grp. Of Boston*, 515 U.S. 557, 573–74 (1995).

[15] Although the poster identifies the Board as its author, it does not state that the employer had no choice but to display it. We suppose an employer could post a statement next to the poster pointing out its compulsory nature. Cf. *Prune Yard Shopping Ctr. v. Robins*, 447 U.S. 74, 87 (1980).

contractor). They argued that the National Labor Relations Act preempted the Executive Order. *UAW*, 325 F.3d at 362. This was their only argument. They did not raise any "free-standing First Amendment claim." *Id.* at 364. We therefore did not reach the question whether the posting requirement violated the contractors' freedom of speech. As to § 8(c), the unions could not plausibly claim that the Executive Order violated this provision. The National Labor Relations Board was not in the picture. That is, there was no prospect of a contractor's being charged with an unfair labor practice for failing to post the required notice. As we put it, "the activities described in § 8(c) do not 'constitute an unfair labor practice,' except by negation, and are not 'protected by' the NLRA, except from the [Board] itself." *Id.* at 365 (emphasis omitted).

We acknowledged in *UAW* that "the right to speak" includes "the right not to speak." *Id.* And we assumed, in light of the Supreme Court's First Amendment decisions so holding "that the § 8(c) right includes the right not to speak." *Id.* But the § 8(c) right was only against the Board's finding an unfair labor practice, or evidence thereof. Beyond that, "an employer's right to silence is sharply constrained in the labor context, and leaves it subject to a variety of burdens to post notices of rights and risks." *Id.*

* * *

We return then to the question with which we began. Suppose that § 8(c) prevents the Board from charging an employer with an unfair labor practice for posting a notice advising employees of their right not to join a union. Of course § 8(c) clearly does this. How then can it be an unfair labor practice for an employer to refuse to post a government notice informing employees of their right to unionize (or to refuse to)? Like the freedom of speech guaranteed in the First Amendment, § 8(c) necessarily protects—as against the Board, *see UAW*, 325 F.3d at 365— the right of employers (and unions) not to speak. This is why, for example, a company official giving a noncoercive speech to employees describing the disadvantages of unionization does not commit an unfair labor practice if, in his speech, the official neglects to mention the advantages of having a union.

We therefore conclude that the Board's rule violates § 8(c) because it makes an employer's failure to post the Board's notice an unfair labor practice, and because it treats such a failure as evidence of anti-union animus in cases involving, for example, unlawfully motivated firings or refusals to hire—in other words, because it treats such a failure as evidence of an unfair labor practice.[19] *See Brown & Root, Inc. v. NLRB*, 333 F.3d 628, 637–39 & n.7 (5th Cir. 2003).

III

[The Court proceeded next to hold that the Board lacked the power to toll the Act's statute of limitations for unfair labor practices where an employer had not complied with the posting rule.]

---

[19] Our conclusion here does not affect the Board's rule requiring employers to post an election notice (which similarly contains information about employee rights) before a representation election, 29 C.F.R. § 103.20. Because the failure to post the required election notice does not constitute an unfair labor practice but may be a basis for setting aside the election, *see id.* § 103.20(d), the rule does not implicate § 8(c).

IV

Because all three of the means for enforcing the Board's posting requirement are invalid, we do not decide whether, as plaintiffs also contend, the Board lacked the regulatory authority to issue subpart A of its rule—the requirements that employers post the notice specified in the appendix to that subpart.   Subpart A clearly is not severable. . . .Here we know that the Board would not have issued a posting rule that depended solely on voluntary compliance. We know this because the Board rejected that regulatory option in the preamble to its final rule. *See* 76 Fed. Reg. at 54,031. Subpart A must therefore fall along with the rest of the Board's posting rule.

* * *

KAREN LeCRAFT HENDERSON, with whom *Circuit Judge* BROWN joins, concurring:

I fully agree with Judge Randolph's analysis of NLRA section 8(c) and wholeheartedly concur in his well-reasoned opinion. *See* 29 U.S.C. § 158(c). Judge Brown and I would also hold, however, that the Board is without authority to promulgate the posting rule under NLRA section 6 as well—the issue Judge Randolph does not reach in light of his reliance on section 8(c).   Section 6 provides: "the Board shall have authority from time to time to make, amend, and rescind, in the manner prescribed by subchapter II of chapter 5 of Title 5, such rules and regulations as may be necessary to carry out the provisions of this subchapter." 29 U.S.C. § 156. Such "general rulemaking authority," although facially broad, "does not mean that the specific rule the agency promulgates is a valid exercise of that authority." *Colo. River Indian Tribes v. Nat'l Indian Gaming Comm'n*, 466 F.3d 134, 139 (D.C. Cir. 2006). Here, I do not believe the posting rule—which creates a new species of unfair labor practice unforeshadowed in the NLRA's text— constitutes a valid exercise of the Board's section 6 authority because the rule is not, as section 6 requires, "necessary" to carry out the express provisions of the Act.

In the Final Rule, the Board claims the posting rule is necessary to carry out sections 1 and 7 of the NLRA, 29 U.S.C. §§ 151, 157. *See* 76 Fed. Reg. at 54,007 (§ 1); *id.* at 54,032 (§ 7). Section 1 consists of four paragraphs of general findings the Congress made to justify regulating the collective bargaining process in order to eliminate and mitigate "substantial obstructions to the free flow of commerce," 29 U.S.C. § 151. Section 7 sets out the general rights "as to organization, collective bargaining, etc. . . .[that e]mployees shall have," *id.* § 157.   Neither section contains any particularized "provision" that the Board can "carry out" by regulation or otherwise. In the past, we have rejected such a "general declaration of policy," by itself, as authority for a specific regulation, observing that " '[a]ll questions of government are ultimately questions of ends and means.' " *Colo. River Indian Tribes*, 466 F.3d at 139 (quoting *Fed'n of Fed. Emps. v. Greenberg*, 983 F.2d 286, 290 (D.C. Cir. 1993)). An agency, as we have stated, is " 'bound, not only by the ultimate purposes Congress has selected, but by the means it has deemed appropriate, and prescribed, for the pursuit of those purposes.' " *Id.* at 139–40 (quoting *MCI Telecomms. Corp. v. Am. Tel. & Tel. Co.*, 512 U.S. 218, 231 n.4 (1994)). And the Congress, in enacting the NLRA, prescribed that the Board use *reactive* means to enforce its policies—namely, through an unfair labor practice proceeding *initiated by a charging party* or by resolving representation and election issues *when so petitioned by a party. See* 29 U.S.C. § 160 (empowering Board "as *hereinafter provided*, to prevent any person from engaging in any unfair labor practice" and thereinafter providing "*[w]henever it is charged* that any person has engaged in or is engaging in any such [ULP], the Board. . .shall have power to issue and cause to be served upon such person a complaint stating the charges"), § 159 (authorizing Board to "investigate" a petition by employees or employer regarding representation and elections "*[w]henever a petition shall have been filed*, in accordance with such regulations as may be prescribed by the Board"), § 161 (setting out Board's "Investigatory powers. . .[f]or the purpose of all hearings and investigations, which, in the opinion of the Board, *are necessary and proper for the exercise of the powers vested in it by sections 159 and 160*) (emphases added). . . .

The Final Rule also claims that, as a practical matter, the posting rule is "necessary" to ensure that employees know both what their rights are under the Act and that the Board protects those rights— thereby enabling employees to exercise them under the substantive provisions of the Act. It further asserts that the Board "has reason to think that most [employees] do not" have such knowledge given "the low percentage of employees who are represented by unions, . . . ; the increasing proportion of immigrants in the work force, who are unlikely to be familiar with their workplace rights; and lack of information about labor law and labor relations on the part of high school students who are about to enter the labor force"—citing as authority three law review articles. Final Rule, 76 Fed. Reg. at 54,006 & nn.3–4; *see also* Appellees/Cross-Appellants Br. 15–16. Even assuming these speculative assertions have some factual basis and, as well, that providing such information is "necessary to carry out" the Act's provisions, there is nothing in the text of the NLRA to suggest the burden of filling the "knowledge gap" should fall on the employer's shoulders. Unions and the NLRB are at least as qualified to disseminate appropriate information—easily and cheaply in this information technology age—and in fact already do so. *See, e.g.*, http://www.nlrb.gov/rights-we-protect (NLRB's explanation of covered employee rights, its protection of concerted activity, employer and employee reciprocal rights and obligations and its jurisdiction over private employers). The NLRA—and section 6 in particular—simply does not authorize the Board to impose on an employer a freestanding obligation to educate its employees on the fine points of labor relations law. *See Chamber of Commerce of U.S. v. NLRB*, 856 F. Supp. 2d 778, 792 n.13 (D.S.C. 2012) ("Here, the Board's interpretation of Section 6 as authorizing the rule does not incorporate any labor-related expertise. *See Hi-Craft Clothing Co.* [*v. NLRB*], 660 F.2d [910,] 918 [(3d Cir. 1981)] ('This is not a question of the Board applying a broad statutory term to a specified set of facts, but is a case of straightforward statutory construction.')").

In sum, given the Act's language and structure are manifestly remedial, I do not believe the Congress intended to authorize a regulation so aggressively prophylactic as the posting rule. . . .

PROBLEMS FOR DISCUSSION

1.   What is the holding in this case? If it is that § 8(c) forbids non-posting to be evidence of an unfair labor practice, then why all the discussion of compelled speech under the First Amendment? If it is that the First Amendment forbids posting, then why all the discussion of § 8(c)?

2.   Is the court's First Amendment analysis correct? If it is, are all the many statutes, state and federal, that require employers to post notices informing their employees of statutory rights unconstitutional? Is the Board's requiring the posting of a remedial notice, an example of which is set out on page 126 of this Supplement, *ultra vires* its remedial power?

3.   In adopting the rule the Board stated it had rejected "relying *solely* on voluntary compliance." 54 Fed. Reg. 54, 031 (italics added). Does it follow that the rule could not be severed from the means the Board adapted to secure compliance in addition to voluntary adherence?

4.   Is the concurrence's depiction of the Labor Board as, essentially, a labor court—a supine body that must await cases to be brought to it before it has any power to act—correct? What differentiates an administrative agency from a court?

Page 92.   Add to Problems for Discussion:

3.   May a company maintain a rule subjecting employees to discharge for violation of any of the following rules:

> a.   "inability or unwillingness to work harmoniously with other employees"?

> 2 Sisters Food Group, Inc., 357 NLRB No. 168 (2011).

> b.   "indulging in harmful gossip" or "exhibiting a negative attitude toward or losing interest in your work assignment"?

> Hyundai America Shipping Agency, Inc., 357 NLRB No. 80 (2011); Copper River of Boiling Springs, 360 NLRB No. 60 (2014) ("lack of respect" and "negative attitude"); Hills and Dales Gen. Hospital, 360 NLRB No. 70 (2014) ("negativity or gossip"); First Transit, Inc., 360 NLRB No. 70 (2014) (variety of conduct rules).

> c.   Any communication transmitted, stored or displayed electronically must comply with the policies outlined in the Costco Employee Agreement. Employees should be aware that statements posted electronically (such as [to] online message boards or discussion groups) that damage the Company, defame any individual or damage any person's reputation, or violate the policies outlined in the Costco Employee Agreement, may be subject to discipline, up to and including termination of employment.

> Costco Wholesale Corp., 358 NLRB No. 106 (2012); Weyerhauser Co., 359 NLRB No. 138 (2013); MCPc, Inc., 360 NLRB No. 39 (2014).

> d.   The Emmett Worth Company has a compelling interest in protecting the integrity of its investigations. In every investigation, Emmett Worth has a strong desire to protect

witnesses from harassment, intimidation and retaliation, to keep evidence from being destroyed, to ensure that testimony is not fabricated, and to prevent a cover-up. To assist Emmett Worth in achieving these objectives, we must maintain the investigation and our role in it in strict confidence. If we do not maintain such confidentiality, we may be subject to disciplinary action up to and including immediate termination.

Banner Health Sys., 358 NLRB No. 93 (2012).

e. for a brokerage and financial services company to require employees to sign the following:

I agree as follows: . . . that I will not solicit or encourage Schwab's employees or Schwab's clients to leave Schwab. . . .

The scope of these obligations, and some of the possible consequences for breaching them, are described in more detail below. . . .

Agreement Not to Solicit. While I work for Schwab and for 18 months after my employment ends, I will not directly or indirectly solicit or induce . . . any Schwab employee or contingent worker to leave his or her employment or engagement with Schwab.

General Counsel Advice Memorandum in the Matter of Charles Schwab Corp., 28–CA–084931 (Sept. 14, 2012).

———

Page 102. Replace the Note following Lechmere:

In Ralphs Grocery v. United Food and Commercial Workers Union Local 8, 290 P.3d 1116 (Cal. 2012), the California Supreme Court held that "the areas outside the individual stores' customer entrances and exits, at least as typically configured and furnished, are not public forums" under California's constitutional free speech clause. However, California's "little Norris-LaGuardia Act"—the Moscone Act of 1975—and another California statute limit the power of the courts to enjoin picketing during a labor dispute by requiring proof of irreparable injury and the lack of another adequate remedy. The California Supreme Court sustained those laws as against First Amendment challenge, that they impermissibly singled out labor speech for protection. One judge dissented on the latter ground.

Page 102. Add to Problems for Discussion, at the End of Question 3(a):

Roundy's Inc. v. NLRB, 674 F.3d 638 (7th Cir. 2012) (store's non-exclusive easement gave the easement holder the power to deny "unreasonable" interference in its use under state law; product boycott, including the display of a rat to protest use of non-union contractors, did not create an unreasonable interference).

Page 103. Add to Problems for Discussion:

5. Mad Dog Casino has contracted with Yo-Yo's, Inc., to run the restaurant located inside the casino. A few of Yo-Yo's off duty employees have gathered at the walkway in front of Yo-Yo's—between the restaurant

and the gaming area—to distribute pro-union handbills to casino patrons and Yo-Yo's customers. Mad Dog's security force has told them they must leave the premises. Has Mad Dog committed an unfair labor practice? New York-New York, LLC v. NLRB, 676 F.3d 193 (D.C. Cir. 2012).

6.   May an employer forbid employees to remain on the property after the end of their work hours? The Continental Group, Inc., 357 NLRB No. 39 (2011).   May it allow them to remain only when "authorized by" a supervisor? American Baptist Homes, 360 NLRB No. 100 (2014).

7.   In the face of planned mass protests at Wal-Mart stores nation-wide on the day after Thanksgiving ("Black Friday") by a coalition of community and activist groups, including unions, the company sent a letter to as many of these as could be identified. The letters stated that non-employees were not permitted on "Walmart owned or controlled" property for the purpose of engaging in, among other things, mass demonstrations, flash mobs, customer disruption, and picketing. The letters also directed the recipients to call the Wal-Mart attorney if they had any questions. Has the company violated § 8(a)(1) by sending these letters? Wal-Mart Stores, Case 12–CA–101200 (Advice Memorandum) (March 6, 2014).

Page 104.   Add to Problem 2:

In Independent Elect. Contractors v. NLRB, 720 F.3d 543 (5th Cir. 2013), a companion case to *Kenmore* involving the same parties, the court refused to enforce the Board's order under § 8(a)(1) on the ground that the Board had adopted a novel theory of which the charged party had no notice and to whom due process was denied. One judge dissented.

Page 119.   Add following the excerpt after The Register-Guard:

[The Board accepted the court's decision as the law of the case and ordered the rescission of the discipline imposed on Ms. Prozanski. The Register-Guard, 357 NLRB No. 27 (2011).]

In Purple Communications, Inc., 21–CA–095151 et. al., the Administrative Law Judge dismissed the complaint asserting that a prohibition on the personal use of the company's electronic communications system was violative of § 8(a)(1). The General Counsel excepted to the decision and asked the Board to overrule *Register Guard*. On April 30, 2014, the Board published an invitation for amicus briefs asking the following questions to be addressed:

1.   Should the Board reconsider its conclusion in *Register Guard* that employees do not have a statutory right to use their employer's email system (or other electronic communications systems) for Section 7 purposes?

2.   If the Board overrules *Register Guard*, what standard(s) of employee access to the employer's electronic communications systems should be established? What restrictions, if any, may an employer place on such access, and what factors are relevant to such restrictions?

3.   In deciding the above questions, to what extent and how should the impact on the employer of employees' use of an employer's electronic communications technology affect the issue?

4.   Do employee personal electronic devices (e.g., phones, tablets), social media accounts, and/or personal email accounts affect the proper balance to be struck between employers' rights and employees' Section 7 rights to communicate about work-related matters? If so, how?

5.   Identify any other technological issues concerning email or other electronic communications systems that the Board should consider in answering the foregoing questions, including any relevant changes that may have occurred in electronic communications technology since *Register Guard* was decided. How should these affect the Board's decision?

2.   ELECTION PROPAGANDA

(c)   Inflammatory Appeals

Page 150.   Add following Problem 2:

Volkswagen, which has a plant in Chattanooga, Tennessee, signed a neutrality agreement with the United Auto Workers (UAW). This was the product of extensive negotiations tied to VW's desire to have a German-style works council in its U.S. operations, as it does elsewhere in the world. A works council is an elected employee body with extensive rights of consultation and co-determination with management. It would be a "labor organization" within the meaning of § 2(5) of the Labor Act and so could not be established unilaterally under § 8(a)(2). The UAW and VW fashioned a framework agreement toward the establishment of a works council created by collective agreement were the UAW to become the employees' collective bargaining representative. In the neutrality agreement VW agreed not to oppose the UAW, to allow it access to the employees in non-work areas and on non-work time, and to arbitrate any dispute over the agreement's application. The UAW agreed, among other things, to make no home visits to employees and to forego striking, picketing, or boycotts in bargaining the collective agreement. The parties also agreed to a Board-run election. The election was held on February 13–14, 2014 and the UAW lost: 712–626.

Before the vote, elected officials from Tennessee issued several statements opposing unionization. These were given extensive coverage in the local media. These included statements that a union victory would result in the state's refusal to extend any additional incentives for VW to expand in Tennessee. Senator (and former Chattanooga mayor) Bob Corker stated that VW had assured him that its plans for expansion were continent on a union loss. The UAW filed objections to the election, Volkswagen Groups of America, Inc., 10–RM–121704, (Feb. 21, 2014), setting out the extensive record of statements and media coverage; but the union then withdrew the objections on the ground that, if successful, the remedy would be a re-run election in which the same campaign could be conducted.

Did this public campaign by elected officials so upset the "laboratory conditions" as to warrant the setting aside of the results? Were you counsel to the union would you have advised your client to object? To withdraw the objections?

B. COMPANY DOMINATION OR ASSISTANCE

Page 184.   Add the following before the Problems for Discussion:

The *Dana* decision was sustained by the Sixth Circuit. Montague v. NLRB, 698 F.3d 307 (6th Cir. 2012). The court treated the crux thusly:

> At the heart of the dispute between the parties is the extent to which the terms in Article 4 are "substantive" because they are "binding." On their face, the terms in Article 4.2.4 are not specific, and that would require further negotiations to reach any level of detail. However, Article 4.2.5. requires arbitration if both parties do not reach the first formal agreement within six months, and that agreement—according to the LOA—must include the provisions discussed in Article 4.2.4. In this way, terms regarding "mandatory overtime" or "compensation," for instance, could become binding. As the entity entrusted with maintaining "industrial peace," however, the Board was within its discretion to allow some substantive terms to be determined between the employer and union prior to recognition, as long as that agreement did not ultimately impact employees' choice regarding union representation. With the LOA in this case, employees may decide if they agree with the general principles that the agreement sets forth as well as if they are willing to risk being bound to any concessions that the union may make during negotiations of the first formal contract. If the employees are not willing to take that risk, then they do not have to select the union as their exclusive bargaining representative. In this instance, the employees at Dana did not select the UAW.

Id. at 316.

Page 184.   Add following the Problems for Discussion:

The facts and issues presented in Mulhall v. Unite Here Local 355, 667 F.3d 1211 (11th Cir. 2012) *cert. granted* (June 24, 2013), *writ dismissed as improvidently granted*, 134 S. Ct. 594 (Dec. 10, 2013), were set out by Justice Breyer, joined by Justices Sotomayor and Kagan, dissenting from the dismissal of the writ:

Section 302(a) of the Labor Management Relations Act, 1947, 61 Stat. 157, as amended, an antibribery provision, makes it a crime for an employer "to pay, lend, or deliver, or agree to pay, lend, or deliver, any money or other thing of value" to a labor union that represents or seeks to represent its employees. 29 U.S.C. § 186(a)(2). Section 302(b) makes it a crime "for any person to request [or] demand . . . , or agree to receive or accept, any payment, loan, or delivery of any money or other thing of value prohibited by subsection (a). § 186 (b)(1). The question in this case is whether an employer violates § 302(a) by making the following promises to a union that seeks to represent its employees: (1) that the employer will remain neutral in respect to the union's efforts to organize its employees, (2) that the union will be given access (for organizing purposes) to nonpublic areas of the employer's premises, and (3) that the union will receive a list of employees' names and contact information (also for organizing purposes). A further question (the other side of the same coin) is whether a union violates § 302(b) by requesting that the employer perform its contractual obligations to fulfill these promises.

The Eleventh Circuit held that these items are "thing[s] of value" and that an employer's promise to "pay" them in return for something of value from the union violates the Act if the employer intends to use the payment to "corrupt" the union; the Eleventh Circuit also held that a union's request that an employer make such a payment violates § 302(b) if the union intends to "extort" the benefit from the employer. 667 F.3d 1211, 1215–1216 (2012). Other Circuits have held to the contrary, reasoning that similar promises by an employer to assist a union's organizing campaign (or merely to avoid opposing the campaign) fall outside the scope of § 302. See Adcock v. Freightliner LLC, 550 F.3d 369 (C.A.4 2008); Hotel Employees & Restaurant Employees Union, Local 57 v. Sage Hospitality Resources, LLC, 390 F.3d 206 (C.A.3 2004). We granted certiorari to resolve the conflict.

The dissenting Justices noted that the writ was dismissed because of the possibility of mootness and the possible lack of standing, neither of which had been briefed. The dissenters would have asked for briefs on these two issues and on a third as well; whether § 302 authorizes a private cause of action for injunctive relief.

PROBLEMS FOR DISCUSSION

1. Return to the discussion of the contretemps in Chattanooga involving efforts by third parties, including elected officials, to urge Volkswagen employees to reject representation by the UAW. Supp. p. 149, *supra*. Three VW employees at Chattanooga, supported by the National Right to Sork Legal Defense Foundation (NRTW), sued VW and UAW for violation of § 302. Burton v. UAW, U.S.D.C. E.D. Tenn. Case No. 1114–EV–76 (March 12, 2014). Does the VW-UAW agreement "pay, lend, or deliver any money or other thing of value" in violation of federal criminal law? The meaning of a "thing of value" was researched and briefed in depth in the *Mulhall* case; the student may wish to read the briefs available on the Supreme Court's web site.

2. The lawsuit was dismissed by the plaintiffs on May 23, 2014, the NRTW explained, as a "strategic decision". What purpose did the suit serve?

3. Does § 302 criminalize a union's threat to strike unless its wage demands are met? Why isn't that extortionate action to secure something of value?

4. How could a neutrality agreement "extort tribute" from an employer or "tamper" with the duty union officers owe to the employees?

5. This agreement, as do most neutrality agreements, contains an arbitration provision to resolve dispute arising under it. In fact, the employer challenged this agreement as violative of § 302 before the arbitrator who considered, analyzed, and rejected the claim. What role should the availability of an arbitration procedure—or the fact of this award—play in deciding whether the agreement violates § 302?

II. SELECTION OF THE REPRESENTATIVE FOR THE PURPOSES OF COLLECTIVE BARGAINING

B. APPROPRIATE BARGAINING UNIT

2. CRITERIA FOR UNIT DETERMINATIONS

Page 248.   Add after American Hospital Ass'n.:

In *Specialty Health Care*, 357 NLRB No.83 (2011), the Board abandoned *Park Manor Medicare Center*, 305 NLRB 872 (1991), under which the Board looked to the background information it developed regarding bargaining units for acute-care facilities in deciding units for non-acute-care facilities. Instead, the Board decided that its general "community of interests" approach to unit determination should apply. It then held that a petitioned-for unit of 53 certified nursing assistants (CNAs) of a nursing home was appropriate in the face of the employer's insistence that only a unit of all 86 of its non-professional service and maintenance employees was appropriate. The Board's taking up of that issue, which included a call for *amicus curiae* briefs, generated a minor political storm in Congress including extensive demands for documentation, from the chairman of the House Committee on Education and the Workforce, and the introduction of legislation to counter the Board's position. The Board's decision was enforced *sub nom.* Kindred Nursing Centers East v. NLRB, 727 F.3d 552 (6th Cir. 2013) (relying on Blue Man Vegas, LLC v. NLRB set out in the main volume at pp. 235–243).

PROBLEMS FOR DISCUSSION

1.   Why would this change in policy occasion such strong political opposition in the House?

2.   Frugal Car Rental operates out of the Greater Siloplex Airport. It employs 109 hourly employees: 31 rental service agents (RSAs), 3 staff assistants, 2 lead staff assistants, 9 return agents, 6 lot agents, 9 service agents, 4 lead service agents, 1 fleet agent, 9 exit booth agents, 2 shuttlers, 21 courtesy bus drivers, 2 lead courtesy bus drivers, 3 mechanics, 4 assistant mechanics, 2 bus mechanics, and 1 building maintenance technician.

An RSAs primary duties are to greet customers, process rental contracts, sell optional services, answer and receive telephone calls, resolve overdue rentals, and respond to customer questions and complaints. Each RSA is responsible for entering information into the Employer's database about the customers, their rental contracts, vehicle upgrades, and additional products sold. A typical RSA completes 378 rental agreements a month. RSAs—and only RSAs—get incentive payments by selling upgrades and additional products. All employees wear uniforms but RSAs are distinctive. The rates of pay, duties, and qualifications for hire of the other employees vary according to the job. Is a petitioned-for unit of only RSAs an appropriate unit? *DTG*

Operations, Inc., 357 NLRB No. 175 (2011). Would a unit of only the mechanics be appropriate?

4. MULTIEMPLOYER AND COORDINATED BARGAINING

Page 263.   Add following the quote to *Sturgis*:

A note on "triangular employment relationships." The development discussed on pages 261–263 on "triangular employment," that is, of the individual who contracts with a supplier of labor who then contracts with a purchaser of labor services, is an unfolding global phenomenon. The economic logic and circumstances in the United States has been developed by David Weil, THE FISSURED WORKPLACE (2014). Many countries are struggling with it. *See generally*, Louisa Corazza & Orsola Razzolini, *The Law's Focus: Who is an Employer? Who is an Employee? in* Elgar Research Handbook in Comparative Labour Law (Matthew Finkin & Guy Mundlak eds.) (in press). On April 30, 2014, the National Labor Relations Board posted an Invitation to File Briefs in Browning-Ferris Indus., 32–RC–109684. The Board seeks address to the following questions:

1. Under the Board's current joint-employer standard, as articulated in *TLI, Inc.*, 271 NLRB 798 *1984), enfd. mem. 772 F.2d 894 (3d Cir. 1985), and *Laerco Transportation*, 269 NLRB 324 (1984), is Leadpoint Business Services the sole employer of the petitioned-for employees?

2. Should the Board adhere to its existing joint-employer standard or adopt a new standard? What considerations should influence the Board's decision in this regard?

3. If the Board adopts a new standard for determining joint-employer status, what should that standard be? If it involves the application of a multifactor test, what factors should be examined? What should be the basis or rationale for such a standard?

PART THREE

NEGOTIATION OF THE COLLECTIVE BARGAINING AGREEMENT

I. EXCLUSIVE REPRESENTATION AND MAJORITY RULE

Page 319.   Add to Problems for Discussion:

4.   The Emmett Worth Company operates a warehouse with 250 employees. Its employee policy manual provides,

> . . . .[I]n certain circumstances, and at management's sole discretion, it may be necessary to impose an action, up to and including termination of employment, without prior notice or counseling and without progressing through each stage of the disciplinary guidelines. Determination of appropriate action will be made on a case-by-case basis based on the nature and severity of the occurrence.

> The Warehouse Workers Union has won a representation election and the parties are in the process of exchanging contract demands. Meanwhile, employee Tania Jones got into an argument with her supervisor. The plant manager, after receipt of the supervisor's demand that Jones be fired, has issued a notice of termination to Jones providing that her short period of service (five years), record of tardiness (two warnings), and what he understood was a threat of physical violence ("You'd better watch your back" is what her supervisor said she said) combined to make termination appropriate. The Union was later given notice of Jones' discharge. Has the Company violated section 8(a)(5)? Alan Ritchey, Inc., 359 NLRB No. 40 (2012).

II. THE DUTY TO BARGAIN IN GOOD FAITH

Page 348.   Add to the Problems for Discussion:

6.   A union representing licensed practical nurses has negotiated a collective agreement with a multi-employer association of nursing homes. The collective agreement deals in detail with shift differentials, staffing levels, floor differentials, health insurance, and the use of non-employee "agency" nurses. It also contains a "most favored nation clause" that provides that should the Union agree to terms with any other nursing home in the metropolitan area that are more favorable to the employer than the instant agreement, the instant agreement will be modified by the incorporation of these terms. A nursing home in the city not an association member has agreed to recognize the Union. The Union has given the Employer a copy of the multi-employer agreement and stated that it was a "basis for negotiation." The Employer has presented the Union with a set of proposals on the above subjects that differ substantially from the multi-employer agreement and are more favorable from the Employer's perspective. The Union has said that it is willing to look at the proposals "as a package," but that it would not agree to terms that would trigger less favorable treatment for the employees in the multi-employer unit. Has the Union bargained in good faith? *Compare* Laurel Bay Health & Rehab. Center v. NLRB, 666 F.3d 1365 (D.C.Cir.2012), *with* Monmouth Care Center v. NLRB, 672 F.3d 1085 (D.C.Cir.2012).

Page 350.   Add to end of the Note on "THE DUTY TO DISCLOSE INFORMATION":

In a time of both recession and intense global competition, in which companies often seek wage and benefits concessions on the stated need to remain competitive, the obligation to disclose financial and other business information has loomed large. From an economic perspective, informational transparency is commonly understood to be an aid to efficient bargaining, just as informational asymmetry can lead to market failure. From a legal perspective, the Supreme Court has grounded good faith in the notion, stated in *Truitt*, that claims made at the bargaining table be honest and therefore testable.

In KLB Industries, Inc., v. NLRB, 700 F.3d 551 (D.C. Cir. 2012), the company, a manufacturer of aluminum extrusions, insisted on a wage concession of 20%, pointing to its loss of customers to Asian competitors. The Union requested the following: (1) a list of all current customers; (2) a copy of all price quotes that the company had provided over the past five years and an indication of which of those quotes had been awarded; (3) a list of all projects outsourced over the past five years that had been handled by bargaining unit employees; (4) a list of all customers who had ceased purchasing from KLB during the last five years; (5) a complete list of prices for KLB's products; (6) market studies concerning the company's products; and (7) a complete calculation of KLB's projected savings from its concessionary wage proposal, including an estimate of overtime. The Company turned over its estimate of wage savings only, omitting the bases for its calculations. It provided none of the other information. The Company also proceeded to lock out the employees over its concessionary bargaining demands.

The Board held the information had to be disclosed and the Court of Appeals agreed. The court noted that the Labor Board had at times tended to conflate "inability to pay" with "unwillingness to pay," but, in this case,

> The union targeted its information request to that competitiveness claim and did not ask the company to open its books and provide generalized financial data concerning profits and management expenses. Thus, the union's information request and the company's concomitant disclosure obligation were narrow.

Id. at 557.

The company had vigorously asserted the need to remain competitive. The Union was not required to accept those assertions at face value. Judge Karen LeCraft Henderson dissented. Unlike her brethren, she did see the company's contention regarding competitiveness as indistinguishable from a statement that it was unwilling to do better, not that it was incapable of doing better.

That issue was taken up by the United States Court of Appeals for the Second Circuit in SDBC Holdings, Inc., v. NLRB, 711 F.3d 281 (2nd Cir. 2013), where a holding company that had purchased the failing Stella D'oro bakery also demanded concessions from the Union. Management told the Union that it hoped to turn the business around and was prepared further to invest to get that done, but that in order to do that costs had to be reduced: it was " 'not in the business to sustain losses.' " The Union demanded that the Company disclose its financial situation, to support the claim of operating losses. The Company agreed only that the Union could see and take notes on, but not copy (or secure a copy of) its last, and rather terse, financial statement.

The court rejected the Board majority's ruling that the company had asserted an "inability to pay" sufficient to trigger a duty to open up the books, for it had consistently maintained that it was willing to put in additional financing in order to turn the company around. The court also discussed the weltered state of the law, in particular the Board's failure to have reconsidered precedents that lent weight to the position taken by the Board's dissent.

Judge Cabranes concurred separately to recommend that the Board revisit the issue, come to grips with its conflicting precedent, and announce a clear, or clearer, position. He emphasized that, according to his reading of *Truitt*, and the gloss of law on it, *inability to pay* does not mean the employer is bankrupt or might be made so by acceding to the union's demands, but rather that it cannot *afford to pay* the union's demands and remain profitable. Id. at 296–297.

Page 356.   Add following Detroit Edison:

The Board has glossed *Detroit Edison* requiring the disclosure of test scores, critical to policing the employer's hiring system, by redacting the test-takers' names without securing personal consent. U.S. Postal Service, 359 NLRB No. 115 (2013).

Page 357.   Add to Problem 3.

See generally Piedmont Gardens, 359 NLRB No. 46 (2012).

Page 358.   Add to the Problems for Discussion:

5.   A collective agreement between a union representing registered nurses and a large metropolitan hospital precludes the use of registered nurses "who are outside the bargaining unit to perform clinical duties normally performed by members of the bargaining unit" except for training or certification purposes. Some nurses have reported to the union's officers the presence of a number of nurse practitioners (NPs)—registered nurses who possess higher credentials—whom they have not seen before. The Union has inquired about them and the hospital has informed the Union that the NPs were independent contractors, not hospital employees. The Union has demanded that the hospital disclose: the "shifts worked by the NPs; their names, dates of hire and/or termination, job duties, departments or areas of work; and full or part-time status". Must the hospital comply? New York and Presbyterian Hospital v. NLRB, 649 F.3d 723 (D.C. Cir. 2011).

Page 369.   Add to the end of Problem 2:

Omit *Hacienda Hotel* (except for the fascinating 15-year history leading up to it and the fact that it was by an equally divided Board). Instead, *see* WKYC-TV, 359 NLRB No. 30 (2012).

III. SUBJECTS OF COLLECTIVE BARGAINING

Page 407.   Add to the end of the note on " 'WAIVER' BY CONTRACT OR PAST PRACTICE":

The issue of waiver is taken up in *Metropolitan Edison Co.*, v. *NLRB*, set out in the Main Volume at pp. 538–543, and again in Part Five, section IV, on the role of the NLRB and the arbitrator when the claim of contractual waiver is made. In anticipation of that discussion, it would be well to set the stage here because, as will appear directly, the courts of appeals are divided on the analytical framework.

The difference in approach between the Labor Board and some of the courts of appeals was taken up by the Second Circuit in Local Union 36, IBEW v. NLRB, 706 F.3d 73 (2d Cir. 2013). A group of gas and electric company technicians who provided customer service had long been assigned company vehicles which they were allowed to keep at home on their off-duty hours (and for which the company deducted certain costs from their pay). The Company unilaterally altered that policy. The Union demanded to bargain about the change and its effects on the employees. The Company refused arguing that the collective bargaining agreement gave it

> the right in its "sole and exclusive judgment" to "regulate the use of machinery, facilities, equipment, and other property of the Company;" the "exclusive right to issue, amend and revise reasonable policies, rules, regulations, and practices;" (Article 8) and "the exclusive and unilateral right to issue, amend, revise or terminate any or all benefits" (Article 24).

The General Counsel issued a complaint of violation of § 8(a)(5) in refusing to bargain about the policy or its effects. But he amended the complaint to assert only the latter. The Board agreed with the ALJ that the Company had unlawfully refused to engage in "effects bargaining" and a unanimous panel of the Second Circuit (in an opinion by Judge Cabranes) agreed. It said the contract did not "cover" the dispute; but explained it this way:

ii. The Waiver Analysis

> Where, as here, the Board's determination regarding waiver is based upon an interpretation of a contract, we begin by making a threshold, *de novo* determination of whether a matter is covered by the contract—meaning that the parties have already bargained over the matter and set out their agreement in the contract. Only if we conclude as a matter of law that the matter was not covered by the contract can we consider whether the Board's finding regarding waiver was supported by substantial evidence.

Put another way, we use a two-step framework to decide whether there has been a valid waiver of the right to bargain over a particular decision or its effects. At the first step, we ask whether the issue is clearly and unmistakably resolved (or "covered") by the contract. If so, the question of waiver is inapposite because the union has already clearly and unmistakably exercised its statutory right to bargain and has resolved the matter to its satisfaction. . . .

If we determine that the applicable CBA does not clearly and unmistakably cover the decision or effects at issue, we proceed to the second step, at which we ask whether the union has clearly and unmistakably *waived* its right to bargain. As noted above, such a waiver "may be found in an express provision in the parties' collective bargaining agreement, or by the conduct of the parties, including their past practices and bargaining history, or by a combination of the two." *United Techs. Corp.*, 884 F.2d at 1575. Whether a party has effectively waived its statutory right to bargain is therefore a mixed question of law and fact.

Under this two-step process, an employer can successfully carry its burden of proof by showing either that the CBA (or any other contract governing the relations between the parties) covers a particular decision, or that the Union has waived its right to bargain over a particular decision. *See Olivetti Office U.S.A.*, 926 F.2d at 187 (noting that "[t]he burden of proving a union waiver rests with the employer."). At either step, however, the contractual indicia of exercise of the right to bargain or proffered proof of waiver must clearly and unmistakably demonstrate the coverage or waiver sought to be proved. *Metro. Edison Co.*, 460 U.S. at 708, 103 S.Ct. 1467; *see Chesapeake & Potomac Tel. Co. v. N.L.R.B.*, 687 F.2d 633; 636 (2d Cir. 1982) ("[A] union's intention to waive a right must be clear before a claim of waiver can succeed.").

iii. The Contractual Coverage
Approach

It bears noting that, although we have used the term "covers," we have not adopted the "contractual coverage" *approach*, which several other Courts of Appeal use. *See, e.g., Bath Marine Draftsmen's Ass'n*, 475 F/3d at 23. While some of our sister Courts of Appeals have decided that, although the Board is obligated to apply the "clear and unmistakable waiver" standard, they "owe [ ] no deference to the Board's choice of standard when the unfair labor practice turns solely on the interpretation of a labor contract,"[10] *id.*, we think that approach is inconsistent with the Supreme Court's holdings in *Metropolitan Edison*, 460 U.S. at 708, 103 S.Ct. 1467, and

---

[10] Compare e.g., Bath Marine Draftmen's Ass'n, 475 F.3d at 25 (adopting the contractual coverage approach); Honeywell Int'l Inc., 253 F.3d at 132; Chi. Tribune Co. v. N.L.R.B., 974 f.2d 933, 937 (7th Cir. 1992); with Local Joint Exec. Bd. Of Las Vegas v. N.L.R.B., 540 F.3d 1072, 1080 & n. 11 (9th Cir. 2008) (noting that the "so-called 'contract coverage' standard" competes with the "clear-and-unmistakable" standard, and reaffirming the Ninth Circuit's commitment to the clear and unmistakable standard).

Mastro Plastics Corp. v. N.L.R.B., 350 U.S. 270, 283, 28, 76 S.Ct. 349, 100 L.Ed. 309 (1956), and our own precedents interpreting those decisions.

Although the "contract coverage" approach aligns with the Supreme Court's admonition that "courts are still the principal sources of contract interpretation," *Litton*, 501 U.S. at 202, 111 S.Ct. 2215, ignoring the "clear and unmistakable waiver" standard undermines our "national labor policy [that] disfavors waivers of statutorily protected rights," *Olivetti Office U.S.A.*, 926 F.2d at 187. Especially in the context of effects bargaining, the "contract coverage" approach can lead to the unwitting relinquishment of rights. Taken to its logical conclusion, the "contract coverage" approach means that a contract granting an employer the unilateral right to make a decision almost always means that the union has also given up the right to bargain about the effects of that decision. *See Enloe Med. Ctr. v. N.L.R.B.*, 433 F.3d 834, 839 (D.C.Cir. 2005) ("It would be rather unusual . . . to interpret a contract as granting an employer the unilateral right to make a particular decision but as reserving the union's right to bargain over the effects of that decision."). As discussed previously, however, a union has a statutory right to bargain over the decision itself *and* the effects that that decision might have upon employees' terms and conditions of employment.

Our two-step analysis preserves the long-standing precedent requiring that the relinquishment of statutory rights be deliberate and obvious, while retaining the judicial authority to interpret contacts *de novo*. We must interpret the relevant contract with particular attention to the heightened waiver standards that apply in the labor context. Just as "[W]e will not thrust a waiver upon an unwitting party," *N.Y. Tel. Co.*, 930 F.2d at 1011, we will not find a contractual *exercise* of the right to bargain over a decision (or its effects) unless the contract clearly and unmistakably demonstrates that the parties bargained with respect to the disputed matter.

Id. at 84–86 (footnotes omitted) (italics in original).

On the merits, the court sustained the Board:

The general right given to Rochester Gas to "regulate the use of [its] machinery, facilities, equipment, and other property," . . . does not explicitly or implicitly include the right to alter the terms and conditions of employment—even if those terms and conditions are related to Rochester Gas's use of its covered property. Although an intent to permit the Company to change its policy regarding vehicles without the need to bargain over the effects of such a decision may be a *plausible* reading of the contract, it is not a *clear and unmistakable* exercise of the Union's bargaining power regarding those effects. Thus, although the CBA reserves to Rochester Gas the right to make the decision to implement the Vehicle Policy Change, we include that it does not clearly and unmistakably "cover" the disputed issue. That is, the CBA does not clearly and unmistakably set out whether (and how) Rochester Gas must account for the effect that the Vehicle Policy Change has on the employee benefits relating to the vehicles. Therefore, at step one of our analysis, we conclude that the Union did not already exercise its statutory right to bargain over the effects of the Vehicle Policy Change.

At step two, we examine the Board's determination that the Union had not waived its right to bargain over the effects of the Vehicle Policy Change. We agree with the Board's finding that the Union did not waive this right, and we hold that this finding is supported by substantial evidence.

Judge Straub concurred, finding the "two-step framework" an "unnerving innovation"—and that the "clear and unmistakable" standard was sufficiently clear and unmistakable.

The court also held that the General Counsel's decision not to issue a § 8(a)(5) complaint for a refusal to bargain about the decision, not only its effects, was not reviewable.

Page 429.   Add to the Problems for Discussion:

4.   Reargear is an automotive parts manufacturer. It has a plant in Illinois whose workforce is represented by the Metal Workers Union (MWU) and one in South Carolina that is not unionized but where the MWU has filed a petition for an election. The week of the election the company announced to its South Carolina workforce that it would be moving about a third of its production from Illinois to South Carolina. (Local political figures in that state hailed the announcement for bolstering the state's economy.) This is the only notice the MWU has had of this decision. The MWU's leadership has consulted you, the union's lawyer. Would you advise the filing of a charge of violation of § 8(a)(5) in Illinois? Of § 8(a)(1) in South Carolina? (Review *Exchange Parts* on page 158 of the casebook.) Both? Would you consider the impact of your decision on the impending election? If so, how would that affect your decision?

PART FOUR

STRIKES, PICKETING AND BOYCOTTS

I. RIGHTS OF EMPLOYEE PROTESTERS UNDER THE NLRA

A. PROTECTED AND UNPROTECTED CONCERTED ACTIVITY

Page 461. Add following to the text discussing Washington Aluminum:

Social Media. Employers often screen job applicants' social media. They also monitor employee use of social media, not only of postings available to the general public but of postings intended to reach a more limited audience. Thus far fourteen states have forbidden employers to request access to applicant or employee social media. *See generally,* Matthew Finkin, PRIVACY IN EMPLOYMENT LAW (4th ed. 2013) and 2014 Supplement. Even where the employer does not monitor non-public postings, recipients—co-workers—may bring the message or messages to the employer's attention..

The Labor Act may bear upon employer monitoring in two ways. The first and most obvious is where a posting critical of the employer or addressing some workplace issue is a basis for discharge or discipline. Where the posting is not an atomistic expression of personal pique but an appeal to co-workers, or a preliminary or anticipatory step toward group protest or action, it would be protected activity. The Board's Acting General Counsel has issued a report dealing with the advice given and the texture of cases in process that concerns that aspect of section 7. General Counsel Memorandum OM 12–59 (May 30, 2012). Facebook postings by two employees expressing concern about working late in an unsafe neighborhood were held to be protected activity. Design Technology Group, LLC, 359 NLRB No. 96 (2013). *But see* Tasker Healthcare Group, General Counsel Advice Memorandum (May 8, 2013).

There is a second aspect of such monitoring that has yet to be presented. It violates the Act not only to monitor employees for their union activity ("surveillance" is the customary term), but also to create the impression of doing so as that would have a chilling effect and so "interfere" in the exercise of section 7 rights. It remains to be seen how routine employer surveillance of social media that would inevitably sweep in expressions of workplace discontent that are or might be preliminary to group action would be treated under this doctrine.

Page 472. Add to Problem 4:

See also Hoodview Vending Co., 359 NLRB No. 36 (2012) (an employee's inquiry of a co-worker—if he had heard that someone would be discharged—was held to be protected concerted activity, one Board member dissenting).

Page 481.   Add to Problems for Discussion:

4.   Bill Smith is a union steward at the Emmett Worth Company. Dewey Dell, the manager of production, has told Smith to come to his office to discuss his "productivity problem." Two days earlier Smith had been asked by a co-worker, Brenda Starr, to accompany her to a meeting with Dell, but Dell had told him to leave as the discussion with Starr was "private." Smith called the Union's business agent and told him that he expected that he, too, would not be allowed to have a witness. The business agent advised him to record the conversation secretly, which he did. Dell learned shortly thereafter that the conversation had been recorded and fired Smith. Has the Company committed an unfair labor practice? Media, LLC v. NLRB, 677 F.3d 1241 (D.C. Cir. 2012). Because state law allows the recording of a conversation where one party to it consents, the recording did not violate state law. Should it make a difference whether the Company prohibited surreptitious recording by employees? That Smith first consulted the Union business agent?

Page 486.   Add Following Eastex:

A NOTE ON WAIVER OF GROUP ARBITRATION

An employer may not condition employment on the waiver of rights protected by the Act. Thus the policy of a non-unionized employer that requires employees to submit all disputes and claims to a system of binding arbitration established unilaterally by it would violate the Act to the extent it would sweep in claims that could be filed with the Board or, arguably, would waive resort to collective self-help. 2 Sisters Food Group, Inc., 357 NLRB No. 168 (2011). *See also* Supply Technologies, LLC, 359 NLRB No. 38 (2012).

Even so, the United States Supreme Court has given strong support to such arbitration systems. (*See* the discussions at pp. 763–765 of the casebook.) In AT&T Mobility v. Concepcion, 563 U.S. 321 (2011), involving a consumer sales agreement, the Court held that the Federal Arbitration Act precluded the states from holding a waiver of participation in a class or group arbitration to be unconscionable and therefore unenforceable. Inasmuch as a consumer transaction was presented no mention was made of the Labor Act.

In D.R. Horton, Inc., 357 NLRB No. 184 (2012), a three-member panel of the Board took up the issue of whether a company arbitration policy which provides the following violates the Labor Act:

- that all disputes and claims relating to the employee's employment with the Company will be determined exclusively by final and binding arbitration;

- that the arbitrator "may hear only Employee's individual claims," "will not have the authority to consolidate the claims of other employees," and "does not have authority to fashion a proceeding as a class or collective action or to award relief to a group or class of employees in one arbitration proceeding"; and

- that the signatory employee waives "the right to file a lawsuit or other civil proceeding relating to Employee's employment with the Company" and "the right to resolve employment-related disputes in a proceeding before a judge or jury."

The Board held that the arbitration policy violated Sections 7 and 8(a) for two reasons: first, by being drafted broadly enough to convey to a reasonable employee that she was giving up her right to file unfair labor practice charges with the Board; and, second, infringing on employee rights to act concertedly for mutual aid and protection by barring employees from pursuing both class or group actions and class or group arbitration. The implications of the second reason are far broader than the first, since, in the employment area, it had the potential to undermine *Concepcion*'s validation of agreements barring class arbitration.

The Board commenced from *Eastex*: that employee engagement in concerted activity for mutual aid or protection extends to concerted activity in any venue or forum from which employees may derive benefit as employees—legislative, judicial, or administrative. It follows that where arbitration substitutes for the courts, the right of concerted activity in that forum would apply as well. The Board next reiterated the longstanding rejection of individual waivers of statutory rights going back to the Act's earliest days. Finally, it saw no conflict between its holding and the Federal Arbitration Act. The Court's FAA jurisprudence is built on the conception of forum substitution: all arbitration contracts do is substitute an arbitrator for a court to apply the same legal standards; that the procedures in the two fora differ is neither here nor there, so long as due process is observed. But, in Labor Act terms the preclusion of collective claims or action is not procedural: "The right to engage in collective action—including collective *legal* action—is the core substantive right protected by the NLRA and is the foundation on which the Act and Federal labor policy rest." (Emphasis in original.)

On appeal, the Fifth Circuit addressed both of the Board's grounds.

D.R. Horton, Inc. v. NLRB

737 F.3d 344 (5th Cir. 2013).

LESLIE H. SOUTHWICK, Circuit Judge:

* * *

. . . [We] conclude that the Board's decision did not give proper weight to the Federal Arbitration Act. We uphold the Board, though, on requiring Horton to clarify with its employees that the arbitration agreement did not eliminate their rights to pursue claims of unfair labor practices with the Board.

* * *

DISCUSSION

[The court first addressed of a number of challenges to the *Horton* Board's authority. It held that it did not have to consider the constitutional validity of Member Becker's recess appointment (the issue later addressed in the Supreme Court's *Noel Canning* decision, *see* Supplement at p. 129)]. . .

III. NLRA Sections 7 & 8(a)(1) and the Federal Arbitration Act

. . . .[T]he Board first determined that the agreement interfered with the exercise of employees' substantive rights under Section 7 of the NLRA, which allows employees to act in concert with each other:

Employees shall have the right to self-organization, to form, join, or assist labor organizations, to bargain collectively through representatives of their own choosing, *and to engage in other concerted activities for the purpose of collective bargaining or other mutual aid or protection,* and shall also have the right to refrain from any or all of such activities except to the extent that such right may be affected by an agreement requiring membership in a labor organization as a condition of employment as authorized in section 158(a)(3) of this title. . . .

The Board deemed it well-settled that the NLRA protects the right of employees to improve their working conditions through administrative and judicial forums.

Taking this view of Section 7, the Board held that the NLRA protects the right of employees to "join together to pursue workplace grievances, including through litigation" and arbitration. The Board concluded that an "individual who files a class or collective action regarding wages, hours or working conditions, whether in court or before an arbitrator, seeks to initiate or induce group action and is engaged in conduct protected by Section 7 . . . central to the [NLRA's] purposes." In the Board's opinion, by requiring employees to refrain from collective or class claims, the Mutual Arbitration Agreement infringed on the substantive rights protected by Section 7.

* * *

[The Board also held that the Agreement violated § 8(a)(1).]

Horton and several amici disagree with this interpretation of Section 7. According to Horton, the NLRA does not grant employees the substantive right to adjudicate claims collectively. Additionally, Horton argues that the Board's interpretation of Sections 7 and 8(a)(1) impermissibly conflicts with the FAA by prohibiting the enforcement of an arbitration agreement.

We give to the Board "judicial deference when it interprets an ambiguous provision of a statute that it administers." *Lechmere, Inc. v. NLRB,* 502 U.S. 527, 536 (1992). . . . Where "an issue . . . implicates its expertise in labor relations, a reasonable construction by the Board is entitled to considerable deference." *Id.* "Deference to the Board 'cannot be allowed to slip into a judicial inertia which results in the unauthorized assumption . . . of major policy decisions properly made by Congress.'" *NLRB v. Fin. Inst. Emps. of Am., Local*1182, 475 U.S. 192, 202 (1986) (alteration in original) (quoting *Am. Ship Bldg. Co. v. NLRB,*

380 U.S. 300, 318 (1965)). Particularly relevant to this dispute is that "the Board has not been commissioned to effectuate the policies of the Labor Relations Act so single-mindedly that it may wholly ignore other and equally important Congressional objectives." *Southern S.S. Co. v. NLRB,* 316 U.S. 31, 47 (1942). "Frequently the entire scope of Congressional purpose calls for careful accommodation of one statutory scheme to another, and it is not too much to demand of an administrative body that it undertake this accommodation without excessive emphasis upon its immediate task." *Id.* "[W]e have accordingly never deferred to the Board's remedial preferences where such preferences potentially trench upon federal statutes and policies unrelated to the NLRA." *Hoffman Plastic Compounds, Inc. v. NLRB,* 535 U.S. 137 (2002).

Section 7 effectuated Congress's intent to equalize bargaining power between employees and employers "by allowing employees to band together in confronting an employer regarding the terms and conditions of their employment," and that "[t]here is no indication that Congress intended to limit this protection to situations in which an employee's activity and that of his fellow employees combine with one another in any particular way." *City Disposal,* 465 U.S. at 835. On the other hand, no court decision prior to the Board's ruling under review today had held that the Section 7 right to engage in "concerted activities for the purpose of . . . other mutual aid or protection" prohibited class action waivers in arbitration agreements.

Board precedent and some circuit courts have held that the provision protects collective-suit filings. "It is well settled that the filing of a civil action by employees is protected activity . . . [and] by joining together to file the lawsuit [the employees] engaged in concerted activity." *127 Rest. Corp.,* 331 NLRB 269, 275–76 (2000). "[A] lawsuit filed in good faith by a group of employees to achieve more favorable terms or conditions of employment *is* 'concerted activity' under Section 7" of the NLRA. *Brady v. Nat'l Football League,* 644 F.3d 661, 673 (8th Cir. 2011). An employee's participation in a collective-bargaining agreement's grievance procedure on behalf of himself and other employees is similarly protected. *City Disposal,* 465 U.S. at 831–32, 835–36.

These cases under the NLRA give some support to the Board's analysis that collective and class claims, whether in lawsuits or in arbitration, are protected by Section 7. To stop here, though, is to make the NLRA the only relevant authority. The Federal Arbitration Act ("FAA") has equal importance in our review. Caselaw under the FAA points us in a different direction than the course taken by the Board. As an initial matter, arbitration has been deemed not to deny a party any statutory right. *See Mitsubishi Motors Corp. v. Soler Chrysler-Plymouth, Inc.,* 473 U.S. 614, 627 (1985). Courts repeatedly have rejected litigants' attempts to assert a statutory right that cannot be effectively vindicated through arbitration. To be clear, the Board did not say otherwise. It said the NLRA invalidates any bar to *class* arbitrations.

Although the Board is correct that none of those cases considered a Section 7 right to pursue legal claims concertedly, they nevertheless emphasize the barrier any statute faces before it will displace the FAA.

The Board presents no cases that have overcome that barrier, and our research reveals very limited exceptions. *See In re Nat'l Gypsum Co.,* 118 F.3d 1056, 1069 (5th Cir.1997) (finding exception to mandatory arbitration necessary to preserve Bankruptcy Code's purpose of creating centralized and efficient bankruptcy court system); *Clary v. Helen of Troy, L.P.,* No. EP–11–CV–284–KC, 2011 WL 6960820, at *7 (W.D. Tex. Dec. 20, 2011) (finding inherent conflict between Jury Act and FAA).

The use of class action procedures, though, is not a substantive right. *See Amchem Prods., Inc. v. Windsor,* 521 U.S. 591, 612–13 (1997); *Deposit Guar. Nat'l Bank v. Roper,* 445 U.S. 326, 332 (1980) ("[T]he right of a litigant to employ Rule 23 is a procedural right only, ancillary to the litigation of substantive claims."). This court similarly has "characterized a class action as 'a procedural device.'" *Reed v. Fla. Metro. Univ., Inc.,* 681 F.3d 630, 643 (5th Cir.2012), *abrogated on other grounds by Oxford Health Plans LLC v. Sutter,* ___ U.S. ___, 133 S. Ct. 2064, 186 L.Ed.2d 113 (2013) (quoting *Blaz v. Belfer,* 368 F.3d 501, 505 (5th Cir.2004)). . . . The Board distinguished such caselaw on the basis that the NLRA is essentially *sui generis.* That act's fundamental precept is the right for employees to act collectively. Thus, Rule 23 is not the source of the right to the relevant collective actions. The NLRA is.

Even so, there are numerous decisions holding that there is no right to use class procedures under various employment-related statutory frameworks. For example, the Supreme Court has determined that there is no substantive right to class procedures under the Age Discrimination in Employment Act, 29 U.S.C. § 621 *et seq.* ("ADEA"), despite the statute providing for class procedures. *Gilmer v. Interstate/Johnson Lane Corp.,* 500 U.S. 20 (1991). Similarly, numerous courts have held that there is no substantive right to proceed collectively under the FLSA, the statute under which Cuda originally brought suit. *Carter v. Countrywide Credit Indus., Inc.,* 362 F.3d 294, 298 (5th Cir.2004); *see also Adkins v. Labor Ready, Inc.,* 303 F.3d 496, 506 (4th Cir.2002); *Kuehner v. Dickinson & Co.,* 84 F.3d 316, 319–20 (9th Cir.1996).

The Board determined that invalidating restrictions on class or collective actions would not conflict with the FAA. The Board reached this conclusion by first observing that when private contracts interfere with the functions of the NLRA, the NLRA prevails. The Board then noted that the FAA was intended to prevent courts from treating arbitration agreements less favorably than other private contracts, but the FAA allows for the non-enforcement of arbitration agreements on any "grounds as exist at law or in equity for the revocation of any contract." 9 U.S.C. § 2. It then reasoned that "[t]o find that an arbitration agreement must yield to the NLRA is to treat it no worse than any other private contract that conflicts with Federal labor law." The Board argues that any employee-employer contract prohibiting collective action fails under Section 7, and arbitration agreements are treated no worse and no better.

In so finding, the Board relied in part on its view that the policy behind the NLRA trumped the different policy considerations in the FAA that supported enforcement of arbitration agreements. The Board considered its holding to be a limited one, remarking that the only agreements affected by its decision were those between employers and employees. The Board recognized that "a party may not be compelled under the FAA to submit to class arbitration unless there is a contractual basis for concluding that the party *agreed* to do so." *Stolt-Nielsen S.A. v. AnimalFeeds Int'l Corp.,* 559 U.S. 662, 684 (2010). Even so, the Board concluded that it was not requiring parties to engage in class arbitration: "So long as the employer leaves open a judicial forum for class and collective claims, employees' NLRA rights are preserved without requiring the availability of class-wide arbitration," and "[e]mployers remain[ed] free to insist that *arbitral* proceedings be conducted on an individual basis."

The Board explained its interpretation of the NLRA as appropriately weighing the public policy interests involved and, to the extent the NLRA and FAA might conflict, suitably accommodating those statutes' interests. Had it found the two enactments to conflict, the Board believed the FAA would have to yield for also being in conflict with the Norris-LaGuardia Act of 1932, which prohibits agreements that prevent aiding by lawful means a person participating in a lawsuit arising out of a labor dispute, and which was passed seven years after the FAA.

We now evaluate the Board's reasoning. We start with the requirement under the FAA that arbitration agreements must be enforced according to their terms. [*CompuCredit Corp. v. Greenwood,* ___ U.S. ___, 132 S. Ct. 665, 669 (2012).] Two exceptions to this rule are at issue here: (1) an arbitration agreement may be invalidated on any ground that would invalidate a contract under the FAA's "saving clause," *AT&T Mobility LLC v. Concepcion,* ___ U.S. ___, 131 S. Ct. 1740, 1746 (2011); and (2) application of the FAA may be precluded by another statute's contrary congressional command, *CompuCredit,* 132 S. Ct. at 669.

The Board clearly relied on the FAA's saving clause. Less clear is whether the Board also asserted that a contrary congressional command is present. We consider each exception.

The first exception to enforcing arbitration agreements is set out in this language found in the FAA, which we will refer to as the "saving clause":

> A written provision in any maritime transaction or a contract evidencing a transaction involving commerce to settle by arbitration a controversy thereafter arising out of such contract or transaction . . . shall be valid, irrevocable, and enforceable, *save upon such grounds as exist at law or in equity for the revocation of any contract.*

9 U.S.C. § 2 (emphasis added).

The Board found that the Mutual Arbitration Agreement violated the collective action provisions of the NLRA, making the saving clause applicable. A detailed analysis of *Concepcion* leads to the conclusion that the Board's rule does not fit within the FAA's saving clause. A California statute prohibited class action waivers in arbitration agreements. *Concepcion,* 131 S. Ct. at 1746, 1753. The Court considered whether the fact that California's prohibition on class-action waivers applied in both judicial and arbitral proceedings meant the prohibition fell within the FAA's saving clause. *Id.* at 1746. The Court said the saving clause was inapplicable. "The overarching purpose of the FAA . . . is to ensure the enforcement of arbitration agreements according to their terms so as to facilitate streamlined proceedings," and "[r]equiring the availability of classwide arbitration interferes with fundamental attributes of arbitration and thus creates a scheme inconsistent with the FAA." *Id.* at 1748. The Court found numerous differences between class arbitration and traditional arbitration. These included that "the switch from bilateral to class arbitration sacrifices the principal advantage of arbitration—its informality—and makes the process slower, more costly, and more likely to generate procedural morass than final judgment." *Id.* at 1751. Class arbitration also *"requires* procedural formality" because "[i]f procedures are too informal, absent class members would not be bound by the arbitration." *Id.* Finally, class arbitration "greatly increases risks to defendants" by removing "multilayered review," resulting in defendants, who might have been willing to accept such risks in individual arbitrations as the cost of doing business, being "pressured into settling questionable claims." *Id.* at 1752. Taken together, the effect of requiring the availability of class procedures was to give companies less incentive to resolve claims on an individual basis. *Id.* at 1750.

Like the statute in *Concepcion,* the Board's interpretation prohibits class-action waivers. While the Board's interpretation is facially neutral—requiring only that employees have access to collective procedures in an arbitral or judicial forum—the effect of this interpretation is to disfavor arbitration. As the *Concepcion* Court remarked, "there is little incentive for lawyers to arbitrate on behalf of individuals when they may do so for a class and reap far higher fees in the process. And faced with inevitable class arbitration, companies would have less incentive to continue resolving potentially duplicative claims on an individual basis." *Id.*

It is no defense to say there would not be any class arbitration because employees could only seek class relief in court. Regardless of whether employees resorted to class procedures in an arbitral or in a judicial forum, employers would be discouraged from using individual arbitration. Further, as *Concepcion* makes clear, certain procedures are a practical necessity in class arbitration. *Id.* at 1751 (listing adequate representation of absent class members, notice, opportunity to be heard, and right to opt-out). Those procedures are also part of class actions in court. As *Concepcion* held as to classwide arbitration, requiring the availability of class actions "interferes with fundamental attributes of arbitration and thus creates a scheme inconsistent with the FAA." *Id.* at 1748. Requiring a class mechanism is an actual impediment to arbitration and violates the FAA. The saving clause is not a basis for invalidating the waiver of class procedures in the arbitration agreement.

We examine next whether the NLRA contains a congressional command to override the FAA. The FAA establishes "a liberal federal policy favoring arbitration agreements." *Id.* at 1749. The FAA's purpose is "to ensure the enforcement of arbitrations agreements according to their terms." *Id.* at 1748. "That is the case even when the claims at issue are federal statutory claims, unless the FAA's mandate has been 'overridden by a contrary congressional command.'" *CompuCredit,* 132 S. Ct. at 669 (quoting *Shearson/American Express Inc. v. McMahon,* 482 U.S. 220, 226 (1987)). If such a command exists, it "will be discoverable in the text," the statute's "legislative history," or "an 'inherent conflict' between arbitration and the [statute's] underlying purposes." *Gilmer,* 500 U.S. at 26. "[T]he relevant inquiry [remains] whether Congress . . . precluded 'arbitration or other nonjudicial resolution' of claims." *Garrett v. Circuit City Stores, Inc.,* 449 F.3d 672, 679 (5th Cir.2006) (quoting *Gilmer,* 500 U.S. at 28).

When considering whether a contrary congressional command is present, courts must remember "that questions of arbitrability must be addressed with a healthy regard for the federal policy favoring arbitration." *Gilmer,* 500 U.S. at 26 (quotation marks and citation omitted). The party opposing arbitration bears the burden of showing whether a congressional command exists. *Id.* Any doubts are resolved in favor of arbitration. *Moses H. Cone Mem'l Hosp. v. Mercury Const. Corp.,* 460 U.S. 1, 24–25 (1983).

There is no argument that the NLRA's text contains explicit language of a congressional intent to override the FAA. Instead, it is the general thrust of the NLRA—how it operates, its goal of equalizing bargaining power—from which the command potentially is found. For example, one of the NLRA's purposes is to "protect[ ] the exercise by workers of full freedom of association . . . for the purpose of negotiating the terms and conditions of their employment or other mutual aid or protection." 29 U.S.C. § 151. Such general language is an insufficient congressional command, as much more explicit language has been rejected in the past. Indeed, the text does not even mention arbitration. By comparison, statutory references to causes of action, filings in court, or allowing suits all have been found insufficient to infer a congressional command against application of the FAA. *See CompuCredit,* 132 S. Ct. at 670–71. Even explicit procedures for collective actions will not override the FAA. *See Gilmer,* 500 U.S. at 32 (ADEA); *Carter,* 362 F.3d at 298 (FLSA). The NLRA does not explicitly provide for such a collective action, much less the procedures such an action would employ. 29 U.S.C. § 157. Thus, there is no basis on which to find that the text of the NLRA supports a congressional command to override the FAA.

We next look for evidence in legislative history of a disavowal of arbitration. We find none. As amicus Chamber of Commerce observes, the legislative history of the NLRA, and its predecessor, the National Industrial Recovery Act of 1933, only supports a congressional intent to "level the playing field" between workers and employers by empowering unions to engage in collective bargaining. The Chamber of Commerce draws attention to the fact that Congress did not discuss the right to file class or consolidated claims against employers, although such a discussion would admittedly have occurred prior to the existence of Rule 23 or the FLSA. Therefore, the legislative history also does not provide a basis for a congressional command to override the FAA.

Neither the NLRA's statutory text nor its legislative history contains a congressional command against application of the FAA. Therefore, the Mutual Arbitration Agreement should be enforced according to its terms unless a contrary congressional command can be inferred from an inherent conflict between the FAA and the NLRA's purpose. *See Gilmer,* 500 U.S. at 26. As explained below, we do not find such a conflict.

First, courts repeatedly have understood the NLRA to permit and require arbitration. *See 14 Penn Plaza LLC v. Pyett,* 556 U.S. 247, 257–58 (2009) (finding that a collective-bargaining agreement's arbitration provision must be honored unless ADEA removes such claims from NLRA's scope); *Blessing v. Freestone,* 520 U.S. 329, 343 (1997) ("[W]e discern[ ] in the structure of the [NLRA] the very specific right of employees to complete the collective-bargaining process and agree to an arbitration clause." (internal quotation marks and citation omitted)); *Richmond Tank Car Co. v. NLRB,* 721 F.2d 499, 501 (5th Cir.1983) (holding that NLRA's policy favors arbitration of labor disputes). As the Board itself acknowledged, "arbitration has become a central pillar of Federal labor relations policy and in many different contexts the Board defers to the arbitration process both before and after the arbitrator issues an award." Having worked in tandem with arbitration agreements in the past, the NLRA has no inherent conflict with the FAA.

Second, there are conceptual problems with finding the NLRA in conflict with the FAA. We know that the right to proceed collectively cannot protect vindication of employees' statutory rights under the ADEA or FLSA because a substantive right to proceed collectively has been foreclosed by prior decisions. *See Gilmer,* 500 U.S. at 32 (ADEA); *Carter,* 362 F.3d at 298 (FLSA). The right to collective action also cannot be successfully defended on the policy ground that it provides employees with greater bargaining power. "Mere inequality in bargaining power . . . is not a sufficient reason to hold that arbitration agreements are never enforceable in the employment context." *Gilmer,* 500 U.S. at 33. The end result is that the Board's decision creates either a right that is hollow or one premised on an already-rejected justification.

We find no clear answer to the validity of the Board's use of the NLRA and FAA's respective enactment dates. Where statutes irreconcilably conflict, the statute later in time will prevail. *See Chi. & N.W. Ry. Co. v. United Transp. Union,* 402 U.S. 570, 582 n. 18 (1971); *see also Lockhart v. United States,* 546 U.S. 142, 148 (2005) (Scalia, J., concurring). The Board determined that the NLRA was the later statute. The FAA was enacted in 1925, then reenacted on July 30, 1947. The NLRA was enacted on July 5, 1935, and reenacted on June 23, 1947. The reenactments were part of a recodification of federal statutes that apparently made no substantive changes. An Act to codify and enact into positive law, Title 9 of the United States Code, entitled "Arbitration", Pub. L. No. 80–282, 61 Stat. 669 (1947). The relevance of the date of enactment is whether a repeal by implication arises. *S. Scrap Material Co., LLC. v. ABC Ins. Co. (In re Southern Scrap Materials Co., LLC.),* 541 F.3d 584, 593 n. 14 (5th Cir.2008). The implication is based on the assumption that Congress is fully aware of prior enactments as it adopts new laws. *Id.* It is unclear whether that assumption has the same force for a recodification.

Of some importance is that the NLRA was enacted and reenacted prior to the advent in 1966 of modern class action practice. *See Ortiz v. Fibreboard Corp.,* 527 U.S. 815, 832–33 (1999). We find limited force to the argument that there is an inherent conflict between the FAA and NLRA when the NLRA would have to be protecting a right of access to a procedure that did not exist when the NLRA was (re)enacted.[10] The dates of enactment have no impact on our decision.

The NLRA should not be understood to contain a congressional command overriding application of the FAA. The burden is with the party opposing arbitration, *Gilmer,*500 U.S. at 26, and here the Board has not shown that the NLRA's language, legislative history, or purpose support finding the necessary congressional command. Because the Board's interpretation does not fall within the FAA's "saving clause," and because the NLRA does not contain a congressional command exempting the statute from application of the FAA, the Mutual Arbitration Agreement must be enforced according to its terms.

We do not deny the force of the Board's efforts to distinguish the NLRA from all other statutes that have been found to give way to requirements of arbitration. The issue here is narrow: do the rights of collective action embodied in this labor statute make it distinguishable from cases which hold that arbitration must be individual arbitration? *See Concepcion,* 131 S. Ct. at 1750–53. We have explained the general reasoning that indicates the answer is "no." We add that we are loath to create a circuit split. Every one of our sister circuits to consider the issue has either suggested or expressly stated that they would not defer to the NLRB's rationale, and held arbitration agreements containing class waivers enforceable. *See Richards v. Ernst & Young, LLP,* 734 F.3d 871, 873–74 (9th Cir.2013); *Sutherland v. Ernst & Young LLP,*726 F.3d 290, 297–98 n. 8 (2d Cir.2013); *Owen v. Bristol Care, Inc.,* 702 F.3d 1050, 1055 (8th Cir.2013).[11]

IV. *Mutual Arbitration Agreement's Violation of NLRA Section 8(a)(1)*

The ALJ found that the Mutual Arbitration Agreement violated Section 8(a)(1) and (4) for including language that would lead employees to a reasonable belief that they were prohibited from filing unfair labor practice charges. The ALJ reached this conclusion by analyzing the Board's decisions in *Bill's Electric, Inc.,* 350 NLRB 292 (2007) and *U-Haul Co. of California,* 347 NLRB 375 (2006), *enforced* 255 Fed. Appx. 527 (D.C. Cir. 2007), both of which found broad and ambiguous judicial waivers unlawful. The Board affirmed the ALJ's Section 8(a)(1) holding on the same grounds.[12] The Board also relied on language in the agreement that all disputes would be resolved by

---

[10] The Board also relied on the Norris–LaGuardia Act ("NLGA") to support its view that the FAA must give way to the NLRA. It is undisputed that the NLGA is outside the Board's interpretive ambit. *See* Lechmere, 502 U.S. at 536. We also conclude that the Board's reasoning drawn from the NLGA is unpersuasive.

[11] A thorough explanation of the strongest arguments in favor of the Board's decision, which embraces the Board's distinctions from earlier Supreme Court pronouncements on arbitrations and adding some of its own, appears in a recent law review article. Charles A. Sullivan & Timothy P. Glynn, Horton *Hatches the Egg: Concerted Action Includes Concerted Dispute Resolution,* 64 ALA. L.REV. 1013 (2013). We do not adopt its reasoning but note our consideration of its advocacy.

[12] Because the Board affirmed the ALJ's holding under Section 8(a)(1), it did not reach Section 8(a)(4).

arbitration, without listing any exception for unfair labor practice charges, and that employees waived the right to file a "lawsuit or other civil proceeding."

The arbitration agreement would violate the NLRA if it prohibited employees from filing unfair labor practice claims with the Board. Even "in the absence of express language prohibiting section 7 activity, a company nonetheless violates section 8(a)(1) if 'employees would reasonably construe the language to prohibit section 7 activity.'" *Cintas Corp. v. NLRB,* 482 F.3d 463, 467 (D.C. Cir. 2007) (citation omitted).

The agreement clearly provides that employees agree to arbitrate "without limitation[:] claims for discrimination or harassment; wages, benefits, or other compensation; breach of any express or implied contract; [and] violation of public policy." It also provides for four exceptions to arbitrations. None of these exclusions refer to unfair labor practice claims.

Horton emphasizes that the agreement refers to "court actions" and "rights to trial in court before a judge or jury," implying that administrative proceedings before the Board are unaffected. The agreement gives different indications too, as it provides that an "arbitrator will not have the authority to order any remedy that a court *or agency* would not be authorized to order." (emphasis added). The agreement also states that each party shall pay costs "that each party would incur if the claim(s) were litigated in a court *or agency* " and that "[t]he arbitrator may award reasonable fees and costs . . . to the prevailing party to the same extent a court *or agency* would be entitled to do." (emphases added).

Most importantly, the Mutual Arbitration Agreement concludes with an employee's acknowledgment that he or she "knowingly and voluntarily waiv[es] the right to file a lawsuit *or other civil proceeding* relating to Employee's employment with [Horton] *as well as* the right to resolve employment-related disputes in a proceeding before a judge or jury." (emphases added). The reasonable impression could be created that an employee is waiving not just his trial rights, but his administrative rights as well.

The ALJ and the Board cite some Board precedents that assist in our analysis. In one, the employer changed an application form to include a requirement that applicants resolve through grievance and arbitration procedures "any legal claims . . . in connection with [the applicant's] rights under Federal or State law." *Bill's Electric,* 350 NLRB at 295–96 (omission in original). An accompanying alternate dispute resolution form was entitled "Arbitration to be Exclusive Procedure for Resolution of All***364*** Disputes." *Id.* at 296. While that form also stated that it did not constitute a waiver of an employee's right to file a charge with the Board, this was not enough to save it: "At the very least, the mandatory grievance and arbitration policy would reasonably be read by affected applicants and employees as substantially restricting, if not totally prohibiting, their access to the Board's processes." *Id.*

Another Board decision invalidated an arbitration agreement that provided for arbitration of "any other legal or equitable claims and causes of action recognized by local, state, or federal law or regulations."

U-Haul, 347 NLRB at 377. The Board "recognize[d] that the language in the arbitration policy [did] not explicitly restrict employees from resorting to the Board's remedial procedures" but that "the breadth of the policy language" would result in employees "reasonably constru[ing] the remedies for violations of the [NLRA] as included among the legal claims . . . covered by the policy." *Id.* The panel rejected the argument that the phrase "court of law" cured the agreement's deficiencies because decisions by the Board could always be appealed to a United States court of appeals. *Id.* at 377–78.

As in *U-Haul,* the Mutual Arbitration Agreement refers to "court," "judge," and "jury," but these references are insufficient to counter the breadth of the waiver created by the phrase "right to file a lawsuit or other civil proceeding." Further, as in *Bill's Electric,* the agreement's use of seemingly incompatible language that refers to court actions in one sentence and agency actions in another, means an employee would reasonably read the agreement as also precluding unfair labor practice charges. Horton distinguishes *Bill's Electric* and *U-Haul* as occurring in the context of union activity, but neither opinion's reasoning was premised on such activity. The Board's finding that the Mutual Arbitration Agreement could be misconstrued was reasonable and the need for Horton to take the ordered corrective action was valid.

* * *

GRAVES, Judge, concurring in part and dissenting in part.

The Mutual Arbitration Agreement (MAA) precludes employees from filing joint, class or collective claims in any forum. I agree with the Board that the MAA interferes with the exercise of employees' substantive rights under Section 7 of the NLRA, which provides, in relevant part, that employees have the right "to engage in other concerted activities for the purpose of collective bargaining or other mutual aid or protection. . . ." 29 U.S.C. § 157.

Further, as the Board specifically found, holding that the MAA violates the NLRA does not conflict with the FAA for several reasons: (1) "the purpose of the FAA was to prevent courts from treating arbitration agreements less favorably than other private contracts." *In re D.R. Horton, Inc.,* 357 NLRB No. 184, 2012 WL 36274, at *11 (2012). "To find that an arbitration agreement must yield to the NLRA is to treat it no worse than any other private contract that conflicts with Federal labor law." *Id.*; (2) "the Supreme Court's jurisprudence under the FAA, permitting enforcement of agreements to arbitrate federal statutory claims, including employment claims, makes clear that the agreement may not require a party to 'forgo the substantive rights afforded by the statute.'" *Id.* at *12. "The right to engage in collective action—including collective *legal* action—is the core substantive right protected by the NLRA and is the foundation on which the Act and Federal labor policy rest." *Id.* (emphasis original); (3) "nothing in the text of the FAA suggests that an arbitration agreement that is inconsistent with the NLRA is nevertheless enforceable." *Id.* at *14. "To the contrary, Section 2 of the FAA . . . provides that arbitration agreements may be invalidated in whole or in part upon any 'grounds as exist at law or in equity for the revocation of any contract.'" *Id.*; and (4) "even if there were a direct conflict between the NLRA and the FAA, there are strong indications that the FAA would have to yield under the terms of the Norris-LaGuardia Act." *Id.* at *16.

I also agree with the Board's holding that Horton "violated Section 8(a)(1) by requiring employees to waive their right to collectively pursue employment-related claims in all forums, arbitral and judicial." *Id.* at *17. The Board made it clear that it was not mandating class arbitration in order to protect employees' rights under the NLRA, but rather was holding that employers may not compel employees to waive their NLRA right to collectively pursue litigation of employment claims in all forums, judicial and arbitral.

As acknowledged by the majority, we give the Board judicial deference in interpreting an ambiguous provision of a statute that it administers. *Lechmere, Inc. v. NLRB,* 502 U.S. 527, 536 (1992). Further, as acknowledged by the majority, there is authority to support the Board's analysis.

For the reasons set out herein, I would deny the petition for review and affirm the Board's decision in toto. Therefore, I respectfully concur in part and dissent in part.

* * *

The Fifth Circuit's upholding the Board on *Horton*'s first ground— that the language in the MAA would lead employees to reasonably believe that they were prohibited from filing unfair labor practice charges—is not without significance. Indeed, assuming the Board continues to adhere to this part of its decision, and it is accepted in other circuits, employers seeking to avoid unfair labor practice charges will have to revise arbitration agreements to make plain—or at least clearer—that employees subject to such agreements retain the right to file charges with the NLRB. This could affect many thousands of workplaces and millions of employees. Moreover, yet unresolved is the question of whether arbitration agreements that run afoul of Section 8(a)(1) for this reason might be deemed invalid in their entirety, thus prompting courts to refuse to enforce such agreements or stay a suit pending arbitration.

But, undoubtedly, the majority's rejection of the second ground is far more important. The opinion is not a model of judicial clarity. The majority fails to explain, for example, the salience of its determination that class actions are "procedural" in nature. For one thing, the holding would appear to sweep in all waivers of concerted dispute resolution, not just class actions. Moreover, Section 7 protects various activities that can be described as procedural, including not only petitioning and organizing, but, as the court acknowledges, also concerted resort to judicial forums. Notably, the majority does not even mention *Eastex* in this discussion, much less address its implications. And the opinion appears adrift elsewhere, including in its discussion of relative enactment dates in light of recodification, as well as in its reliance on judicial approval of arbitration provisions in collective bargaining agreements—a context well understood to be far removed from the individual employment contract at issue in the case.

Ultimately, however, after discussing *Concepcion* and rejecting the argument that Section 7's protection for concerted activity fits squarely within the FAA's own savings clause, the majority concluded that the general thrust of the NLRA is not sufficient to override the FAA's command in favor of arbitration. In the court's view, something more explicit or more clearly evincing an inherent conflict is needed for a later-enacted statute such as the NLRA to trump the FAA's mandate. Do you agree with the majority that Section 7's protection for concerted activity fails to overcome this presumption? Is such a presumption itself sound?

Still, the Fifth Circuit's decision is unlikely to be the last word on whether arbitration policies containing waivers of class or joint actions in individual employment contracts contravene federal labor policy. Although, as the majority notes, court challenges to arbitration systems that preclude group claims relying collaterally on the Board's *D.R. Horton* decision have been almost uniformly rejected, ALJs considering such arbitration policies in unfair labor practice proceedings have continued to follow the Board's reasoning. And it will be interesting to see how the present Board will treat the matter, in light of the Board's traditional willingness to abide by the policy of nonacquiescence.

Furthermore, while the majority brushed aside the Norris-LaGuardia Act (in part because the Board does not have authority to enforce it), Section 2 of the Act contains its own guaranty of the right of concerted activity for mutual aid and protection. That provision, which is directed at courts (not the Board), would seem to be applicable despite the *D.R. Horton* decision; that is, section 3 of Norris-LaGuardia (at p. 5 of this Supplement) provides that any "undertaking" in conflict with section 2's guaranty of the right of concerted activity for mutual aid or protection is "declared to be contrary to the public policy of the United States." Thus, other courts confronting challenges to the enforceability of arbitration agreements or motions to enforce such agreements will have the opportunity to address this matter. *See* Matthew Finkin, *The Meaning and Contemporary Vitality of the Norris-LaGuardia Act*, ___ Neb. L. Rev ___ (in press).

PROBLEM FOR DISCUSSION

The Fifth Circuit did not address the broader implications of its holding, including the potential impact of the FAA on other types of concerted activity. On its face, Section 2 of the FAA reaches beyond concerted pursuit of legal claims, covering a contract term "to settle by arbitration a *controversy* thereafter arising out of such contract or transaction . . . ." Consider for example how this provision might apply to the circumstances in NLRB v. Washington Aluminum Co., 370 U.S. 9 (1962) (Casebook, p. 461), where the Supreme Court affirmed the Board's finding that seven workers who had left work together to protest the shop's bitterly cold conditions had engaged in protected concerted activity. In light of the Fifth Circuit's decision, could an employer like Washington Aluminum require that all employees agree, as a condition of employment, to submit complaints or disputes—i.e., "controversies"—over conditions in the shop exclusively to individualized, binding arbitration? Even if courts were to somehow conclude that, unlike the treatment of concerted legal action, an employer could not compel individual arbitration in this context (or discipline employees for failing to adhere to the arbitration mandate), do you think the mere presence of such a clause might chill employees from exercising their Section 7 rights because they could reasonably interpret it to prohibit making a joint demand, protesting as a group, or walking out together? If so, what does this suggest about the Fifth Circuit's conclusion that there is no inherent conflict between the NLRA and the FAA?

Page 503.   Add to the end of Problem 3:

See also Fortuna Enterprises, LP v. NLRB, 665 F.3d 1295 (D.C. Cir. 2011) (concerning a 90-minute sit-in by hotel employees demanding to meet with management over a supervisor's suspension).

* * *

Page 503.   Add at the end of Problem 6:

See also Medco Health Solutions of Las Vegas, Inc., v. NLRB, 701 F.3d 710 (D.C. Cir. 2012).

Page 503.   Add to Problems for Discussion:

7. Blastcom is a service provider for DirecTV. It is not unionized. Its service technicians install and service that equipment. The attachment of an active telephone line to the system gives the customer more options, but at a cost. DirecTV notified Blastcom that it would charge it for installations that did not include these attachments. Blastcom told its service technicians that their pay was to be reduced unless they persuaded customers to buy the package. The policy was implemented resulting in loss of income; and when the technicians protested they were advised either not to tell the customer that the added service was being attached or that the equipment would not work without it, which was a lie. One of their number contacted a local TV station and a group were invited to appear and recount their story on the air, which they did: they described the new policy, their loss of income, their protest, management's response and their acting pursuant to the advice they were given, i.e. lying to customers to make the sale. They were discharged. Has the Company violated the Labor Act? Mastec Advanced Technologies, 357 NLRB No. 17 (2011).

B. EMPLOYER RESPONSES TO CONCERTED ACTIVITIES

Page 523.   Add following Great Dane Trailers:

On April 20, 2011, the Acting General Counsel of the NLRB caused a complaint of unfair labor practice to issue against the Boeing company. *Boeing Company*, Case No. 19–CA–32431. It identifies several Boeing executives and alleges that they made "coercive statements" that they would remove work from the company's unionized Puget Sound facility to its non-union South Carolina facility because of union strikes. *E.g.*, that a statement

> in a quarterly earnings conference call that was posted on Boeing's intranet website for all employees and reported in the Seattle Post Intelligencer Aerospace News and quoted in the Seattle Times, made an extended statement regarding "diversifying [Respondent's] labor pool and labor relationship," and moving the 787 Dreamliner work to South Carolina due to "strikes happening every three to four years in Puget Sound."

that an

> October 28, 2009, memorandum entitled "787 Second Line, Questioners and Answers for Manager," informed employees, among other things, that its decision to locate the second 787 Dreamliner line in South Carolina was made in order to reduce Respondent's vulnerability to delivery disruptions caused by work stoppages.

and that the Company did just that. The complaint alleges that the Company "decided to transfer its second 787 Dreamliner production line of 3 planes per month from the [bargaining] Unit to its non-union site in North Charleston, South Carolina."

The complaint asserts that this conduct violates sections 8(a)(1) and (3) by restraining or coercing employees in the exercise of section 7 rights and "is also inherently destructive of" those rights. As a remedy, the Acting General Counsel will be seeking an Order requiring the company

> to have the [bargaining] Unit operate its second line of 787 Dreamliner aircraft assembly production in the State of Washington, utilizing supply lines maintained by the Unit in Seattle, Washington, and Portland, Oregon, area facilities

Ten Republican Senators wrote a public letter of protest to the Board's Acting General Counsel cautioning him that the issue would be taken up in hearings on his nomination to the position. In addition, on Sept. 15, 2011, the House passed H.R. 2587, the "Protecting Jobs from Government Interference Act," which would have amended section 10 (c) of the Labor Act to provide that the Labor Board

> shall have no power to order an employer (or seek an order against an employer) to restore or reinstate any work, product, production line, or equipment, to rescind any relocation, transfer, subcontracting, outsourcing, or other change regarding the location, entity, or employer who shall be engaged in production or other business operations, or to require any employer to make an initial or additional investment at a particular plant, facility, or location.

However, Boeing and the Union came to an agreement and the complaint was settled.

––––––––––––

PROBLEMS FOR DISCUSSION

1. Reconsider the Boeing complaint in light of *Adkins Transfer* and the notes following it at pp. 201–207 of the main volume. Assume the factual allegations in the complaint are proved. (The General Counsel of Boeing had strongly contested the facts in a six-page letter to the Acting General Counsel of May 3, 2011.) Would Boeing's decision violate the Act? Would it violate the Act if the decision was to locate a new line in South Carolina, not to transfer one from a unionized facility?

2. Why did the General Counsel allege that Boeing's decisions are "inherently destructive" of section 7 rights? Are they?

II. CONSTITUTIONAL LIMITATIONS ON GOVERNMENT REGULATION

B. PICKETING AND FREEDOM OF COMMUNICATION

Page 572.   Add to the note following Carpenters Local No. 1506 (Eliason & Knuth of Arizona, Inc.):

The Board, by vote of 3–1, extended the Act's protection to the display of a large inflated rat and the stationing of a union member to leaflet near the targeted site's vehicle entrance. Sheet Metal Int'l Ass'n, Local 15 (Galencare, Inc.), 356 NLRB No. 162 (2011).

III. THE NATIONAL LABOR RELATIONS ACT

A. ORGANIZATIONAL AND RECOGNITION PICKETING

Page 600.   Add to Problems for Discussion:

5. ConMed is a medical contractor operating clinics at correctional facilities. It operates the clinic at the Urbana State Prison. A union has secured majority support from all the clinic's employees at Urbana State except office clericals, physicians, and supervisors, and has demanded recognition. The Company has refused. Twenty of these clinic employees have picketed for thirty minutes demanding union recognition. No notice was given to the Federal Mediation and Conciliation Service under § 8(g) of the Act. Were this not a medical facility, would it be permissible to discharge these employees? Should it make a difference that the employer *is* a medical facility? Consider § 8(g) and the treatment of § 8(g) in § 8(d) in the statutory section. Correctional Med. Services, Inc., 356 NLRB No. 48 (2010).

B. SECONDARY PRESSURE

1.   UNDER THE TAFT-HARTLEY ACT

Page 608.   Add to Problems for Discussion:

8.   The Emmett Worth Company is a fencing contractor. It hires subcontractors for its jobs and performs the function of "construction manager." If there is a project agreement that requires only union contractors, Emmett Worth will contract with unionized subcontractors; but, absent that restriction it will hire non-union subcontractors. The Laborers District Council has asked Emmett Worth to sign an agreement with it that Emmett Worth will agree to a contract under section 8(f) of the NLRA for its workers and that it will subcontract only with contractors who are unionized. Emmett Worth has refused. Phyllis Pickett and her son have incorporated Pickett Fences to do fence installation. As most of the work in the area is subject to project agreements, she has asked the Laborers Union to sign a section 8(f) agreement. When the Laborers learned that Ms. Pickett intended to accept jobs from Emmett Worth (which would be unionized as per her section 8(f) agreement with the Union) it refused nevertheless to execute a section 8(f) agreement with her. Emmett Worth has filed a charge of violation of § 8(b)(4)(ii)(B). You are the General Counsel. Will you issue a complaint? Will you seek an injunction under section 10(*l*)? What arguments would you expect to confront? How would you deal with them? Estimate the likelihood of success.

PART FIVE

ADMINISTRATION OF THE COLLECTIVE AGREEMENT

III. JUDICIAL ENFORCEMENT OF COLLECTIVE AGREEMENTS

Page 713.   Add to Problems for Discussion:

4.   The Company has a unionized plant in Paris, Illinois, and a non-union facility in Kentucky. The collective agreement in Illinois ran from November 3, 2009 to November 2, 2012. In early 2012, the Company informed the Union that due to declining business conditions it needed to consolidate the operations: one of the plants would have to be closed. After extensive negotiations the Union agreed to immediate economic concessions in return for the following agreement:

> None of these items will be implemented unless Paris is the plant chosen to remain in operation after the consolidation. If Paris is NOT the chosen facility, it will continue to operate under the current contract.

The agreement also provided that:

> It is mutually agreed between the company and union bargaining teams that the items revised through this process will not be subject to change in the next contract negotiations.

In September, 2012, the Company announced that it was consolidating its operations in Paris and began to do so. In October, negotiations for a new collective agreement commenced. The parties deadlocked and in mid-November the Union struck. The Company then announced that it was reversing its prior decision: it would close the Paris facility and consolidate in Kentucky. The Union has sued in federal district court under § 301 seeking a preliminary injunction staying the plant closing and an order compelling the Company to arbitrate the decision to close under the expired collective agreement. The Company has moved for summary judgment. How should the court rule? Cf. UAW v. ZF Boge Elastmetall LLC, 649 F.3d 641 (7th Cir. 2011).

Page 718.   Add after the reference to Michigan Family Resources:

Despite what would seem to be the unmistakable teaching of *Enterprise Wheel* and the cases set out in the next section of the Main Volume, some lower courts insist on reading collective agreements as commercial contracts and to treat arbitrators as magistrates subject to judicial oversight for their parsing of contractual language. *Compare* Northern States Power Co., Minn. v. IBEW Local 160, 711 F.3d 900 (8th

Cir. 2013), *with* Albemarte Corp. v. United Steel Workers, 703 F.3d 821 (5th Cir. 2013); *compare* Alcan Packaging Co. v. Graphic Communications Conference, 729 F.3d 839 (8th Cir. 2013). *with* Reyco Granning LLC v. Teamsters Local No. 245, 735 F.3d 1018 (8th Cir. 2013).

IV. The Role of the National Labor Relations Board and the Arbitrator During the Term of a Collective Agreement

A. Conduct Which Allegedly Violates Both the Contract and the Labor Act

Page 758.   Add following the discussion of GC 11–05:

PROBLEM FOR DISCUSSION

Employee Wood was dismissed for distributing a union flyer. The Company asserted that she had done so on work time. The Union pursued her discharge as without just cause under the collective agreement. It also filed a charge of violation of section 8(a)(3) on which the General Counsel issued a complaint. The Arbitrator held the discharge was not for just cause and ordered reinstatement but without back pay because Ms. Wood had lied to management about when she distributed the flyer and lied about it as well in the arbitration. Should the Board defer to the arbitrator's award? Shands Jacksonville Med. Center, 359 NLRB No. 104 (2013).

On February 7, 2014, the Board posted a Notice and Invitation to File Briefs in Babcock & Wilcox Constr. Co., Case 28–CA–022625, requesting address to the following:

1. Should the Board adhere to, modify, or abandon its existing standard for post-arbitral deferral under *Spielberg Mfg. Co.*, 112 NLRB 1080 (1955), and *Olin Corp.*, 268 NLRB 573 (1984)?

2. If the Board modifies the existing standard, should the Board adopt the standard outlined by the General Counsel in GC Memorandum 11–05 (January 20, 2011) or would some other modification of the existing standard be more appropriate: e.g., shifting the burden of proof, redefining "repugnant to the Act," or reformulating the test for determining whether the arbitrator "adequately considered" the unfair labor practice issue?

3. If the Board modifies its existing post-arbitral deferral standard, would consequent changes need to be made to the Board's standards for determining whether to defer a case to arbitration under *Collyer Insulated Wire*, 192 NLRB 837 (1971); *United Technologies Corp.*, 268 NLRB 557 (1984); and *Dubo Mfg. Corp.*, 142 NLRB 431 (1963)?

4. If the Board modifies its existing post-arbitral deferral standard, would consequent changes need to be made to

the Board's standards for determining whether to defer to pre-arbitral grievance settlements under *Alpha Beta*, 273 NLRB 1546 (1985), *review denied sub nom.*, *Mahon v. NLRB*, 808 F.2d 1342 (9th Cir. 1987); and *Postal Service*, 300 NLRB 196 (1990)?

PART SEVEN

LABOR AND THE ANTITRUST LAWS

Page 862.   **Add to Problem for Discussion:**

2.   On March 11, 2011, the National Football Players Association notified the National Football League that it disclaimed any further interest in representing the teams' players in collective bargaining. The following day, the League imposed a lock-out excluding all team members from access to or use of team facilities or personnel and denying compensation and health benefits. Several players sued the league to enjoin the lock-out under anti-trust law and a federal district court issued an injunction against it. Did the court have jurisdiction to issue the injunction under the Norris-LaGuardia Act? Brady v. National Football League, 644 F.3d 661 (8th Cir. 2011).

PART EIGHT

FEDERALISM AND LABOR RELATIONS

I. PREEMPTION OF STATE LABOR LAW: AN OVERVIEW

Page 893.   Add at the end of Problem 6:

Consider the role of a judge via-à-vis a jury in deciding whether union speech in the context of a labor dispute was uttered with such "malice" as to lose the qualified privilege the law accords. *Compare* Brandon v. Coupled Prods., LLC, 975 N.E. 2d 382 (Ind. App. 2012), *with* Spacecon Specialty Contractors, LLC v. Bensinger, 713 F.2d 1028 (10th Cir. 2013).

Page 894.   Add to Problems for Discussion:

9.   In the course of a union's organizing campaign it asked employees to sign a permission allowing the union "to use my name and likeness in" the union's publications and to sign a statement, "I support the union." The union used these photos on a flyer captioned, "WE'RE VOTING YES!" The union won the election; but one of the employees whose face was displayed has complained that the flyer misrepresented her actual intention: while she was sympathetic to the union's larger goals, she never disclosed how she actually intended to vote. The Company has filed an objection to the election. Is a hearing required? (Return to *Midland Life* at pp. 138–148.) Durham School Servs., 360 NLRB No. 108 (2014). Assume the employee has sued the union in state court for "false light" invasion of privacy—for presenting her publicly in such a way as to misrepresent her intentions—and the union moves to dismiss on preemption grounds. How should the court rule?

Page 910.   Add to end of Problems for Discussion:

May a city require grocery stores that change ownership to hire from the complement of incumbent employees and retrain them for a 90-day period (subject to dismissal for cause and to a written evaluation at the conclusion of the 90-day period)? Cal. Grocers Ass'n v. City of Los Angeles, 254 P.3d 1019 (Cal. 2011). May the City do much the same for employees in the "hospitality business"—hotels, motels, bed & breakfast with at least 25 rooms? Rhode Island Hospitality Ass'n v. City of Providence, 667 F.3d 17 (1st Cir. 2011).

If an employer observes the terms of the above "displaced worker" law for 90 days, hiring most of the prior employer's unionized workforce, must it bargain with the union at that point—or may that determination turn on the percentage of its workforce that had been unionized after the close of the 90-day period? Paulson v. GVS Properties, LLC, 904 F.Supp.2d 282 (E.D.N.Y. 2012).

II. SPECIFIC APPLICATIONS: REPRESENTATION, BARGAINING AND CONCERTED ACTIVITIES

A. SELECTION OF BARGAINING REPRESENTATIVE

Page 911.   Add to Problems for Discussion:

The following provision was added to Oklahoma Stat. tit. 40, § 701, effective November 1, 2011:

> A.   Except as provided by subsection B of this section, any contract or agreement between a minor and a union is not a valid contract or agreement and shall be null and void for any purpose including, but not limited to, official recognition by a union for purposes of intent or interest by a minor to join, vote, or consent to any action of the union.

> B.   Any contract or agreement between a minor and a union shall be signed and adjoined by the parent or legal guardian of the minor. The minor, or parent or legal guardian of the minor, shall have the right to rescind the contract or agreement within ninety (90) days of the date of the contract or agreement.

> C.   Any funds received by a union in an attempt to contractually obligate a minor, without meeting the provisions set forth in subsection B of this section, shall be fully refunded to the minor within thirty (30) days after receipt of written notice from the minor, or parent or legal guardian of the minor. If the full amount of funds received by the union has not been refunded to the minor, or parent or legal guardian of the minor within thirty (30) days, the full amount of funds due shall double each successive thirty-day-period until such refund is made in full to the minor, or parent or legal guardian of the minor.

About 25% of supermarket and grocery store employees in the state are under the age of 18. Is this law federally preempted?

C. ENFORCEMENT OF COLLECTIVE AGREEMENTS

Page 944.   Add to the end of Problem 1:

Compare McKnight v. Dresser, Inc., 676 F.3d 426 (5th Cir.2012).

Page 944.   Add to Problem 3 after Cramer:

Compare Haggins v. Verizon New England, Inc., 648 F.3d 50 (1st Cir. 2011).

Page 944.   Add to Problems for Discussion:

5.   The state's Wage Payment Act defines a "wage" as all amounts at which labor rendered is compensated "which are due to an employee under any employer policy or contract". The law requires all employees to be informed at the time of hire of the "wages agreed upon." All wages due must be paid promptly on a set periodic basis.

Cogburn Farms is a chicken processor. At the time of hire each employee is given an Employee Handbook. One part, headed "Time Card

Administration", stated that "[t]he purpose of the time card is to insure an accurate record of all hours you work in order for you to receive correct payment of wages"; that "[y]ou are required to punch in and out on your own time card according to your schedule"; and that "[i]t is our policy that all work performed by you will be while you are 'on the clock.'" The handbook further specified that "[y]ou must be dressed for work when punching in or out"; that "[e]mployees are to be at their work-stations ready and dressed for work at their scheduled starting time and are to remain at their work-stations until the scheduled quitting work time"; and that "[y]ou will be paid for all time worked per your schedule."

The workers at Cogburn Farms are represented by a union. The collective bargaining agreement sets out wage rates, states that the basic work day is 8 hours and the work week 40 hours, and contains a grievance-arbitration procedure. The collective agreement does not provide how compensable time will be calculated, but for many years, through successive collective agreements, the Company has paid employees on the basis of "line time"—that is, the time actually spent by employees processing chickens on the production line, not "clock time"—that is, time spent from the moment the employee "swipes in" on the employer's time card system. "Line time" did not include time spent donning and doffing protective gear, walking to and from the production area, or washing gear before and after work.

A group of employees has sued Cogburn farms for violation of the state's Wage Payment Act. They claim that: (1) that they were not notified at the time of employment that they would not be paid "line time" and were instead led to believe that they would be paid "clock time;" (2) that this understanding became part of the agreed-upon terms and conditions of their employment; and (3) that Cogburn Farms therefore owed them unpaid wages for the difference between "clock time" and "line time." The Company moved to dismiss on grounds of § 301 preemption. How should the court rule? Barton v. House of Raeford Farms, Inc., 745 F.3d 95 (4th Cir. 2014).

Page 948.   Add following the discussion of Can-Am Plumbing:

See also J.A. Crossen, 359 NLRB No. 2 (2012).

PART NINE

THE INDIVIDUAL AND THE UNION

I. THE RIGHT TO FAIR REPRESENTATION

C. THE INDIVIDUAL AND HIS GRIEVANCE

Page 991.   Add following the text:

See Cameron v. Chang-Craft, 251 P.3d 1008 (Alaska 2011), on the jury's role when the challenged conduct falls along the spectrum laid out by the Ninth Circuit.

Page 1000.   Add to Problems for Discussion:

Does a union's breach of its duty of fair representation in declining to take an employee's grievance to arbitration excuse the employee of the need to exhaust an intra-union appeal? Chapman v. UAW, 670 F.3d 677 (6th Cir. 2012).

II. UNION SECURITY AND THE ENCOURAGEMENT OF UNION ACTIVITY

A. UNION SECURITY AND THE USE OF UNION DUES

Page 1016.   Add to Problems for Discussion:

2(a).   In *Harris v. Quinn*, 573 U.S. ___, 134 S.Ct. 2618 (2014), the Supreme Court held, in a 5–4 decision, that requiring the payment of agency fees by non-union personal assistants who provide in-home care to disabled individuals through Illinois's Medicaid-waiver programs violates the First Amendment. In so holding, the majority first refused to extend to the personal assistants the portion of *Abood* permitting non-union state employees to be compelled to pay the agency fees for collective-bargaining-related costs. It found the assistants to be "partial public employees," who, among other things, are mostly answerable to their customers instead of the state, do not enjoy many of the rights of full-fledged public employees, and are subject to collective bargaining on their behalf that is sharply limited in scope. Thus, in the majority's view, *Abood*'s rationale supporting a fee mandate for full-fledged public sector workers—the union's robust role in negotiating and administering a CBA on more than limited terms, settling disputes, and processing grievances—is not applicable in this context. The Court went on to conclude that requiring the non-union assistants to pay fees to the union did not serve a compelling state interest that could not be achieved through means significantly less restrictive of associational freedoms.

The future implications of *Harris* are unclear. The holding itself is expressly limited to "partial public employees" like the home-care personal assistants at issue in the case; it therefore applies to neither full-fledged public employees nor private sector workers. Still, the decision certainly will affect agency fee mandates in similar home-care worker programs in other states and may affect other work arrangements that might be found to fall into the yet-undefined "partial public" category. Moreover, the majority opinion contains strong criticism of *Abood*'s reasoning, suggesting that these five justices might be willing to overturn that decision in a later case. Anticipating this possibility in a strongly worded response, the four dissenting justices not only disagreed on *Abood*'s applicability to the fee at issue in the case, but also emphasized that the rule in *Abood* is deeply entrenched and the basis on which thousands of contracts between public sector workers and government agencies are premised. The majority's reasoning does not appear to threaten agency fees in the private sector.

Page 1017.   Add to Problems for Discussion:

7.   May a state disallow the deduction from wages of any political contributions? May it also exempt charitable organizations or health care organizations or retirement or benefits funds from that prohibition? *Compare* Ysursa v. Pocatello Educ. Ass'n, 555 U.S. 353, 129 S.Ct. 1093, 172 L. Ed.2d 770 (2009), *with* UFCW v. Brewer, 817 F. Supp. 2d 1118 (D.Ariz. 2011).

Page 1033.   Add to Problems for Discussion:

2.   May a union require objectors annually to renew their objections in order to qualify for a reduced obligation? United Auto Workers Local 376 (Colt's Mfg. Co.), 356 N.L.R.B. No. 164 (2011).

3.   As a union sends an annual *Hudson* notice to the bargaining unit, must it re-send that notice if it adopts a temporary mid-term assessment to raise money for political purposes? Knox v. SEIU Local 1000, ___ U.S. ___, 132 S.Ct. 2277, 2012 (U.S. Sup. Ct. 2012) (public-sector employees basing claim on First Amendment).

B. STATE RIGHT-TO-WORK LAWS

Page 1034.   Add to the first paragraph:

In 2012, Indiana adopted a right-to-work law. PL2–2012 amending Indiana Code § 22–6–6 (2012 Supp.). Michigan enacted a right-to-work law as well. Mich. Comp. L. § 423.14 (2012 Supp.).

III. DISCIPLINE OF UNION MEMBERS AND THE NATIONAL LABOR RELATIONS ACT

Page 1062.   Add to Problems for Discussion:

3.   Since 1977, the NLRB has held that it violates § 8(b)(1)(A) for a union to discipline a member for complying with an employer's safety rules, notably a rule requiring employees to report safety violations— which may lead to the discipline or discharge of another employee. Is that statutory application sound? International Union of Operating Engineers, Local 513 v. NLRB, 635 F.3d 1233 (D.C. Cir. 2011).

PART TEN

RECONSIDERING THE LABOR ACT IN THE CONTEMPORARY CONTEXT

III. LABOR LAW REFORM

Page 1087.   Add to footnote "c":

The "75th Anniversary Symposium" referred to is at 26 ABA J. LAB. & EMP. L. No. 2 (2011).